Weollege

D0443035

DISCARDED

The Art of Growing Older

ALSO BY WAYNE BOOTH

The Rhetoric of Fiction
Now Don't Try to Reason with Me: Essays and Ironies for a Credulous Age
A Rhetoric of Irony
Modern Dogma and the Rhetoric of Assent
Critical Understanding: The Powers and Limits of Pluralism
The Harper & Row Rhetoric (with Marshall Gregory)
The Company We Keep: An Ethics of Fiction
The Vocation of a Teacher

Editions
The Knowledge Most Worth Having
The Harper & Row Reader (with Marshall Gregory)

The ART of GROWING OLDER

Writers on Living and Aging

*Selected, and with Personal Reflections,
by Wayne Booth*

THE UNIVERSITY OF CHICAGO PRESS
Chicago and London

Acknowledgments of Permissions appear on page 319.

The University of Chicago Press, Chicago 60637
The University of Chicago Press, Ltd., London

Copyright © 1992 by Wayne Booth

All rights reserved. Originally published 1992
University of Chicago Press Edition 1996
Printed in the United States of America
02 01 00 99 98 97 96   6 5 4 3 2 1

Library of Congress Cataloging-in-Publication Data

Booth, Wayne C.
    The art of growing older : writers on living and aging / selected, and with
personal reflections, by Wayne Booth.
        p.   cm.
    Originally published: New York : Poseidon Press, ©1992.
    Includes bibliographical references and index.
    ISBN 0-226-06549-9 (pbk.: alk. paper)
    1. Aging—Literary collections.   I. Title.
PN6071.A48A78   1996
808.8'0354—dc20   96-28550
                                                            CIP

♾The paper used in this publication meets the minimum requirements of the
American National Standard for Information Sciences—Permanence of Paper for
Printed Library Materials, ANSI Z39.48-1984.

This book is printed on acid-free paper.

To Phyllis

Contents

Illustrations

It is surprising that stories about old people
should make bright reading.
  —Carol Bly

The old are us.
  —Ronald Blythe

The compensation of growing old, Peter Walsh
thought, coming out of Regent's Park, and holding his
hat in hand, was simply this: that the passions remain
as strong as ever, but one had gained—at last!—the
power which adds the supreme flavour to existence,—
the power of taking hold of experience, of turning it
round, slowly, in the light.
  —Virginia Woolf

To tell the truth, Cephalus, I [Socrates] answered, I
enjoy talking with very old people. They have gone
before us on a road by which we too may have to
travel, and I think we do well to learn from them what
it is like, easy or difficult, rough or smooth.
  —Plato's *Republic*

Old men ought to be explorers
Here and there does not matter
We must be still and still moving
Into another intensity
For a further union, a deeper communion
Through the dark cold and the empty desolation. . . .
                    In my end is my beginning.
  —T. S. Eliot

You need only claim the events of your life to make
yourself yours.
  —Florida Scott-Maxwell, at eighty

Introduction: Feeling Older

"You're only as old as you feel." All of us have said it or heard it. We may even believe it, at least on the mornings when we're feeling especially young. But what exactly is an *old* feeling? And how do you go about trying to *feel* young? Is this feeling I have now the feeling of growing old? What will it feel like when I'm *really* old? And how—to paraphrase that lovely epigraph from the "elderly" Florida Scott-Maxwell, interviewed by Ronald Blythe—how can I "claim" the implacable event of my growing older in any way that will make my self *mine?*

This book is a collection of the best poems and meditations I've found addressing such questions. Most of my selections qualify as what we call "literature" or "poetry"; whether precisely true or not, they are to me beautiful. (I wonder what it would take to convince you, in these rushing times, to read everything here very slowly? Almost every piece will profit from being read aloud.) Some few are not, I confess, strikingly well formed, but they seem true enough to shine through even the plainest prose: the solemn works of quite unpoetic philosophers, or the undoctored recollections and meditations of folks who do not think of themselves as the least bit literary. The pains and joys, the fears and hopes that all of us feel as we discover—at twenty-five or forty or seventy— that we are growing older, maybe even old, are not confined to those who, like the poets, implicitly claim to represent our feelings.

Aging in itself worries us moderns more than it worried our ancestors. They had other troubles to think about, especially the threat of early, painful, terrifying disease and death. They all had good reason to fear that they would die fairly soon. Why fear old age when early death was much more probable? As Montaigne put the point, about four and a half centuries ago, chiding his readers for worrying about old age,

What an idle fancy it is to expect to die of a decay of powers brought on by extreme old age, and to set ourselves this term for our duration, since that is the rarest of all deaths and the least customary! We call it alone natural, as if it were contrary to nature to see a man break his neck by a fall, be drowned in a shipwreck, or be snatched away by the plague or a pleurisy, and as if our ordinary condition did not expose us to all these mishaps. . . . We ought perhaps rather to call natural what is general, common, and universal. . . . Death of old age is a rare, singular, and extraordinary death, and hence less natural than the others. . . . It is a very rare privilege of hers [Nature's] to make us last that long.

As Montaigne concedes, some few folks in his time do live on —fortunately or unfortunately. Of course their chances of living long varied greatly, like ours, depending on their social class, where they lived, and whether there happened to be a devastating plague in their neighborhood. But they could *all* assume, until quite recently, that though they had squeaked through to thirty or forty, the odds were against their reaching sixty—Montaigne didn't make it—let alone what we consider old age.

"Reaching the age of 80 [in the Renaissance] was akin to a sporting triumph"—so Georges Minois summarizes the earlier demographics of old age. The same could be said of our great-grandparents; they felt in their bones that death was just around the corner. Death, not being really old, was the great threat, the great denier, the great mystery that opened onto further and—for all sinners—much more terrifying mysteries: either annihilation or eternal torment. Consequently, though a few of them lived into their seventies or eighties or even beyond, and though some of those rare birds wrote about the pains and losses and consolations of old age, far more wrote about just plain death, that monstrous skeleton with his reaping scythe. They often preached that the best way to live was to live somehow with him—he was always male —and they went on and on writing about and to him, in poem after poem, sermon after sermon, painting after painting, century after century.

Sometimes they wrote like John Donne in his "Holy Sonnets," hailing the possibility of salvation in the afterlife in tones that for some critics have seemed radically unconvincing.

> Death be not proud, though some have called thee
> Mighty and dreadfull, for thou art not soe,
> For, those, whom thou think'st, thou dost overthrow,
> Die not, poore death, nor yet canst thou kill mee.
> From rest and sleepe, which but thy pictures bee,
> Much pleasure, then from thee, much more must flow,
> And soonest our best men with thee doe goe,
> Rest of their bones, and soules delivery.
> Thou'art slave to Fate, chance, kings, and desperate men,
> And dost with poyson, warre, and sicknesse dwell,
> And poppy or charmes can make us sleepe as well,
> And better than thy stroake; why swell'st thou then?
> One short sleepe past, wee wake eternally,
> And death shall be no more. Death thou shalt die.

Others wrote about death in sheer terror—or simulated terror —as in this splendid anonymous poem from the fifteenth century (I have cut a couple of stanzas).

> In what estate so ever I be
>   *Timor mortis conturbat me.*
>
> As I went on a merry morning,
> I heard a bird both weep and sing,
> This was the tenor of her talking:
>   *Timor mortis conturbat me. . . .*
>
> "When I shall die, I know no day;
> What country or place I cannot say;
> Wherefore this song sing I may:
>   *Timor mortis conturbat me. . . .*

Lucas van Leyden, *St. Jerome* (1521). Ashmolean Museum, Oxford.

"Wake I or sleep, eate or drink,
When I on my last end do think,
For greate fear my soul do shrink:
    Timor mortis conturbat me.

"God grant us grace him for to serve,
And be at our end when we sterve [die],
And from the fiend he us preserve.
    Timor mortis conturbat me."

Though such conturbation will not be encountered much in this book, it is worth dwelling on here as a contrast with what we will meet. We turn-of-the-millennium folk may still fear death, but most of us can be fairly sure that we'll experience old age, and that it will bring woes that the young do not even suspect. It is true that modernity has threatened us with new agents of sudden death: the automobile, gangs armed with Uzis, new plagues. And though the old fear of hellfire has faded, the thought of annihilation, total oblivion, can still feel terrifying. Here is Irving Howe, writing after a lifetime of proud unbelief:

Past sixty, I think frequently about death. Sometimes I think in response to bodily messages: an arrow through the chest, a creaking in the hips. Sometimes I think out of greediness for time: another book to be finished, another tyrant's end to be celebrated. So people delude themselves into supposing their hunger for life has some objective validity. The truth is, one simply wants.

I think about death because it seems proper at this point in life, rather like beaming at the children of younger friends. But how absurd to suppose there is any sort of propriety in such matters! Perhaps I mean that the time has come to get ready for what no one can ever be ready for. The contemplation of death, says Montaigne, helps us "withdraw our soul outside of us and set it to work apart from the body, which is a sort of apprenticeship and likeness of death." A wonderful sentence, but who can follow its disciplines?

This thinking about death is a decidedly curious experience since, think as one may, it yields no thoughts. Who would care to add a line to Montaigne? In the end I hope not to disgrace myself with panic or a deathbed conversion, but as for thoughts about death—rattle this skull as you wish, you won't find any. But perhaps what we call thinking about death is not really thinking at all. It seems more like a slow unclenching of the will, a readiness to wait for the angel at the door. This much acknowledged, one submits to the wand of comedy: not all your wit nor guile can help.

I think about death because I fear extinction, total and endless. My fear is not equally intense from day to day; apparently the deepest terrors are as short-lived as the keenest ecstasies. But even when dulled, my fear persists. The thought that I won't be here in, say, the year 2000 hardly troubles me; what troubles me is the thought of never coming back. A fatal heart attack next week seems far less frightening than eternal extinction. This precious consciousness of mine, coaxed through so many trials and now at last showing a few signs of worth: must all this now end as nothing?

A serious person who has spent a lifetime without religious faith must accept the idea of eternal nonbeing. Having taken pride in skepticism, I must have the courage of its consequences. That doesn't, however, keep me from a bemused interest in notions of reincarnation, since no one would mind a thousand-year sleep if at the end, knuckle to one's eye, there were a prospect of waking.

—Irving Howe, from *A Margin of Hope*

"Statistics show," Howe might want to say to anyone worrying about growing old, "that your chances of dying—sooner or later—are infinitely greater. Why not concentrate—if you are looking for something to worry about—on the certain rather than the merely possible?''

But it is just those statistics that have placed us in an unprecedented world. For the first time in history, authors and their readers, of whatever age, have good statistical reason to feel in their threatened bones the coming of age. And to many of us, the condition of being old, or even of seeming old, feels more threatening than death itself.

To many of you I must appear to be there already—at seventy-one. But you wouldn't even be reading this book, whether you are forty or eighty, unless you were already aware of just how rapidly you're moving toward—well, what names should we use for that point beyond being young, beyond what we fondly hoped, in our fifties and sixties, would turn out to have been our middle years? We're all here together, getting older and older, moving on and on and feeling pretty certain that before long we'll find other people calling us senior citizens, or even worse. And we have been learning to fear that future point where we will have left behind whatever is golden about the "golden years" and moved on into that enigmatic time when *old* age has taken over, when sheer survival from day to day becomes the main business, when the eyes and ears and knees and hips and memory no longer work as they should.

Though you may never get *that* old, you've no doubt seen actuarial reports proclaiming that you will almost certainly live far longer than your parents did; a large percentage of people in all "advanced" nations now do. And they—we—are only lately beginning to develop the kind of rich literary coping that was concentrated upon dying in earlier centuries. The one major form of suffering that Jesus Christ did not take upon himself was growing old—and nobody until this very moment seems to have commented on his fortunate escape.

We rightly hail poets like William Butler Yeats, who in poem after poem faced the facts as he does in "The Tower," published in his early sixties:

> What shall I do with this absurdity—
> O heart, O troubled heart—this caricature,
> Decrepit age that has been tied to me
> As to a dog's tail? . . .

Most of us honor them even more, though, when they go on, as Yeats usually does, to explore various consolations and celebrations that can—sometimes—redeem the condition. Like Yeats, we'll move quickly in this book beyond the losses and the fears they generate in order to savor what can be said about the consolations and celebrations of life after one has left behind the country where young folks dwell. Yeats describes that country in nostalgic tones as he opens another of his most famous poems, "Sailing to Byzantium":

> That is no country for old men. The young
> In one another's arms, birds in the trees
> —Those dying generations—at their song,
> The salmon-falls, the mackerel-crowded seas, .
> Fish, flesh, or fowl, commend all summer long
> Whatever is begotten, born, and dies.
> Caught in that sensual music all neglect
> Monuments of unageing intellect.

We'll meet that wonderful poem in full on page 154—and then go on with Yeats to explore those redeeming "monuments" of art and mind. They were not the only resources Yeats turned to, as he experienced more and more of the losses that aging brings. He tried out in verse as in life a broad variety of cures, consolations, and celebrations available to those who have left that country of "sensual music" behind; he even attempted to restore the sensual music by experimenting with monkey glands. But he never took the dishonest route of claiming that the losses are not real, and I emulate him here by beginning in Part I with a sharp look at the worst that can be said about our losses. Though all of us can defer some of them for a while, and some of us will avoid all of them by dying early, for most of us they will be real, and the art of growing older includes the art of resisting all comforters who try to pretend that being older is no different from being younger. In a culture that worships youth as ours does, it is too easy to accept the view of the glossy advertisements: your worth diminishes with every sign that you are no longer young.

It is not easy, though, to explain just why being able to see through that kind of hypocrisy about aging is itself one of the possible rewards of aging. The words "give up" in the following poem by Kelly Cherry may worry us, but doesn't her kind of honesty, like her craft, prove that she herself has still conserved one glorious possibility—the making of good poetry?

Lines Written on the Eve of a Birthday

It is the loss of possibility
That claims you bit by bit. They take away
Your man, the children you had hoped would be.
They even take brown hair and give you gray
Instead. You ask if you can save your face
But that is part of their plan—to strip you
Of your future and put the past in its place.
They don't stop there. They take the skies' deep blue
And drain it off; the empty bowl they leave
Inverted, white as bone. They dust the trees
With strontium, but they keep up their sleeve
The biggest trick of all, the one that sees
    You give up in the end. It is the loss
    Of possibility that murders us.

To face the losses honestly doesn't mean that we cease to fear them. We all hear ourselves saying things like "It's not death that scares me; it's getting old"; "I'm making my collection of pills *now*, so I'll have them *then*"; "I've been trying to talk my wife into our making out living wills"; "I've just bought that new book *Final Exit*, produced by the Hemlock Society." On good days we may try to deal humorously with what we know and fear; we'll come to some humor later. But in doing so we will not want to forget just how prominent a role fear of aging plays—perhaps even in the need to tell jokes about it.

W. H. Auden prayed—and he was a man who prayed seriously —that when he reached seventy he could be taken neatly and cleanly with a heart attack. (He also could joke cheerfully about aging: see his "Doggerel by a Senior Citizen" on page 229). I have a seventy-five-year-old friend whose fantasy, he says, is to intervene in some cruel mugging and thus get himself killed as a hero. Why? Why of course to avoid old age by dying with his boots on. Maybe I've missed something, but I've not found anyone in earlier periods who felt or talked in quite this way.

We are not the first to figure out that immortality in this world would be disastrous. As Jonathan Swift long ago realized, to prolong life indefinitely would be torture. When Gulliver gets carried away about the good fortune of those strange immortals, the Struldbruggs, and holds forth on what must be the wonders of immortality, his Luggnuggian friend quickly disabuses him: he's seen what actually happens to those immortals. The question, he tells the innocent Gulliver,

> was not whether a Man would chuse to be always in the Prime of Youth, attended with Prosperity and Health; but how he would pass a perpetual Life under all the usual Disadvantages which old Age brings along with it.

He admits that most people answer the question badly: everybody seems to desire "to put off Death for sometime longer: . . . he rarely heard of any Man who died willingly, except he were incited by the Extremity of Grief or Torture." He then goes on to show just what happened to those who had the badge of immortality planted on their foreheads from birth:

> They commonly acted like Mortals, till about Thirty Years
> old, after which by Degrees they grew melancholy and dejected, increasing in both till they came to Fourscore. . . .
> When they came to Fourscore Years . . . they had not only all
> the Follies and Infirmities of other old Men, but many more
> which arose from the dreadful Prospect of never dying. They
> were not only opinionative, peevish, covetous, morose, vain,
> talkative; but uncapable of Friendship, and dead to all natural
> Affection, which never descended below their Grand-children. Envy and impotent Desires, are their prevailing Passions. . . . They have no Remembrance of any thing but what
> they learned and observed in their Youth and Middle Age, and
> even that is very imperfect. . . . The least miserable among
> them, appear to be those who turn to Dotage, and entirely
> lose their Memories; these meet with more Pity and Assistance, because they want many bad Qualities which abound in
> others.

Now *that* is a modern man, speaking to us moderns; a man who has thought about age and death, a man who has discovered, before his time, as it were, that it's harder to deal with aging than with death itself. George Bernard Shaw, at ninety-two an equally modern man, thought that to believe in genuine immortality would be to believe in an "unimaginable horror." Yet nearly everybody tries to prolong life, even those of us who know what Swift and Shaw knew: it's folly to try very hard.

So here we are, in what many are calling a "belated" time, aware of truths that Swift thought were so novel and uninviting that they required heavy satire to sink them home. And what do we talk about? Much of the time, it is true, we still talk about how we can make sure that we will grow older and older. More often we talk about how bad it feels to grow old. And sometimes—not often enough in my view—we talk about what we can do to make aging not just endurable but a form of life worthy of celebration.

Generally we talk about it poorly—just as we talk poorly about other important matters. By now we have scores, perhaps hundreds, of books on age and aging. Most of these are by social scientists, scholars of aging for whom our time has invented the label "gerontologist." Too many of these write in a style that does not deserve reproduction in a book like this. So instead of collecting useful essays *about* aging, as many of those mentioned in my notes have done, I offer here that more eloquent kind of talk: the "poetry" (some of it not in verse) that has come to men and women as they have felt, regardless of their chronological age, the losses and fears of aging and have struggled for the possible rewards to be gleaned from those mysterious turnings.

In other words, I've chosen to concentrate on how growing older *feels,* as expressed by the aging, not as *imagined* by youngsters. The world the Beatles inhabited as they sang their mocking lyric "When I'm 64" is no country for old folks, delightful as satires like theirs may still seem when we hear them with youth in our hearts. Though I quote, for example, a few Greek and Roman satirists, we move quickly beyond them; they seem all to be Beatles-like youths earning reputations by outdoing each other with repugnant portraits of old people—and especially of old women. With a few exceptions, like Shakespeare in his early forties imagining himself into the mind of King Lear, I save the creations of those who still think they are young for some other collector. It may be the bias of a seventy-one-year-old, but to me the transmutation of one's own pain and fear into beauty requires more sheer imaginative courage than any portrayal by a young poet of others' aging, impressive as that creative act can be.

It is true that the widespread new interest in aging has led many younger writers to imagine themselves quite wonderfully into the souls of the old: Anne Tyler's *Dinner at the Homesick Restaurant;* Dorothy Sennett's anthology, *Full Measure: Modern Short Stories on Aging,* with stories by Saul Bellow, Richard Stern, Grace Paley, and Nadine Gordimer, Philip Roth's *Patrimony,* and scores of others. But in my view we have insufficiently savored the profundity and astonishing vitality found in laments and celebrations written or spoken by *those who know*—those who, as they write, are deeply aware that they almost certainly will go on growing older, much older.

This is our fate—mine as collector, yours as my readers, the authors' as our guides. And we'll hear first their widely divergent accounts of the losses and miseries, in Part I, and then their astonishingly diverse answers to the laments, in Part II.

My emphasis on the aging themselves explains why I've included so few quotations from tragic drama. Almost everybody who has responded to my request for suggestions has turned up pithy summations spoken by powerful characters in formal tragedies. These often appear in books of famous quotations, attributed to their authors as if what the character thought, at his or her moment of greatest despair, was the author's final summation: " 'Life . . . is a tale / Told by an idiot, full of sound and fury, / Signifying nothing.' —Shakespeare." " 'The best fortune in life is never to be born.' —Sophocles." Well, no, not quite Shakespeare or Sophocles; rather Macbeth and one of Sophocles' choruses at a given moment in contemplating an especially tragic selection from "life." Go on and read other statements by other characters; read on and find what the chorus says in *Oedipus at Colonus.* Indeed, even the despairing quotations often reveal, on a closer look, a vision that transcends despair. Macbeth, in his utter misery, says:

> . . . My way of life
> Is fall'n into the sere, the yellow leaf;
> And that which should accompany old age,
> As honour, love, obedience, troops of friends,
> I must not look to have; but in their stead,
> Curses, not loud but deep, mouth-honour, breath,
> Which the poor heart would fain deny, and dare not.

Repeat that please. What are you saying "should" accompany old age, according to normal, everyday, non-tragic expectations?

. . . honour, love, obedience, troops of friends . . .

That is what Macbeth, in his misery, and perhaps even Shakespeare, think is what people take for granted as what "should" accompany old age.

The same double vision can be detected in Jaques's famous lines, in *As You Like It,* about the ages of life:

> . . . The sixth age shifts
> Into the lean and slippered pantaloon,
> With spectacles on nose and pouch on side,
> His youthful hose, well saved, a world too wide
> For his shrunk shank; and his big manly voice,
> Turning again toward childish treble, pipes
> And whistles in his sound. Last scene of all,
> That ends this strange eventful history,
> Is second childishness and mere oblivion,
> Sans teeth, sans eyes, sans taste, sans everything.

Jaques is not Shakespeare; he is Shakespeare's notion of a shrewd and eloquent melancholic. Such quotations, powerful as they are, will not quite serve our purposes here.

The experience of aging can come, as our poets will remind us, long before anyone would think of calling us old. Some sensitive folks are touched with the first twinges in their twenties and thirties. The young and vigorous Matthew Arnold lamented, "Here I am thirty, and three-parts iced over." Milton started worrying about the lost years at twenty-three.

How soon hath Time the suttle theef of youth,
Stoln on his wing my three and twentieth yeer!
My hasting dayes flie on with full career,
But my late spring no bud or blossom shew'th.

—John Milton

Philip Larkin feared the losses even before he wrote about them, in his mid-twenties.

"On Being Twenty-six"

I feared these present years,
    The middle twenties,
When deftness disappears,
And each event is
Freighted with a source-encrusting doubt,
    And turned to drought.

I thought: this pristine drive
    Is sure to flag
At twenty-four or -five;
And now the slag
Of burnt-out childhood proves that I was right.
    What caught alight

Quickly consumed in me,
    As I foresaw.
Talent, felicity—
These things withdraw,
And are succeeded by a dingier crop
    That come to stop; . . .

—and he goes on for six more stanzas, clutching at a "putrid infancy" that "forbids"—well, it's a bit hard to decipher exactly what his lost childhood does forbid.

Like Larkin, Byron felt the Big Threat early:

ON THIS DAY I COMPLETE MY THIRTY-SIXTH YEAR

'Tis time this heart should be unmoved,
  Since others it hath ceased to move:
Yet, though I cannot be beloved,
  Still, let me love!

My days are in the yellow leaf;
  The flowers and fruits of love are gone;
The worm, the canker, and the grief
  Are mine alone!

The fire that on my bosom preys
  Is lone as some volcanic isle;
No torch is kindled at its blaze—
  A funeral pile. . . .

—George Gordon, Lord Byron

And he then in effect announces a plan to go off to Greece and get himself killed, before real old age strikes: "Seek out . . . / A soldier's grave, for thee the best" . . .

Christina Rossetti felt old in her early thirties ("Dead Before Death," page 109). Many such authors manage to sound more doom-ridden, in what to me looks like their youth, than does many an oldster—Malcolm Cowley at eighty, say, discussing age in deft and humorous prose (pages 49–50), or Yeats, in his mid-seventies, grappling, in "The Wild Old Wicked Man," with what it's like to be "a wild old man in the light," but still "a young man in the dark."

You may wonder, "Why bother? What's the point of a book that has so many painful reminders of what is to come?" I have a somewhat better answer than simply to say "Misery loves company," though I know that it does. I find most of the works I collect here, even the ones hammering home the losses, more inspiriting than depressing. They exhibit a vitality that belies the claim that aging is all decline. To see a fine poet making great poetry out of how it feels to age is already to combat the worst effect of aging, which is the desire to give up, to say that life is not now and perhaps never was worth living. Dwelling with the quiet voices we hear in these pages may not be quite as invigorating as listening to young poets roar their passions. But even young readers should be able to listen to these voices with profit: They are the steady, controlled voices of men and women who have, after all, gone on coping, coping by means of their well-wrought language even when their bodies have begun to fail.

To any young folks, then, who happen to stumble into this book and suspect that it is not for them, we can thus say: Just like the good people quoted here, all of whom were once as young as you, you'll surprisingly soon join the over-thirties, and then, quicker than lightning, the over-forties, and then suddenly, in all probability—just have a look again at those actuarial tables—you'll find yourself in your seventies, or eighties, or even your nineties. *Then* you'll see; *then* you'll know.

We needn't wait for them. We have already enough company, here on the other side of youth, to keep *us* alive and kicking. As Cicero put it, just two millennia ago, addressing a friend who obviously had also been thinking about the art of growing older:

> I think it good to write something on old age to be dedicated to you. For I would want to ease somewhat our burden of old age, which, if it is not already pressing hard upon us, certainly is fast approaching. . . . For me, writing this book has been so delightful that it has not only erased all the petty annoyances of old age but has also made old age soft and pleasant.

Cicero was in his early sixties when he wrote that. At seventy-one, which doesn't feel at all to me like *old* age, I can say the same to you: Join me, friends, in this distinctively modern adventure, the *almost* certain journey into old age.

A FINAL NOTE ABOUT SOURCES:

Our authors here come from many different centuries and cultures, but since most of their questions, and many of their "answers," are universally pertinent, I've chosen not to bother about distinctions of historical period: you will find thrown together here ancient Chinese, Egyptians, Greeks and Romans, authors from many centuries who wrote in Arabic, French, English, Italian, and German, and living men and women. Indeed, I see us all as belonging to one grand company working these matters out together.

Still, if, like me, you are a bit unclear about just when the famous and not-so-famous authors lived, you may want some dates, and you'll find plenty of them in the notes beginning on page 317. But when you consult them, do keep in mind a fine paradox underlying much of this collection. On the one hand, I embrace Robert Penn Warren's advice to those seeking happiness in old age—"We must not count years." Yet I provide hundreds of countings, some of them perhaps even accurate, about when the authors lived and how old they were when they wrote. (Often one cannot tell, exactly, since the poem finally printed in 1840 may have been written in 1835 or 1820.)

Some of you who accept the advice, offered by a few authors in Part II, to revive your curiosity, may wish that I had provided a full bibliography of works about aging. To have done so would have turned this into another kind of book. But you can make a good start on a reading program that can well last for the rest of your life by consulting first the books I praise as I go along and then the booklists provided by the ten works I list following the endnotes, page 331. Spend a year on those lists, and first thing you know you'll have become an expert and people will start calling you a gerontologist.

PART I

Facing the Facts: Losses, Fears, Lamentations

Age will not be defied.
—Francis Bacon

Age, I do abhor thee, youth, I do adore thee.
Crabbed age and youth cannot live together . . .
Youth is full of pleasance, age is full of care.
—Shakespeare, *The Passionate Pilgrim*

On Friday, Lendl played the tortoise to Edberg's hare.
He was always a step slow. And he was 30 years old.
He will not get quicker.
—News account of Ivan Lendl's defeat by Stefan
Edberg in the 1990 Wimbledon tournament

To be an old man is evil for people in every respect.
—Egyptian papyrus

Empty, my mind, of web and dust;
Of diamond too, and sharpened gold;
Of everything, and if you must,
Of my own self, grown old and cold.
—Mark Van Doren, nearing seventy

who may tell the tale
of the old man?
weigh absence in a scale?
mete want with a span?
the sum assess
of the world's woes?
nothingness
in words enclose?
—Samuel Beckett, in his mid-forties

When I began browsing for this collection, I expected to find more sentimental denials of the problems of aging than open-hearted and unconsoled expressions of loss or pain. I had noticed in booklists a lot of works with titles such as *Going Like Sixty; Going Strong; Golden Age Exercises; Aging Successfully; Live Longer and Enjoy It;* and *How to Make the Rest of Your Life the Best of Your Life.* I had read a fair number of aggressively cheerful assertions about how lovely old age can be, few of them as well-made as Robert Browning's Rabbi Ben Ezra's:

> Grow old along with me!
> The best is yet to be,
> The last of life, for which the first was made:
> Our times are in His hand
> Who saith, "A whole I planned,
> Youth shows but half; trust God; see all, nor be afraid!"

That was written when Browning was approaching fifty. Does the Rabbi speak for Browning? Maybe. We must again be cautious about attributing to authors what were in fact views they have imagined for their characters.

No doubt we should exercise the same caution when we read the innumerable denials of the "old" in "old age" that we find on many a Hallmark card and in many an article in popular magazines and Sunday newspaper supplements. For all we know, they have been written by oldsters feeling desperate about life but hoping to earn a buck by giving members of the aging market the cheering words they think they want to hear. We'll come to a few such suspect denials in Part II.

I did find an abundance of one-sided claims that if we just pull up our socks, learn a few appropriate setting-up exercises, and smile, all will be well. But I was a bit surprised by how much there is of just plain lamentation, cursing, and mourning. Some of it is pretty grim, unredeemed by any special vision or verbal richness that might justify publishing it even once, let alone reprinting it here. Many egoists have apparently felt that the simple shock of waking one morning to *feel old* is itself justification for saying to the world, "Look, the unthinkable has happened to me, me of all people!" I don't want to read much of that kind of thing, and I see no point in inflicting it on others. Yet I also have hoped to avoid here even a hint of dishonest denial.

"Grow old along with me! / The *best* is yet to be"? Well, maybe. Best in what sense? Will you, Rabbi Ben Ezra, cut my toenails when I can no longer reach them? Will you be patient with my memory lapses? On the other hand, can *I* promise to be totally forgiving and solicitous when *you* fall and break your hip, or become incontinent?

Perhaps no one who honestly faces aging avoids moments when any expression of good cheer will seem hypocritical. Alexander Pope, who had a good eye for hypocrisy, said that "when men grow virtuous in their old age, they only make a sacrifice to God of the devil's leavings." When we're really down in the doleful dumps, any pretense at cheerfulness is likely to seem about as empty as "Have a good day!" spoken by an IRS agent. Living through our worst moments, we usually don't manage to express them. How could we possibly even try, *at the time?* To express the feeling, to express it with sufficient grace to justify the effort, one must wait a bit, wait until enough energy returns for some recollecting in tranquillity.

All of which is simply to warn you not to take the Jeremiahs you will meet in Part I with quite the degree of seriousness that they seem to take themselves with. The flesh-and-blood authors who composed these laments were not precisely the suffering speakers who seem to be whining and groaning in utter despair. They are actually the better-organized, more energetic complainers who are obviously coping in at least this one major dimension of life; they can pull themselves together, face that blank sheet of paper, and *say* something *well*—and that's not what utterly despairing people manage to do. In other words, the *implied* speakers of the composed words are almost always to some degree less able to cope, more fully buried in the moment of negation, than the *actual* authors who penned the words. In effect, the flesh-and-blood authors are using their despairing surrogates to combat whatever immobilizing despair they are not quite feeling fully *now* but felt last week, or fear that they may feel again tomorrow. While they are quite certain, at the time of writing, that the only honest statement must be negative, they are caught in the great paradox of creativity: to speak to, or about, or against the *nothingness* is to make *something* and to demonstrate that making is one of life's possibilities.

The paradox is underlined, at least tacitly, whenever the lamenter rises to wit, or indeed to any kind of genuine eloquence. Turning fifty-nine, Kenneth Burke wrote to his lifelong friend, Malcolm Cowley, who had written of *his* symptoms of physical decline.

> What bad observer or corrupt reporter ever gave you the notion that I am "quite spry"? I am dying on my feet—and . . . the only way I can live long enough is by taking long enough to die. Meanwhile, know that I could match you, symptom for symptom, any time. . . .

Such playfulness shows too much vitality to stand for real despair.

This paradox is seemingly denied whenever the complainer simply blares out the miseries, without attempting poetic grace. Here is John Berryman, at thirty, writing to his mother: "my talent lost, like my hair, sex crumbling, like my scalp. . . . Every day I wish to die." This is about as sour as a thirty-year-old can get, even when hoping to hurt his mother. Still, one can see this poet unable to resist making *something* out of his misery: the parallel similes may be feeble, but they show more marks of coping than would an undoctored moan. And that same paradox flashed out in every despairing poem Berryman wrote—until it was decisively turned to a kind of clarity when he jumped to his death in his fifty-eighth year (see his poem, "No," page 126).

There is a story in my family of my grandfather's sister, Aunt May Talmadge, who in her eighties was asked one day by the president of the Mormon Church, "How do you feel, May?" Now, as wife of one of the twelve apostles who was just barely subordinate to President Heber J. Grant in leading the Church, she would have been expected to reply with some pious conventional cover-up. What she actually said, the family believes, was, "Heber, old age is a son-of-a-bitch."

Whenever that story is told we all laugh—in theory one does not use strong language addressing the "prophet." I don't know whether Aunt May laughed as she swore. I suspect that she must have, because I often heard her tell a good funny story about the family, sometimes in fairly strong language. But if she laughed, it was not because she thought that old age is *not* a son-of-a-bitch. She knew in her bones that she spoke the truth, just as De Gaulle spoke the truth when copying, without attribution, Chateaubriand's claim that "Old age is a shipwreck!" (In what ancient text, I wonder, did Chateaubriand find it?) There are moments in every aging life that feel unredeemable—properly described by the one adjective in Genesis, referring to the centenarian Abraham: "old and well *stricken* in age." The author of Genesis doesn't explain how the old guy, already *stricken,* managed to plug on to the age of 175, begetting children all along the way. The point is that the readers of Genesis could be expected to accept without question the word "stricken" as the proper adjective for the condition of an old man.

So we should get the losses and lamentations out on the table early, with a promise never to deny them, whatever happens in Part II.

· · ·

The most obvious losses are of everyday physical powers and pleasures. These are no doubt noticed earliest by athletes, like Lendl being called, in my epigraph, old at thirty. But even the most inactive among us begin to notice, at forty, or fifty, or sixty, that some physical powers are not what they used to be: the number of push-ups declines, the mountain trails seem steeper (especially on the way down), tennis doubles seem more attractive than singles, men find that erections come less frequently and deflate more rapidly, women experience menopause and realize that, for good or ill, the choice of having a child has been withdrawn. Just when, in the face of these changes, we begin to call ourselves *old* will depend—yes, we can say it again—on how we feel. But there will come a time when a list like the following famous one, compiled by Malcolm Cowley, will speak to each of us that unequivocal message: You are, finally, undeniably, irrevocably old.

The new octogenarian feels as strong as ever when he is sitting back in a comfortable chair. He ruminates, he dreams, he remembers. He doesn't want to be disturbed by others. It seems to him that old age is only a costume assumed for those others; the true, the essential self is ageless. In a moment he will rise and go for a ramble in the woods, taking a gun along, or a fishing rod, if it is spring. Then he creaks to his feet, bending forward to keep his balance, and realizes that he will do nothing of the sort. The body and its surroundings have their messages for him, or only one message: "You are old." Here are some of the occasions on which he receives the message:

· when it becomes an achievement to do thoughtfully, step by step, what he once did instinctively
· when his bones ache
· when there are more and more little bottles in the medicine cabinet, with instructions for taking four times a day

- when he fumbles and drops his toothbrush (butterfingers)
- when his face has bumps and wrinkles, so that he cuts himself while shaving (blood on the towel)
- when year by year his feet seem farther from his hands
- when he can't stand on one leg and has trouble pulling on his pants
- when he hesitates on the landing before walking down a flight of stairs
- when he spends more time looking for things misplaced than he spends using them after he (or more often his wife) has found them
- when he falls asleep in the afternoon
- when it becomes harder to bear in mind two things at once
- when a pretty girl passes him in the street and he doesn't turn his head
- when he forgets names, even of people he saw last month ("Now I'm beginning to forget nouns," the poet Conrad Aiken said at 80)
- when he listens hard to jokes and catches everything but the snapper
- when he decides not to drive at night anymore
- when everything takes longer to do—bathing, shaving, getting dressed or undressed—but when time passes quickly, as if he were gathering speed while coasting downhill. The year from 79 to 80 is like a week when he was a boy.

—Malcolm Cowley

Can there be any reader here—of the over-sixties, say—who cannot add to this list? Discussions of physical loss are by no means always as playful as Cowley's. François Villon may have enjoyed writing the following description of age by an old female helmet vendor, but it can hardly be called cheerful. Was Villon himself still feeling young?

This is what human beauty comes to:
The arms short, the hands shriveled,
The shoulders all hunched up.
The breasts? Shrunk again.
The buttocks gone the way of the tits.
The quim? aagh! As for the thighs,
They aren't thighs now but sticks
Speckled all over like sausages.

—François Villon

Such physical revulsion can be found in every historical period. Here is Juvenal—don't ask me how old he really was, but he had obviously experienced some aging himself.

But with what ever-present sorrow age prolongs its hour—
face deformed and hideous and unlike itself,
skin transformed, a wrinkled hide,
        cheeks in hanging folds—
behold in the Numidian shades a venerable baboon!
Young men are not all the same,
        one is handsome, one a beau,
one is stronger than another. In old age it's all the same—
lips that quiver when they speak,
        hairless head and drivelling nose,
toothless jaws that cannot chew.
                        They're a burden to their wives,
to their children—and themselves. . . .

One has a pain in the shoulder, one has back-ache,
        one has arthritis.
One has lost both his eyes—
        and the one-eyed man is king.
One has to take his food
        from the fingers of an attendant—

© DOROTHEA LANGE COLLECTION, OAKLAND MUSEUM OF CALIFORNIA. CITY OF OAKLAND. GIFT OF PAUL S. TAYLOR.

Dorothea Lange, *Ex Slave with Long Memory, Alabama, 1937.*

he who a few years ago
    used to gasp at the sight of supper
      gapes like a poor little swallow
        awaiting titbits from mum.

Worse than these troubles of body is degeneration of mind. . . .
Memory goes—the names of his household,
    the faces of friends
blotted out, or where he had dinner last night,
    his own children.
So he cuts them out of his will and leaves the lot
    to some harlot
whose practised professional look,
    the very breath of her mouth
comes of standing for years sentenced to a Circus archway.

Or should a man still retain his intellectual powers
then all the more must he suffer for what he has to endure,
the funerals of his children, the pyre of his most beloved
or of his brothers and sisters,
    and carry their lamented urn.
This above all is the cross the long-lived hero must bear
to grow old and go on growing old,
    when the rest of his world is gone,
in a house of constant mourning almost daily renewed,
in grief's perpetual shadow and black sorrowing vestments.

Nestor the king of Pylos, according to Homer, example
set for all time of age not much less than the crow's.
Happy indeed to be able in tens to number his years,
happy indeed to put off for more than a century death—
at least to have tasted new wine at the vintage so often.
But wait a little, my friend, and hear what Nestor himself
had to say of the laws of Fate and the too long skein of his life.
"Why?" he asked every friend. "What have I done
that me such cruel immortality consumes?"

                                —Juvenal

And here is Seneca:

Wherever I turn, I find indications that I am getting old. I was visiting a suburban estate of mine and complaining about the expense of the dilapidated building. My caretaker told me that this was not the fault of neglect on his part—he was doing everything, but the fact was that the building was old. In fact this house was built under my own supervision—what will happen to me, if stones of the same age as myself are in such a crumbling state? I was upset at what he said and took the next suitable opportunity for an outburst of anger. "These plane-trees are obviously not being looked after," I said. "There are no leaves on them; the branches are all knotted and parched, and the bark is flaking off those squalid trunks. That would not happen if someone was digging round them and giving them water." He swore by my own soul that he was doing whatever possible, that there was no respect in which his efforts were falling short—but they were old. Between ourselves, I planted them myself; I saw their first growth of leaves. I went up to the entrance. "Who," I said, "is that decrepit fellow? How suitable that he should have been moved to the door—he is clearly waiting to move on. Where on earth did you get hold of him? What possessed you to steal a corpse from someone else?" But the fellow said to me, "Don't you recognize me? I am Felicio—you used to give me puppets at the Saturnalia. I am the son of your manager Philositus; I was your playmate when I was little." "The man is absolutely mad," I said. "Now he has turned into a little boy and play-mate of mine. It could be true, though—he is as toothless as a child."

If we were to judge old age simply by what such famous classical Romans had to say about it, the topics we would find most used are the following, in order of frequency (take a deep breath or else skip this quotation):

dirty, sallow complexion, stinking breath, smelling like a goat, grey-haired, pot-bellied, slanting-jawed, flat-footed, untidy, shabby, sickly, ragged and aged, bent-double, shaky, loose-lipped, groaning and of damnable shape . . . ugly old thing, withered, worn-out, flabby, and fossilized.

A similar list of adjectives that our own culture applies to the elderly—a list usually somewhat subtler but just as nasty—could be constructed by anyone who watches our television sit-coms or reads our comic strips with a critical eye. When advertisers can profit from presenting as comical the spectacle of an elderly woman who has fallen and can't get up, we have come a long way from those cultures that anthropologists tell us considered it a great achievement to grow old.

As you might expect, the physical loss most often lamented is loss of sexual power—usually the male's. For centuries, one commonplace of poetry about marriage was the lament of the lusty young wife over the old husband's failure to deliver. Chaucer's Wife of Bath regales the pilgrims, in her Prologue from *The Canterbury Tales,* with an account of just how it was with three old husbands (her other two were young; Chaucer himself was "only" in his mid-forties when he wrote the *Tales,* but as I've said before, in his time that was clearly "getting on").

> They could indeed with difficulty hold
> The articles that bound them all to me;
> (no doubt you understand my simile).
> So help me God, I have to laugh outright
> Remembering how I made them work at night.
> And faith I set no store by it, no pleasure
> It was to me.

Chaucer's "Miller's Tale" and "Merchant's Tale" are full of jokes about this loss, described somewhat less jokingly by the Reeve in his Prologue.

> The strength to play that game
> Is gone, though we love foolishness the same.
> What we can do no more we talk about
> And rake the ashes when the fire is out. . . .
> Desire never fails, and that's the truth
> For even now I have a coltish tooth,
> Many as be the years now dead and gone
> Before my tap of life began to run.
> Certain, when I was born, so long ago,
> Death drew the tap of life and let it flow.
> And ever since the tap has done its task,
> And now there's little but an empty cask.
> My stream of life's but drops upon the rim.
> An old fool's tongue will run away with him
> To chime and chatter at monkey tricks that's past;
> There's nothing left but dotage at the last.

> —Geoffrey Chaucer

Though modern writers tend not to dwell quite so much on repulsive or embarrassing physical detail, many of them have seen the problem of aging pretty much as Yeats did in his most negative moods: how can I live, tied as I am to "this caricature, Decrepit age" (see page 30). For Adrienne Rich, living in such a "damaged body" presents the problem of how to connect that body's pain to "the pain of the body's world":

18

The problem, unstated till now, is how
to live in a damaged body
in a world where pain is meant to be gagged
uncured   un-grieved-over   The problem is
to connect, without hysteria, the pain
of any one's body with the pain of the body's world
For it is the body's world
they are trying to destroy forever
The best world is the body's world
filled with creatures   filled with dread
misshapen so   yet the best we have
our raft among the abstract worlds
and how I longed to live on this earth
walking her boundaries   never counting the cost

—Adrienne Rich

As Rich suggests, the losses can scarcely be seen as merely
physical. "The art of losing" extends outward indefinitely until it
can no longer feel like an art at all: it becomes swallowed in sheer
anger:

16

It's true, these last few years I've lived
watching myself in the act of loss—the art of losing,
Elizabeth Bishop called it, but for me no art
only badly-done exercises
acts of the heart forced to question
its presumptions in this world   its mere excitements
acts of the body forced to measure
all instincts against pain
acts of parting   trying to let go
without giving up   yes   Elizabeth   a city here
a village there   a sister, comrade, cat
and more   no art to this but anger

—Adrienne Rich

Such pain and anger produced by loss after loss is for some faced best with irony, as in the poem by Elizabeth Bishop that Rich alludes to:

ONE ART

The art of losing isn't hard to master;
so many things seem filled with the intent
to be lost that their loss is no disaster.

Lose something every day. Accept the fluster
of lost door keys, the hour badly spent.
The art of losing isn't hard to master.

Then practice losing farther, losing faster:
places, and names and where it was you meant
to travel. None of these will bring disaster.

I lost my mother's watch. And look! my last, or
next-to-last, of three loved houses went.
The art of losing isn't hard to master.

I lost two cities, lovely ones. And, vaster,
some realms I owned, two rivers, a continent.
I miss them, but it wasn't a disaster.

—Even losing you (the joking voice, a gesture
I love) I shan't have lied. It's evident
the art of losing's not too hard to master
though it may look like (*Write* it!) like disaster.

—Elizabeth Bishop

As "One Art" shows, the transitions from physical losses to subtler forms of loss can be considerably more diverse and interesting than any mere litany of decayed faces and limbs. While the middle-aged John Updike is waiting for his aging mother as she is examined by the doctor in a medical center, he stumbles on the signs of his, and our, condition.

In my embarrassment I wandered off and pondered the marvelous devices offered in this medical center for the use and easement of old age—canes and braces and pans and wheelchairs, and toilet seats thickened like a clubfoot's shoe, and long canelike pincers to retrieve what can no longer be bent over for: a veritable armory as complex as a medieval knight's, our Grail now simply the indefinite prolongation of life.

So far the threat is indeed physical. But Updike goes on to observe in himself

. . . the very traits that used to irritate me in men of late middle age whom I have known: a forgetfulness, a repetitiveness, a fussiness with parcels and strings, a doddery deliberation of movement mixed with patches of inattention and uncertainty that make my car-driving increasingly hazardous and—other younger drivers indicate with gestures and honking—irritating to others. I feel, also, an innocent self-absorp-

tion, a ruminativeness that makes me blind and deaf and indif-
ferent to the contemporary trends and fads that are so crucial
to the young, invested as these passing twitches are with their
own emerging identity and sexuality.

—John Updike

Fortunately, like a fair number of the authors whose portraits of
loss deserve inclusion here, Updike goes on to celebrate the compensations, as we shall see in Part II.

Samuel Johnson, who seems never to have been very young,
found it worth his while as he was turning forty to translate and
rework the Tenth Satire of Juvenal that we saw on pages 52–53.
The resulting lament helped make him famous—a fact that doesn't
fit very well with the frequent modern claim that the eighteenth
century was a time of naïve optimism.

THE VANITY OF HUMAN WISHES

Enlarge my life with Multitude of Days,
In Health, in Sickness, thus the Suppliant prays;
Hides from himself his State, and shuns to know,
That Life protracted is protracted Woe.
Time hovers o'er, impatient to destroy,
And shuts up all the Passages of Joy:
In vain their Gifts the bounteous Seasons pour,
The Fruit Autumnal, and the Vernal Flow'r,
With listless Eyes the Dotard views the Store,
He views, and wonders that they please no more;
Now pall the tastless Meats, and joyless Wines,
And Luxury with Sighs her Slave resigns.
Approach, ye Minstrels, try the soothing Strain,
Diffuse the tuneful Lenitives of Pain:
No Sounds alas would touch th'impervious Ear,
Though dancing Mountains witness'd *Orpheus* near;

Nor Lute nor Lyre his feeble Pow'rs attend,
Nor sweeter Musick of a virtuous Friend,
But everlasting Dictates croud his Tongue,
Perversely grave, or positively wrong.
The still returning Tale, and ling'ring Jest,
Perplex the fawning Niece and pamper'd Guest,
While growing Hopes scarce awe the gath'ring Sneer,
And scarce a legacy can bribe to hear;
The watchful Guests still hint the last Offence,
The Daughter's Petulance, the Son's Expence,
Improve his heady Rage with treach'rous Skill,
And mould his Passions till they make his Will.
    Unnumber'd Maladies his Joints invade,
Lay Siege to Life and press the dire Blockade;
But unextinguish'd Av'rice still remains,
And dreaded Losses aggravate his Pains;
He turns, with anxious Heart and cripled Hands,
His Bonds of Debt, and Mortgages of Lands;
Or views his Coffers with suspicious Eyes,
Unlocks his Gold, and counts it till he dies.
    But grant, the Virtues of a temp'rate Prime
Bless with an Age exempt from Scorn or Crime;
An Age that melts with unperceiv'd Decay,
And glides in modest Innocence away;
Whose peaceful Day Benevolence endears,
Whose Night congratulating Conscience cheers;
The gen'ral Fav'rite as the gen'ral Friend:
Such Age there is, and who shall wish its End?
    Yet ev'n on this her Load Misfortune flings,
To press the weary Minutes flagging Wings:
New Sorrow rises as the Day returns,
A Sister sickens, or a Daughter mourns.
Now Kindred Merit fills the sable Bier,
Now lacerated Friendship claims a Tear.
Year chases Year, Decay pursues Decay,
Still drops some Joy from with'ring Life away;

New Forms arise, and diff'rent Views engage,
Superfluous lags the Vet'ran on the Stage,
Till pitying Nature signs the last Release,
And bids afflicted Worth retire to Peace.

—Samuel Johnson

A major worry of creative folks is naturally the loss of creativity. Many poets write fine stuff lamenting their loss of the capacity to write fine stuff. Here's Philip Larkin again, at age sixty, thirty-four years after that lament we read on page 37. Does his Muse seem, as he claims, really asleep or dead?

DEAR CHARLES, MY MUSE, ASLEEP OR DEAD

Dear CHARLES, My Muse, asleep or dead,
Offers this doggerel instead
To carry from the frozen North
Warm greetings for the twenty-fourth
Of lucky August, best of months
For us, as for that Roman once—
For you're a Leo, same as me
(Isn't it comforting to be
So lordly, selfish, vital, strong?
Or do you think they've got it wrong?),
And may its golden hours portend
As many years for you to spend.

One of the sadder things, I think,
Is how our birthdays slowly sink:
Presents and parties disappear,
The cards grow fewer year by year,
Till, when one reaches sixty-five,
How many care we're still alive?
Ah, CHARLES, be reassured! For you
Make lasting friends with all you do,
And all you write; your truth and sense

We count on as a sure defence
Against the trendy and the mad,
The feeble and the downright bad.
I hope you have a splendid day,
Acclaimed by wheeling gulls at play
And barking seals, sea-lithe and lazy
(My view of Cornwall's rather hazy),
And humans who don't think it sinful
To mark your birthday with a skinful.

Although I'm trying very hard
To sound unlike a birthday card,
That's all this is: so you may find it
Full of all that lies behind it—
Admiration; friendship too;
And hope that in the future you
Reap ever richer revenue.

—Philip Larkin

Sometimes as authors talk of their lost powers, it's a bit hard to pin down precisely what they think they've lost. What is it, exactly, that John Ruskin is lamenting in this eloquent passage?

As the time of rest, or of departure, approaches me, not only do many of the evils I had heard of, and prepared for, present themselves in more grievous shapes than I had expected; but one which I had scarcely ever heard of, torments me increasingly every hour.

I had understood it to be in the order of things that the aged should lament their vanishing life as an instrument they had never used, now to be taken from them; but not as an instrument, only then perfectly tempered and sharpened, and snatched out of their hands at the instant they could have done some real service with it. Whereas, my own feeling, now, is that everything which has hitherto happened to me, or been done by me, whether well or ill, has been fitting me to take greater fortune more prudently, and do better work more thoroughly. And just when I seem to be coming out of school —very sorry to have been such a foolish boy, yet having taken a prize or two, and expecting to enter now upon some more serious business than cricket,—I am dismissed by the Master I hoped to serve, with a—"That's all I want of you, sir."

—John Ruskin

In a way, Ruskin's loss is indeed of powers he once had, yet is he not surreptitiously boasting a bit about the knowledge he has gained? I wish I could put the same question to Walter Savage Landor as he sighs, at age sixty-nine, about a whole range of failing powers that no doubt stand for the loss of poetic skill mentioned explicity in the first stanza.

Yes; I write verses now and then,
But blunt and flaccid is my pen,
No longer talkt of by young men
        As rather clever:

In the last quarter are my eyes,
You see it by their form and size;
Is it not time then to be wise?
        Or now or never.

Fairest that ever sprang from Eve!
While Time allows the short reprieve,
Just look at me! would you believe
        'Twas once a lover?

I can not clear the five-bar gate,
But, trying first its timber's state,
Climb stiffly up, take breath, and wait
        To trundle over.

Thro' gallopade I can not swing
The entangling blooms of Beauty's spring:
I cannot say the tender thing,
                        Be 't true or false,

And am beginning to opine
Those girls are only half-divine
Whose waists yon wicked boys entwine
                        In giddy waltz.

I fear that arm above that shoulder,
I wish them wiser, graver, older,
Sedater, and no harm if colder
                        And panting less.

Ah! people were not half so wild
In former days, when, starchly mild,
Upon her high-heel'd Essex smiled
                        The brave Queen Bess.

                        —Walter Savage Landor

Kelly Cherry, whose lamentation we met in the Introduction,
tries a different metaphor for the mind's losses.

Used:
The Mind-Body Problem

My mind grows cold
and sluggish. No antifreeze salesman
will ever rev her up again.
She's too old

for new parts.
She stands in an empty lot
remembering those bright, false starts
everyone else forgot

so quickly.
As snow packs in around the wheels,
she becomes her abandoned body,
knows how it feels

to reflect the winter sun
in the dent on the door
she will not open
anymore.

—Kelly Cherry

Walt Whitman, turning seventy, worries in poem after poem about his losses and about whether lamentations about them will filter into his "daily songs"—as indeed they are doing as he writes!

As I Sit Writing Here

As I sit writing here, sick and grown old,
Not my least burden is that dulness of the years, querilities,
Ungracious glooms, aches, lethargy, constipation, whimpering,
   ennui,
May filter in my daily songs.

Queries to My Seventieth Year

Approaching, nearing, curious,
Thou dim, uncertain spectre—bringest thou life or death?
Strength, weakness, blindness, more paralysis and heavier?
Or placid skies and sun? Wilt stir the waters yet?
Or haply cut me short for good? Or leave me here as now,
Dull, parrot-like and old, with crack'd voice harping, screeching?

—Walt Whitman

Walt Whitman, September 1887. Museum of the City of New York.

Often the lament is not so much for declining powers as for lost opportunities for employing them, as in Cherry's "loss of possibility." Almost everyone I know who is over sixty confesses, when I get up my courage and ask about regrets, to a deep sense of unfulfilled promise. Oh, the things I could have done, if only . . . If only I had been brought up right, if only my parents had sent me to better schools, if only I hadn't been so lazy, if only I hadn't worked so generously on other people's problems, if only I had been from another ethnic background. . . . "I've lived my whole life wrong," my aging colleague T. W. mourns. "If only I had resisted *that* temptation, or accepted *that* offer . . . but instead I've puttered about with . . ." He can go on at length like that, and it seems never to cross his mind that if the same chances arose now, he'd probably muff them once again.

I can't help thinking that the time he spends in such mourning is simply a further waste of his still lively gifts. As he talks I catch myself feeling superior: you won't find *me* indulging in that kind of petty lament. Yet I can too easily fall into the same aridities: If only I had gone to a good high school, where I might have learned some history, some languages, some math, some philosophy. If only I hadn't spent so much time trying to decide just how much of Mormonism to scuttle or cling to. If only I had finished writing that novel, *Farrago,* which was a post-modernist work at least thirty years ahead of its time . . . or taken that job in Washington. I even catch myself lamenting, as I struggle with thumb position on the cello, the years spent on the clarinet through high school and college. I could have learned thumb position *then!*

That's the form the lament takes in those of us who were slow starters. For those who were in any degree prodigies, the complaints can be even sharper. Consider Kenneth Burke, who must once have been just about the most obviously brilliant and learned college freshman Columbia University ever saw, and who became for many of us the most important American critical theorist of this century, a man who certainly had his fair share of acclaim. Listen to how it felt to him, as he meditated at age seventy-one on the death of the then much more famous Edmund Wilson.

© ELKE WALFORD, FOTOWERKSTATT HAMBURGER KUNSTHALLE/ALTBAU.

Camille Corot, *Old Man Playing Cello* (1874). Hamburger Kunsthalle.

Wilson is a lucky guy. I envy anybody who no longer has to worry about this damnable choice between hanging on and clearing out. Yes, he was competent. But I think that a part of his reputation was due to his being a journalist. His great trick, lots of the time, was not in being a critic, but in giving you the news about books—and people could read the news without reading the books. I believe *Axel's Castle* [Wilson's first book of criticism] came out the same year as *Counter-Statement* [Burke's first critical work]. An ironic fact is that, after the article I did on him for the *New Republic* and showed to him but never published (owing to our battles about my refusal to cut it in half), he did his thing on *The Turn of the Screw*. Without knowing of his, I did one, too . . . I couldn't do a damn thing about mine. For it was enough like his for people to say that I owed mine to his. And the piece was so much my own, the thought was intolerable. So, it still rots in manuscript. . . . The article on him by Roger Straus . . . makes me realize all over again what an incompetent mess I . . . ah, shit. [Burke's ellipses]

Ah, yes: ah, shit. "That new list of the best poets of 1991 doesn't include me." "Why doesn't that bastard Simperson mention me in his book on Swinburne?" "What an incompetent mess I have made of my career!" If only, if only . . . If only I hadn't wasted time before my powers began to decline. Here is Cowley, competing in his turn with his close friend Burke.

The big problem now is that with somewhat declining vigor . . . somewhat increasing deafness, and sleepiness in the afternoons, and a less sharp eye for other people's conduct—I still have to create or put together a body of work while there is still time.

The fear that one is no longer any good at what one used to be good at, or that "I will cease to be/Before my pen has gleaned my teaming brain" (that's how Keats's sonnet about the fear begins) is increased in old age by the discovery, often spared to the young, that nobody's praise can be trusted. It's true that nobody's praise can be fully trusted at any age. But with aging, the grounds for trust necessarily diminish. You begin to notice, or to suspect, that when people praise you they often do it with an implied qualifier. "You're looking wonderfully young." "Your last book was really marvelous (considering you wrote it at seventy-five)." "I loved your speech (in fact I can't think of anyone over eighty who can speak as well)." One's response is complicated by the feeling that sometimes these days you actually do a better job than you could have done at fifty or forty or thirty: you know more, you have had more experience with various pitfalls. But you cannot know, when people say good things about you, whether they mean them or not.

I note an article in *The Chronicle of Higher Education* praising "A Self-taught Folk Artist Who Began Drawing at 85." I look at the illustrations and find myself thinking, "Well, for someone who started at eighty-five, yeah, these are O.K." And then I think of my forty years of apologizing for my cello playing with the same line: "You know, I didn't take it up until I was thirty-one." "You play marvelously—*considering!*"

Sometimes the reservations are quite clear on the surface: "You really maintain your figure very well." That "really" lets me know that what the flatterer means is "as compared with other people your age." Young women tell you you look wonderful, that they just love your shirt and tie, that they admire your hair—and you hear the qualifications pouring out beneath the praise: for an old duffer like you, you do pretty well; you've kept quite a lot of your hair. "I only hope I can be as vigorous as you are when I'm your age." Well, all I can do is think, but not say, "I hope so too." But as I think it, must I not also think further along the lines that Laurence Lerner traces with lovely interweaving?

It Is Time

It is time that I admitted I am old
—Or getting old, at least. It's time my friends
Stopped challenging me to feats of memory
Or games of tennis. They're not so young themselves.
Every sinew is charged with the same message:
The creak of a disintegrating body.

By now I catch every hint dropped by my body.
I can hear it saying: Look, I am just as old
As you are. When the brain sends a message
With its usual insistence to its deferential friends,
Muscle and limb, they do not bestir themselves
As eagerly as they've done within living memory.

I'll console myself by inspecting my memory.
Where are those great achievements of my body—
The times my legs found their way by themselves
Over wet rock; among yew trees, red and old
And twisted; in soft sand, far from my friends,
Exhausted and frightened, unable to send a message?

Now listen: this is an important message.
Find some way to lodge it in memory.
Visible in the averted eyes of friends
Are the facts you haven't admitted about your body.
Mark how their voices are different from of old:
Their words twist awkwardly around themselves.

Can the facts of a life somehow arrange themselves
To convey, for once, a significant message?
Not just: Once I was young and soon I shall be old.
Not just: Sitting on the pot is my earliest memory.
But the sense that in the structure of your body
You and the world, at last, have made friends.

Sooner or later even my closest friends
Will think about nothing except themselves.
Each will have trouble enough with his own body,
His head filled with one repetitive message:
"One day you will not even be a memory,
And admitting this will not keep you from growing old."

This is an old story: loss of friends,
Loss of memory; these words themselves,
With their empty message, outlasting soul and body.

—Laurence Lerner

As Lerner says, the loss of powers and opportunities and trust is made worse by the loss of friends. They die off. They die off at an increasing rate, "Till," to quote Larkin again,

. . . when one reaches sixty-five,
How many care we're still alive?

Some years ago, long before I'd thought very much about all this, I met my sixty-seven-year-old colleague James Cate in the hall and asked—knowing that he had been retired against his wishes: "What are you up to these days, Jimmie?"

His sour/witty reply, delivered in his heavy Southern accent, is almost a poem in itself:

"Conductin' funerals!"

Here's Wordsworth, writing in his mid-sixties:

EXTEMPORE EFFUSION
UPON THE DEATH OF JAMES HOGG

When first, descending from the moorlands,
I saw the Stream of Yarrow glide
Along a bare and open valley,
The Ettrick Shepherd was my guide.

When last along its banks I wandered,
Through groves that had begun to shed
Their golden leaves upon the pathways,
My steps the border minstrel led.

The mighty Minstrel breathes no longer,
'Mid mouldering ruins low he lies;
And death upon the braes of Yarrow,
Has closed the Shepherd-poet's eyes:

Nor has the rolling year twice measured,
From sign to sign, its stedfast course,
Since every mortal power of Coleridge
Was frozen at its marvellous source;

The rapt One, of the godlike forehead,
The heaven-eyed creature sleeps in earth:
And Lamb, the frolic and the gentle,
Has vanished from his lonely hearth.

Like clouds that rake the mountain-summits,
Or waves that own no curbing hand,
How fast has brother followed brother,
From sunshine to the sunless land!

Yet I, whose lids from infant slumbers
Were earlier raised, remain to hear
A timid voice, that asks in whispers,
"Who next will drop and disappear?"

Our haughty life is crowned with darkness,
Like London with its own black wreath,
On which with thee, O Crabbe! forth-looking,
I gazed from Hampstead's breezy heath.

As if but yesterday departed,
Thou too art gone before; but why,
O'er ripe fruit, seasonably gathered,
Should frail survivors heave a sigh?

Mourn rather for that holy Spirit,
Sweet as the spring, as ocean deep;
For Her who, ere her summer faded,
Has sunk into a breathless sleep

No more of old romantic sorrows,
For slaughtered Youth or love-lorn Maid!
With sharper grief is Yarrow smitten,
And Ettrick mourns with her their Poet dead.

—William Wordsworth

Lord Byron, whom we met as he turned thirty-six (page 38), was able even in his mid-twenties to sound like an old man bereft of all former friends and feeling "alone on earth." His readers could not understand how one so young could make "Childe Harold" sound so troubled by aging:

> What is the worst of woes that wait on age?
> What stamps the wrinkle deeper on the brow?
> To view each loved one blotted from life's page,
> And be alone on earth, as I am now.
> Before the Chastener humbly let me bow,
> O'er hearts divided and o'er hopes destroy'd:
> Roll on, vain days! full reckless may ye flow,
> Since Time hath reft whate'er my soul enjoy'd,
> And with the ills of Eld mine earlier years alloy'd.

If one can believe Charles Lamb's lament, written when he was still in his early twenties, every last one of his friends has already "departed," alive or dead.

THE OLD FAMILIAR FACES
(January, 1798)

I have had playmates, I have had companions,
In my days of childhood, in my joyful school-days,
All, all are gone, the old familiar faces.

I have been laughing, I have been carousing,
Drinking late, sitting late, with my bosom cronies,
All, all are gone, the old familiar faces.

I loved a love once, fairest among women;
Closed are her doors on me, I must not see her—
All, all are gone, the old familiar faces.

I have a friend, a kinder friend has no man;
Like an ingrate, I left my friend abruptly;
Left him, to muse on the old familiar faces.

Ghost-like, I paced round the haunts of my childhood.
Earth seemed a desart I was bound to traverse,
Seeking to find the old familiar faces.

Friend of my bosom, thou more than a brother,
Why wert not thou born in my father's dwelling?
So might we talk of the old familiar faces—

How some they have died, and some they have left me,
And some are taken from me; all are departed;
All, all are gone, the old familiar faces.

—Charles Lamb

The loss is naturally worst when it is of the one best friend.
Here is Kenneth Burke again, writing of the death of his wife.

Dear Malcolm,

Poor Shorty is gone. She left in her sleep last night. At
least, she escaped the year or two of hell-on-earth that was in
store for her, had the disease run its "normal" course.

A good deal of my reason for existence has gone with her.
And, I fear, also a sizable portion of my reason. For her companionship worked constantly to redeem me from my nature
as a born loser.

It is so good to be surrounded by one's family at such a
time. It does help.

There will be no funeral. This is our understanding; this
is our deal; and it goes for all of us. We will deal with our
grief in our own way.

In a tangle,
K.B.

Almost as painful as the actual death of friends is the perception of their physical decline—indeed their loss of the graces that helped charm you into friendship years ago. Browning, in his early forties, speaks through the voice of one who has just heard "A Toccata of Galuppi's":

"Dust and ashes!" So you creak it, and I want the heart to scold.
Dear dead women, with such hair, too—what's become of all the gold
Used to hang and brush their bosoms? I feel chilly and grown old.

Thomas Hardy, at eighty-eight (!), gives us no reason to suspect that he has any need for an alter ego like Browning's. The sour, witty unmasking here seems unequivocally his own.

FAITHFUL WILSON

"I say she's handsome, by all laws
Of beauty, if wife ever was!"
Wilson insists thus, though each day
The years fret Fanny towards decay.

Though we tend to be more tolerant of, and perhaps to ignore, the decline of our own physical charms, it can be even more painful when we see it in the light of our unflagging desire to be loved. Robert Graves felt it, in his early sixties, and expressed it with a self-portrait as unflattering as his worst enemy might have drawn:

The Face in the Mirror

Gray haunted eyes, absent-mindedly glaring
From wide, uneven orbits; one brow drooping
Somewhat over the eye
Because of a missile fragment still inhering,
Skin deep, as a foolish record of old-world fighting.

Crookedly broken nose—low tackling caused it;
Cheeks, furrowed; coarse gray hair, flying frenetic;
Forehead, wrinkled and high;
Jowls, prominent; ears, large; jaw, pugilistic;
Teeth, few; lips, full and ruddy; mouth, ascetic.

I pause with razor poised, scowling derision
At the mirrored man whose beard needs my attention,
And once more ask him why
He still stands ready, with a boy's presumption,
To court the queen in her high silk pavilion.

—Robert Graves

Thomas Hardy beat him to it, about three decades before penning "Faithful Wilson":

I Look into My Glass

I look into my glass,
And view my wasting skin,
And say, "Would God it came to pass
My heart had shrunk as thin!"

For then, I, undistrest
By hearts grown cold to me,
Could lonely wait my endless rest
With equanimity.

But Time, to make me grieve,
Part steals, lets part abide;
And shakes this fragile frame at eve
With throbbings of noontide.

—Thomas Hardy

But it is high time for me to drop all this intrusive accompaniment, at least for the time being. Here is a brief miscellany of uninterrupted laments for the losses, beginning with Matthew Arnold's comprehensive summary of where we have been so far. Since Arnold was still in his mid-forties when he wrote it, with almost two decades of productive life ahead of him, we can see it as further evidence that "growing old" is better thought of as "growing older."

Growing Old

What is it to grow old?
Is it to lose the glory of the form,
The lustre of the eye?
Is it for beauty to forego her wreath?
—Yes, but not this alone.

Is it to feel our strength—
Not our bloom only, but our strength—decay?
Is it to feel each limb
Grow stiffer, every function less exact,
Each nerve more loosely strung?

Yes, this, and more; but not
Ah, 'tis not what in youth we dream'd 'twould be!
'Tis not to have our life
Mellow'd and soften'd as with sunset-glow,
A golden day's decline.

'Tis not to see the world
As from a height, with rapt prophetic eyes,
And heart profoundly stirr'd;
And weep, and feel the fulness of the past,
The years that are no more.

It is to spend long days
And not once feel that we were ever young;
It is to add, immured
In the hot prison of the present, month
To month with weary pain.

It is to suffer this,
And feel but half, and feebly, what we feel.
Deep in our hidden heart
Festers the dull remembrance of a change,
But no emotion—none.

It is—last stage of all—
When we are frozen up within, and quite
The phantom of ourselves,
To hear the world applaud the hollow ghost
Which blamed the living man.

—Matthew Arnold

2 SAMUEL
Chapter 19, Verses 32–39

Now Barzillai was a very aged man, even fourscore years old:
and he had provided the king of sustenance while he lay at
Mahanaim, for he was a very great man.

And the king said unto Barzillai, Come thou over with
me, and I will feed thee with me in Jerusalem.

And Barzillai said unto the king, How long have I to live,
that I should go up with the king unto Jerusalem?

I am this day fourscore years old: and can I discern between good and evil? can thy servant taste what I eat or what

I drink? can I hear any more the voice of singing men and singing women? wherefore then should thy servant be yet a burden unto my lord the king?

Thy servant will go a little way over Jordan with the king: and why should the king recompense it me with such reward?

Let thy servant, I pray thee, turn back again, that I may die in mine own city, and be buried by the grave of my father and of my mother. . . .

And all the people went over Jordan. And when the king was come over, the king kissed Barzillai, and blessed him; and he returned unto his own place.

—2 Samuel 19:32–39

He who carries on too long dies disgusted; his old age is painful, he is in need. Wherever he turns, he sees enemies; he is plotted against. He has not gone away in time; he has not had a fine death. . . . Old age, you are the enemy of humankind, you ravage all the beauty of its forms, you transform the splendour of its limbs into heaviness, speed into slowness.

—Menander, as reported by Minois

O sovreign my Lord! Oldness has come; old age has descended. Feebleness has arrived; dotage is here anew. The heart sleeps wearily every day. The eyes are weak, the ears are deaf, the strength is disappearing because of weariness of heart, and the mouth is silent and cannot speak. The heart is forgetful and cannot recall yesterday. The bone suffers old age. God is become evil. All taste is gone. What old age does to men is evil in every respect.

—Ptah Hotep, vizir to Pharaoh Izezi (around 2450 b.c., at age 110, in the fifth dynasty)

FROM *THE BOOK OF COMMON PRAYER*

For when thou art angry all our days are gone: we
      bring our years to an end, as it were a tale that
      is told.
The days of our age are three score years and ten;
      and though men be so strong that they come to
      fourscore years: yet is their strength then but
      labour and sorrow; so soon passeth it away, and
      we are gone.

FROM ALICE JAMES'S DIARY
FEBRUARY 2ND, 1892

This long slow dying is no doubt instructive, but it is disappointingly free from excitements: "naturalness" being carried to its supreme expression. One sloughs off the activities one by one, and never knows that they're gone, until one suddenly finds that the months have slipped away and the sofa will never more be laid upon, the morning paper read, or the loss of the new book regretted; one revolves with equal content within the narrowing circle until the vanishing point is reached, I suppose.

Vanity, however, maintains its undisputed sway, and I take satisfaction in feeling as much myself as ever, perhaps simply a more concentrated essence in this curtailment. If I could concern myself about the fate of my soul, it would give doubtless a savor of uncertainty to the fleeting moments, but I never felt so absolutely uninterested in the poor, shabby, old thing. The fact is, I have been dead so long and it has been simply such a grim shoving of the hours behind me as I faced a ceaseless possible horror, since that hideous summer of '78, when I went down to the deep sea, its dark waters closed over me and I knew neither hope nor peace; that now it's only the shrivelling of an empty pea pod that has to be completed.

A little while ago we had rather an amusing episode with the kind and usually understanding Tuckey [James's doctor], who was led away into assuring me that I should live a good bit still—I was terribly shocked and when he saw the havoc that he wrought, he reassuringly said: "but you'll be comfortable, too," at which I exclaimed: "Oh I don't care about that, but boo-hoo, it's so *inconvenient!*" and the poor man burst into a roar of laughter. I was glad afterwards that it happened, as I was taken quite by surprise, and was able to test the sincerity of my mortuary inclinations. I have always *thought* that I wanted to die, but I felt quite uncertain as to what my muscular demonstrations might be at the moment of transition, for I occasionally have a quiver as of an expected dentistical wrench when I fancy the actual moment. But my substance seemed equally outraged with my mind at Tuckey's dictum, so mayhap I shall be able to maintain a calm befitting so sublimated a spirit!—at any rate there is no humbuggy "strength of mind" about it, 'tis simply physical debility, 'twould be such a bore to be perturbed.

March 4th, 1892

I am being ground slowly on the grim grindstone of physical pain, and on two nights I had almost asked for K.'s lethal dose, but one steps hesitantly along such unaccustomed ways and endures from second to second; and I feel sure that it can't be possible but what the bewildered little hammer [i.e., her heart] that keeps me going will very shortly see the decency of ending his distracted career; however this may be, physical pain however great ends in itself and falls away like dry husks from the mind, whilst moral discords and nervous horrors sear the soul. These last, Katharine has completely under the control of her rhythmic hand, so I go no longer in dread. Oh the wonderful moment when I felt myself floated for the first time into the deep sea of divine *cessation,* and saw all the dear old mysteries and miracles vanish into vapour! That first experience doesn't repeat itself, fortunately, for it might become a seduction.

Katharine can't help it, she's made that way, a simple embodiment of Health, as Baldwin called her, "the New England Professor of doing things."

—Alice James, *The Diary*

He who has lived sixty years has lived all that lay before him. . . . If he desires food, he cannot eat as he is used to. If his heart desires his wife, for her the time of desire never comes.

—Egyptian papyrus, first century A.D.

HENRY JAMES TO W. MORTON FULLERTON

34 De Vere Gardens W.
25*th* February 1897

My dear Fullerton.

Forgive a communication, very shabby and superficial. It has come to this that I can address you only through an embroidered veil of sound. The sound is that of the admirable and expensive machine that I have just purchased for the purpose of bridging our silences. The hand that works it, however, is not the lame *patte* which, after inflicting on you for years its aberrations, I have now definitely relegated to the shelf, or at least to the hospital—that is, to permanent, bandaged, baffled, rheumatic, incompetent obscurity. May you long retain, for yourself, the complete command that I judge you, that I almost see you, to possess, in perfection, of every one of your members. Your letter about my contribution to that flurry of old *romantique* dust was as interesting to me as some of the sentiments it breathed couldn't fail to make it. All thanks for it—all thanks for everything; even for the unconscious stroke by which, in telling me how you have grown up since the day when her acquaintance (Mme. Sand's) was inevitable, you add to the burden of my years. Of course I knew you had; but I am cursed with a memory of my earlier time that beguiles me with associations at which I am able to see young friends, even the most "arrived," address a blank, un-influenced stare. If I could wish you to be anything in any particular but what you are, I should wish you to have been young when *I* was. Then, don't you see, you would have known not only the mistress of *ces messieurs,*—you would almost, perhaps, have known *me.* And now you will never catch up! Neither shall I, however, my dear Fullerton—since it comes to that—if I give too much time to our gossip. I have so much less of that than you to do it in. . . .

—Henry James

MY PICTURE LEFT IN SCOTLAND

I Now thinke, Love is rather deafe, then blind,
    For else it could not be,
        That she,
Whom I adore so much, should so slight me,
    And cast my love behind:
I'm sure my language to her, was as sweet,
        And every close [test] did meet
    In sentence, of as subtile feet,
        As hath the youngest Hee,
  That sits in shadow of *Apollo's* tree.
  Oh, but my conscious feares,
        That flie my thoughts betweene,
    Tell me that she hath seene
    My hundreds of gray haires,
    Told seven and fortie yeares.
  Read so much wast, as she cannot imbrace
  My mountaine belly, and my rockie face,
And all these through her eyes, have stopt her eares.

—Ben Jonson

FROM *PARADISE LOST*

"I yield it just," said *Adam,* "and submit.
But is there yet no other way, besides
These painful passages, how we may come
To Death, and mix with our connatural dust?"
    "There is," said *Michael,* "if thou well observe
The rule of 'Not too much,' by temperance taught
In what thou eat'st and drink'st, seeking from thence
Due nourishment, not gluttonous delight,
Till many years over thy head return:
So may'st thou live, till like ripe Fruit thou drop
Into thy Mother's lap, or be with ease
Gathered, not harshly plucked, for death mature:
This is old age; but then thou must outlive
Thy youth, thy strength, thy beauty, which will change
To withered, weak, and grey; thy Senses then,
Obtuse, all taste of pleasure must forgo
To what thou hast, and for the Air of youth,
Hopeful and cheerful, in thy blood will reign
A melancholy damp of cold and dry
To weigh thy spirits down, and last consume
The Balm of Life."

—John Milton

SONG

Oh roses for the flush of youth,
    And laurel for the perfect prime;
But pluck an ivy branch for me
    Grown old before my time.

—Christina Rossetti (composed as a
song when she was only nineteen)

OLD AGE

Another winter,
And here am I,
By the side of the stove,
Dreaming that a woman might dream of me,
That I might bury in her breast
A secret she would not mock;
Dreaming that in my fading years
I might spring forth as light,
And she would say:
This light is mine;
Let no woman draw near it.

      Here by the side of the stove,
      Another winter,
      And here am I,
      Spinning my dreams and fearing them,
      Afraid her eyes would mock
      My bald, idiotic head,
      My greying, aged soul,
      Afraid her feet would kick
      My love,
      And here, by the side of the stove,
      I would be lightly mocked by woman.
Alone,
Without love, or dreams, or a woman,
And tomorrow I shall die of the cold within,
Here, by the side of the stove.

—Buland al-Haydari

What, then, is life if love the golden is gone? What is pleasure?
  Better to die when the thought of these is lost from my heart:
the flattery of surrender, the secret embrace in the darkness.
  These alone are such charming flowers of youth as befall
women and men. But once old age with its sorrows advances
  upon us, it makes a man feeble and ugly alike,
heart worn thin with the hovering expectation of evil,
  lost all joy that comes out of the sight of the sun.
Hateful to boys a man goes then, unfavored of women.
  Such is the thing of sorrow God has made of old age.

—Mimnermus

From Euripides' *Herakles*

Youth is what I love
Age weighs on my head like a burden
Heavier than the rock of Etna
It draws a curtain of darkness before my eyes.
Not the wealth of an Eastern throne,
Not a palace full of gold
Would I take in exchange for youth.
Youth is most precious in prosperity,
Most precious in poverty;
Age is miserable, tainted with death:
I hate it. Away with it, let the sea swallow it!
Why must the curse of age fall on men's homes and cities?
Away to the winds with it!

—Euripides

From *Oedipus at Colonus* (*the chorus*)

None but a fool would scorn life that was brief.
None but a fool would cleave to life too long:
For when an old man draws his lingering breath
Beyond his fitting season, pain and grief,
The harsh years' harvesting, upon him throng
And joy is but a phantom of the past.
Then soon or late the doom of Hades, death,
Comes with no dance, no lyre, no marriage song,
And all alike delivers at the last. . . .
Not to be born surpasses thought and word.
Next best is to have seen the light of day
And then to return whence we came.
Once the light foolishness of youth is past,
What trouble is beyond the range of man?
What heavy burden must he not bear?
Jealousy, faction, quarrelling, fighting—
The bloodiness of war, the grief of war.
And in the end he comes to a strengthless age,
Abhorred by all men, alone, without friends,
Lonely in that complete twilight
In which he must live with every bitterness.
This is the case, not just for me,
But for this blind and ruined old man.
Consider some desolate northern beach;
The breaking waves make flow
This way and that in the storms of winter;
So it is with him;
The wild force breaking over him
From head to foot, and on and on forever;
Now from the setting of the sun,
Now from the noonday glow;
Now from the night and the north.

—Sophocles (written in his late eighties)

JOGGER

Entered in an event
For which he hasn't trained,

His body is pushing beyond
The limits of the body:

That flat, muscular stomach
So many sit-ups drew taut

(But his sweatsuit is shredded by moths)
Swags over his belt in a bulge.

And what's going on with his features?
They each have a will of their own.

They've decided they're not fully grown,
They're getting too big for themselves—

The nose is thicker, the skin
On the chin wants to hang, so hangs down.

And the face is creased and padded
In a parcel of furrows and folds.

Somewhere under addenda
Of belly and rump and jowl

Strides the crisp youth and slender
Who used to run a quick mile

As if he were still the same
Though what he ran toward became him.

He's within hail of the finish,
His record is writ in flesh.

—Daniel Hoffman

The epistolary part of my [New Year's] "festivities" this year will be cursory. Why? Because my friends are not very numerous any more. And because my work seems a little sour to me. And then, these "festivities" only recall the absentees —and in particular, Pierre, our Marguerite . . . My wits are lacking today. Is this because I'll be seventy-seven in thirty-one days? Or because I have just been arranging in what I call my cemetery of affections the little pen drawing of Marguerite's tombstone? A little of both . . .

—Colette, *Letters*

LAST HOUSECLEANING

Empty, my mind, of web and dust;
Of diamond too, and sharpened gold;
Of everything, and if you must
Of my own self, grown old and cold.

—Mark Van Doren

FROM *AS WE ARE NOW*

Days have gone by. It must be October, mid-October I think, because the leaves are flying fast. The great maples are skeletons against the sky. The beeches are still a marvelous greenish-yellow, a Chinese yellow, I have always thought. Pansy, now the nights are cold, sometimes comes to sleep with me, and slips out (clever cat) before anyone has stirred. The only time I weep is when she is there, purring beside me. I, who longed for touch, can hardly bear the sweetness of that little rough tongue licking my hand.

There is nothing to say any longer. And I am writing only because Lisa is to bring Eva today. Harriet doesn't want them to see me as I was—dirty hair I hardly bothered to comb, an old woman, a grotesque miserable animal. She washed my hair and it is drying now. This time she was gentle, thank God. I suppose she can be because I am just a passive bundle. She brought me a clean and, for once, properly ironed nightgown. I do not dress very often any more. I feel safer in bed.

It must be mid-November. The leaves are all gone. Harriet found Pansy on my bed and now locks her out every night. The walls close in on every side. I do not remember things very clearly . . . is my brother John still alive? Where has Anna gone?

—May Sarton

ECCLESIASTES, CHAPTER 1

The words of the Preacher, the son of David, king in Jerusalem.

2 Vanity of vanities, saith the Preacher, vanity of vanities; all is vanity.

3 What profit hath a man of all his labour which he taketh under the sun?

4 One generation passeth away, and another generation cometh: but the earth abideth for ever.

5 The sun also ariseth, and the sun goeth down, and hasteth to his place where he arose.

6 The wind goeth toward the south, and turneth about unto the north; it whirleth about continually, and the wind returneth again according to his circuits.

7 All the rivers run into the sea; yet the sea is not full; unto the place from whence the rivers come, thither they return again.

8 All things are full of labour, man cannot utter it: the eye is not satisfied with seeing, nor the ear filled with hearing.

9 The thing that hath been, it is that which shall be; and that which is done is that which shall be done: and there is no new thing under the sun.

10 Is there any thing whereof it may be said, See, this is new? it hath been already of old time, which was before us.

11 There is no remembrance of former things; neither shall there be any remembrance of things that are to come with those that shall come after.

12 I the Preacher was king over Israel in Jerusalem.

13 And I gave my heart to seek and search out by wisdom concerning all things that are done under heaven: this sore travail hath God given to the sons of man to be exercised therewith.

14 I have seen all the works that are done under the sun; and, behold, all is vanity and vexation of spirit.

15 That which is crooked cannot be made straight: and that which is wanting cannot be numbered.

16 I communed with mine own heart, saying, Lo, I am come to great estate, and have gotten more wisdom than all they that have been before me in Jerusalem: yea, my heart had great experience of wisdom and knowledge.

17 And I gave my heart to know wisdom, and to know madness and folly: I perceived that this also is vexation of spirit.

18 For in much wisdom is much grief: and he that increaseth knowledge increaseth sorrow.

—Ecclesiastes 1

Readers will have noticed that through all of these powerful lamentations runs that paradox with which I began: The better you express the losses, the less you've lost. To hold back the losses, to capture the beauty that was, is to turn the loss into something else: a triumph of the imagination. Here is Wallace Stevens, in his early seventies, offering us his *Lebensweisheitspielerei,* which can be crudely translated as a "dalliance on the subject of wisdom about life and its losses." Since his portrait of the "dwindled sphere" in effect hails its grandeur, it makes a telling transition to the consolations and celebrations of Part II.

LEBENSWEISHEITSPIELEREI

Weaker and weaker, the sunlight falls
In the afternoon. The proud and the strong
Have departed.

Those that are left are the unaccomplished,
The finally human,
Natives of a dwindled sphere.

Their indigence is an indigence
That is an indigence of the light,
A stellar pallor that hangs on the threads.

Little by little, the poverty
Of autumnal space becomes
A look, a few words spoken.

Each person completely touches us
With what he is and as he is,
In the stale grandeur of annihilation.

—Wallace Stevens

PHOTO #20056.

G. Wharton James, *Gabrielino Woman at San Gabriel, CA* (ca. 1900).
Courtesy of the Southwest Museum, Los Angeles.

Wright Morris, *Uncle Harry Entering Barn.*
The Home Place, 1947.

PART II

Cures, Consolations, Celebrations

To know how to grow old is the master work of wisdom, and one of the most difficult chapters in the great art of living.
—Henri Frédéric Amiel

I wish once more to mention
That I like what I see.
—Gertrude Stein
at fifty eight

I'm growing old, I delight in the past!
—Matisse at seventy-one

To be seventy years young is sometimes far more cheerful and hopeful than to be forty years old.
—Oliver Wendell Holmes

In the past few years I have made a thrilling discovery . . . that until one is over sixty one can never really learn the secret of living.
—Ellen Glasgow

I had forgiven enough
That had forgiven old age.
—William Butler Yeats

From the letters which were written [when I was young], I can easily see what advantages and disadvantages come with every time of life, to balance those of earlier and later periods. In my fortieth year, I was as clear and decided on some subjects as at present, and, in many respects, superior to my present self; yet, now, in my eightieth, I possess advantages which I would not exchange for these.
—Goethe

What, then, is to be done? What do our guides, openly didactic or shy, have to say about that? How are we to live with all of these losses, many of them inevitable? How, other than simply by expressing our feelings about them as vividly as possible, do we cope with where we are and where we're headed?

Perhaps the first thing to be said is that most older people most of the time are not as miserable as Part I might seem to imply. Those who are what Bernice Neugarten calls the "young-old"—retired but still relatively healthy—do often experience some "golden" years. According to Ronald Blythe, an "Age Concern" survey in 1976 "proved that old people are far happier than their image suggests." Only about seven or eight in a hundred said that they felt lonely most of the time and that they had nothing to look forward to.

Well, maybe so. Faced by such claims on a bad day, I would certainly want to have a look at the actual questions asked. In any case, we all know that sooner or later everyone is likely, at least on occasion, to join those miserable loners, and then the question "What is to be done?" cuts as sharply as ever.

The strongly confident, unequivocal answers to such a question—you should do just this, you should think just that—are mostly not much fun to read, though we'll look at some of the better ones in a moment. Their authors either haven't faced aging honestly enough to earn our confidence or they have bought into some formula that may have helped *them* but that may feel inaccessible to *us:* join this church, give up that bad habit, follow this or that diet, chant this or that mantra.

The others—the less preachy affirmations that honestly acknowledge the troubles they spring from—are too diverse to allow neat ordering. In a way, the best ones seem to say "Don't put me into some collection where I'll be labeled with terms that may fit others. I don't consider myself a decisive statement of 'loss' or of 'cure' or of 'consolation' or of 'celebration.' Just read me, read *me* alone, because in me you'll find justice done to the complexities of how it feels to age." They flatly repudiate any efforts, by me or by the more systematic gerontologists, to classify us who are "older" into a few stereotypes.

In fact it is their variety—their rich resistance to classification —that has impressed me most. They underline Carol Bly's warning against thinking about "characters aged 61–100 as if they were only case studies to do with old age, not people."

So my first temptation, in turning from the losses, was simply to honor the idiosyncrasies of the following "answers" by printing them accurately and lovingly—alphabetically, perhaps, or even helter-skelter, like the miscellaneous items at the end of Part I: Here is this fine one, and here's another, and then here is this beauty, and this one . . . Isn't this lovely, all this exuberant creative stuff blooming out of the muck and mire and gloom we've just been through? Who would want to invent pigeon-holes for the subtlety of Wallace Stevens's "Lebensweisheitspielerei" (page 95), or of Adrienne Rich's "One Life"?

ONE LIFE

A woman walking in a walker on the cliffs
recalls great bodily joys, much pain.
Nothing in her is apt to say
My heart aches, though she read those words
in a battered college text, this morning
as the sun rose. It is all too
mixed, the heart too mixed with laughter
raucousing the grief, her life
too mixed, she shakes her heavy
silvered hair at all the fixed
declarations of baggage. I should be dead and I'm alive

don't ask me how; I don't eat like I should
and still I like how the drop of vodka
hits the tongue. I was a worker and a mother,
that means a worker and a worker
but for one you don't pay union dues
or get a pension; for the other
the men ran the union, we ran the home.
It was terrible and good, we had more than half a life,
I had four lives at least, one out of marriage
when I kicked up all the dust I could
before I knew what I was doing.
One life with the girls on the line during the war,
yes, painting our legs and jitterbugging together
one life with a husband, not the worst,
one with your children, none of it just what you'd thought.
None of it what it could have been, if we'd known.
We took what we could.
But even this is a life, I'm reading a lot of books
I never read, my daughter brought home from school,
plays where you can almost hear them talking,
Romantic poets, Isaac Babel. A lot of lives
worse and better than what I knew. I'm walking again.
My heart doesn't ache; sometimes though it rages.

—Adrienne Rich

The trouble is that to throw them all into one hopper would
violate my own feelings. They don't all set out to do the same
thing, and they don't all fit my various moods with equal warmth
and comfort. Though many of them insist on being left in the final
hopper, Part III, "A Further Harvest," others fall without too
much kicking and screaming into three groups: cures, consolations, and celebrations. Works in each group range widely in the
degree to which they openly exhort or claim to teach. Some modern critics have claimed that a poem's quality depends on how well
it avoids (or disguises) any kind of didacticism. Without troubling

to explain just why I think these critics wrong—I've done that in
The Company We Keep—I've felt free to honor the skillful exhorters as much as those who aspire to a purer surface.

Whether the cures, consolations, and celebrations are openly
preachy or not, the dividing lines are fuzzy, and I invite you as you
read to play the game of re-sorting: just what happens to our
experience of Frost's "Provide, Provide," for example (page 132),
if we think of it not as some kind of recommendation for a cure
but as a celebration, or even as an implicit lament belonging in
Part I?

In ordering the pieces roughly according to a plot of affirmation—from those I see as least helpful to those that do most for me
—I don't intend a ranking of literary quality from feeblest to
strongest, any more than I see a flat difference in quality between
parts I and II. Though the truths they offer count, poems earn only
part of their quality with those truths. Many a poem I might label
"true" or "correct" or even "wise" can move me much less than
some sour snarl—one of A. E. Housman's gems, perhaps—to
which I may want to say "Yes, you're beautiful and I want to
preserve you, *but . . .*" or "You've said that too many times already," or even "Come off it, man; you've got it all wrong. Try
thinking it through one more time—but thank you, anyway, for
calling the shots as you see them and for putting it all so well!"

Some readers will surely want to reject the organization of the
comfortings that follow. They might want to ask, in a "post-
modernist" move that would throw me back upon my own principles: Is this entire book attempting to be a celebration? If, as is
obvious, it somehow embraces most of the poems of Part II more
wholeheartedly than most of those of Part I, and if it culminates in
celebration, is the book then at heart a denial of loss? Or perhaps
even a disguised religious exhortation?

If it is indeed some kind of celebration, which of the "answers"
we're coming to does it really celebrate most vigorously? I can
only reply: "If that question could be easily answered, I could have
eliminated at least two-thirds of the book." There is no one answer
to any question about aging. It is the glory of our human history

—and here the word "our" is intended to cover all cultures that have a heritage of poetry about growing older—that it provides us not with any one answer but with manifold experiences that in their very existence "demonstrate" gains as well as losses.

So here they are, then, four kinds of "answers" to Part I:

Denials, assertions that simply ignore what we have seen. These are the whistlers-in-the-dark who would use words as a narcotic or analgesic: a path through cheerfulness to oblivion. Though I give only a few of these, I suspect that if we collected all of the published statements about how to deal with old age, this kind would constitute the largest heap. (Of course if we could collect *all* of the statements, published and *spoken,* the picture might then be reversed. The largest heap would then probably be made up of plain, unadorned laments like my great-aunt's "old age is a son-of-a-bitch" and Chateaubriand's "old age is a shipwreck.")

Cures, offered by those who recognize the losses and consider them, at least for the moment, as symptoms of a disease to be combatted. They use words as an alternative to the vast medical research programs that now promise, at least once a week in the "Lifestyle" section of the morning newspaper, some new cure for this or that "geriatric" condition or symptom. Most of them urge us to drag ourselves out of bed, get dressed in our Sunday suits, and go out there and *do something,* anything, rather than sit around lamenting the inevitable. For them, the problems of old age are essentially like those everybody meets in earlier stages of life: the challenge is to take circumstances that can be threatening and *make* something of them, since experience shows that vigorous work or play can absorb us and make life *for the time being* worth living.

Consolations, offered by would-be comforters as some sort of mitigation or compensation, with or without some degree of denial or suppression of the horrors. There is no cure, they seem to say, but why fuss about that, when if you will just open your eyes and heart, you will find this and this and this comfort? You may, indeed, discover ways in which being older has made life better.

Celebrations, sung by those who rejoice in the condition of *being* old or *growing* old. These *embrace life while aging,* seeing it not as a curse or a disease but as a different kind of (often ambiguous) blessing. They search their experiences and discover genuine advantages to being older, and celebrate the discovery of new territory to be explored. Implicitly muttering, "The future be damned," they sing about the present in tones that may sometimes sound—to the really miserable—like dishonest denial. The difference is that their celebrations are enacted in full acknowledgment of all that we heard in Part I.

Let me repeat that these groups flow in and out of one another in elusive ways. My placements shift under me as my own moods change from day to day. A proffered cure may seem one day like annoying denial and the next like just what will do the trick. To publish a celebration is implicitly to exhort others to take up a new cure. To recommend any action as a cure is to imply that life is still, even in its aging forms, worth celebrating.

We can dramatize this point by returning for a moment to Part I to ask the authors we met there, "Just what did you energetic Jeremiahs think you were giving us when you sent your fine-tuned words to the printer? Were you trying to make us feel worse? Were you merely trying to make us admire you for your honesty, even if your blunt statements made us feel suicidal? Or did you feel, in your troubled hearts, that the gift of an honest statement by a fellow sufferer was itself the best friendship-offering you could create?"

"What did you, Christina Rossetti, imagine yourself as doing when you formalized your pain in the following poem? You were, after all, not yet twenty-five, writing not for publication. And what were you hoping to do for or to us, your readers, when you published it in your aging decline as you reached thirty-two?"

DEAD BEFORE DEATH

Ah! changed and cold, how changed and very cold!
　With stiffened smiling lips and cold calm eyes:
　Changed, yet the same; much knowing, little wise;
This was the promise of the days of old!
Grown hard and stubborn in the ancient mould,
　Grown rigid in the sham of lifelong lies:
　We hoped for better things as years would rise,
But it is over as a tale once told.
All fallen the blossom that no fruitage bore,
　All lost the present and the future time,
All lost, all lost, the lapse that went before:
So lost till death shut-to the opened door,
　So lost from chime to everlasting chime,
So cold and lost for ever evermore.

—Christina Rossetti

"What did you, Yusuf al-Khal, as a modern Arabic poet (born 1917), think you were doing for *me* when you portrayed, at the horrifyingly old age of fifty-seven, the 'chill wave' overwhelming our faces?"

OLD AGE

We wipe the chill wave from our faces
And tell ourselves the story of spring:
How the breeze smiles,
The birds sing,
The trees dance;
How the seed stretches its roots in the soil
And bears fruit.
We tell ourselves the story of autumn,
When the shadows are bowed
And evening lengthens,
Then suddenly a star appears,

Or a moon shines,
And when the fence falls,
The fields stretch out naked,
As far as the eye can see.
We tell ourselves the story of summer,
Which comes to us on the wings
Of a warm melody,
Or the leap of a joyous swallow,
While we gather the crop,
Or recall the halt of a cloud,
Here and there in the distance.
We wipe the chill wave from our faces
And tell ourselves the seasons' story.
But the wave sinks deep in our veins and vanishes.
We think it vanishes,
Yet, suddenly, it appears—
Here, in a hair turned white,
There, in a lip turned dry.

—Yusuf al-Khal

To me the answer to such questions depends largely on just how fully imagined each lament is. A blurted complaint—"Old age stinks"; "To be old is to be miserable"—offers the miserable oldster at best a bit of company, and sour company at that. Add the slightest touch of rhetorical richness—of wit or clever invective or moving description—and the author offers me not just companionship but a picture of one way to cope. "Old age is a son-of-a-bitch"—now there my great aunt showed herself as someone making something of her condition; she was enlivening her present, regardless of its miseries and regardless of what the future was to bring. Hearing her curse, even if I had not known her in life as someone fun to talk with, I'd imagine her as someone I'd like to visit with for a while.

When Chateaubriand said "Old age is a shipwreck," he was

not just complaining; he was celebrating the pleasures of metaphor, still available to him in his old age *now*—and thus to us, *now*, with him long in his grave. A beautifully constructed lament, like Rossetti's, a powerfully angry or witty evocation of the miseries, like Yusuf al-Khal's, reveals a form of mastery that in itself copes with the horrors.

Indeed most of the laments in Part I were created—I must underline again—with a force that refutes their surface message: "I am old, feeble, miserable, dying." Well, yes, I believe you, since you insist. But how, then, do you manage to pull yourself together and offer me a poem, or even just a metaphor, about it. When you put verbal vitality into your lamentation, something quite different occurs from your surface meaning—as we saw with the vicious descriptions of physical loss by Villon and Juvenal, or the more muted confessions to other losses by Kelly Cherry and Matthew Arnold.

When you put your whole soul into it like that, I cannot quite believe in your total helpless and hopeless gloom—not in the same way I believe flat statements like, "I am utterly miserable" or "I am going to commit suicide." In one way, of course, I believe you more: you have made me feel your misery more actively, and so have drawn me into it. On the other hand, even when your poem is not your very best work, it shows you obviously alive, wonderfully alive, more alive than some of the ostensibly more cheerful folks we turn to now.

What do the denials look like? The Golden Years are Golden. The best is yet to be. Life begins at forty . . . or fifty . . . or sixty . . . or seventy. . . . When the going gets tough, the tough get going. And once again: You're only as old as . . .

The shoddiest of such denials are no doubt the advertisements for various ways to disguise aging. Bloomingdale's offers the world a full-page ad for "Youth-Lift," a product of the "Skin Care Institute." The page is dominated by a line drawing of the head and shoulders of a woman who looks about twenty but who is lightly marked with little red dots at the points where aging is likely to show; these are labeled "Brow Furrows" (24 dots),

"Crow's-Feet" and "Eye Lines" (14 dots), and on down the drawing to "Laugh Lines," "Neck Lines" and "Décolletage," each with its share of threatening red blotches. As a flat denial of the truth revealed by these dots, we see at the top of the page, in large letters, the full truth:

BECAUSE IT DOESN'T MATTER HOW OLD YOU ARE. IT ONLY MATTERS HOW OLD YOU LOOK. *YOUTH LIFT.* IT SMOOTHS AWAY THE APPEARANCE OF WRINKLES *INSTANTLY.*

This line of defense is not new; it does not depend on an advertising culture that is aware of the new floods of aging folk. An Egyptian papyrus of more than four thousand years ago promises a "book for making an old man into a youth," and then delivers only a recommendation of "oil of fenugreek for baldness and unsightly spots." Everyone knows about the legend of the fountain of youth, which Ponce de León searched for in the New World, only to discover that center for well-heeled retirees, Florida. Did those who hoped to find the fountain hope for genuine youth, or did they believe that "it only matters how old you *look*"?

Though we could no doubt find bare-faced (or wrinkle-faced) deniers in every culture, ancient or modern, most advisers in previous cultures sound more like Seneca: not "disguise your wrinkles," but "change your attitude."

Men are disturbed not by things but by principles and notions which they form concerning things. Death, for instance, is not terrible else it would have appeared so to Socrates. But the terror consists in our notion of death that it is terrible.

If we substitute "old age" for "death," we find here the kind of advice that we'll meet a lot of later on: not strict denial but an effort at psychological or spiritual therapy.

Obviously, most non-commercial deniers really hope to console us, or even to celebrate honestly the new possibilities that aging uncovers. They want passionately to resist moaning about the losses; they want to help us say "yes" to life—even to life as lived in old age. When they are reporting a genuine pleasure in the moment of writing, or even a sense of happiness about their lot, we no doubt can rejoice with them, even when they make us cringe, as they often do, by their banality. But when they simply close their eyes and assert, "I'm younger than I ever was," their effort to console will usually fail. They make us feel the way a friend of mine felt after reading an early draft of these consolations, without having read first the lamenters of Part I. Tom O'Shea, an amateur boxer and high school teacher, wrote in a letter to me,

> I hope your book will help me deal with the *terror* of aging, the loss of energy, humor, orgasm. Do you know I'm starting to find it *difficult* to get out of bed in the morning. Working out is not a mindless pleasure any more; it's an effort, a chore, a forcing. . . . I'm not interested in reading sentimental slop —especially poems—about *my life, my death.* It's maddening to see a serious, personal, immanent state not seriously, honestly, bravely, addressed. I want you to be harsh, naked, alone. I want you to listen to a bag lady as well as Byron. . . . I want you to help me negotiate the mine-field . . . (Sorry, that mine-field metaphor doesn't work out.) . . . Do you plan to include modern statements like "Our Mother gives birth astride the grave"?

When we're feeling like that, almost any form of affirmation may seem like denial. Even when we're in more positive moods, statements that obviously lie about reality will fail. When the character Hardcastle, in Goldsmith's *She Stoops to Conquer,* says, "I love every thing that's old; old friends, old times, old manners, old books, old wines," we know that he's talking through his hat— that is, he's being exposed by Goldsmith as a "character"—amiable, perhaps even lovable, but a bit obtuse. No thoughtful person could really mean what Hardcastle says; we can too easily think of old things that nobody loves: old soup, old garbage, decrepit horses, ramshackle furniture, old (that is, failing) eyesight and hearing, burnt-out electrical appliances, rotting cut flowers. . . .

At best he has offered us an eccentricity that simply shuts out reality; there can be little consolation in it.

Here's a little poem that was written by a lively affirmer, Minnie Hodapp, at the age of ninety-two. Despite my admiration for its sprightly good cheer, it gives me less comfort than many a poem that openly curses.

I HAVEN'T LOST MY MARBLES YET!

Beloved Senior Citizens,
   I wonder if you know
That I was just a babe in arms
   Some ninety years ago.
And one thing more, lest I forget
   I haven't lost my marbles yet!

I take my walk around the block
   And pause to greet a friend,
With such a stock in goodly talk
   Our visits never end.
I have no time to fume or fret;
   I haven't lost my marbles yet!

I sometimes feel a bit bereft
   Of youthful eyes and ears—
But when I think of all that's left
   My trouble disappears.
So life goes on without upset
   'Cause I ain't lost no marbles yet.

Oliver Wendell Holmes (the elder) is equally banal, but his skill with verse perhaps rescues him:

THE OLD PLAYER

Call him not old, whose visionary brain
Holds o'er the past its undivided reign.
For him in vain the envious seasons roll
Who bears eternal summer in his soul.

—Oliver Wendell Holmes

Our literature is full of such blunt assertions, and we rightly make heroes of those who, like Holmes, carry on into their eighties asserting that "To be seventy years young" is not to be old. But we all know that to be seventy is *less often* cheerful and hopeful than to be forty, and Holmes's statement, uttered (with tongue in cheek?) at a birthday party, simply ignores that fact.

Of course we have no way of knowing just how anyone has really felt when writing words of good cheer. Can the eighty-five-year old Cornaro, the sixteenth-century Venetian nobleman, really mean it when he makes the following boast?

I think my present age, although it is very advanced, the pleasantest and the finest of my life. I would not exchange my age and my life for the most flourishing youthfulness.

Admittedly such a claim does depend on what kind of child hood or youth is being compared. I know people who might well mean what Cornaro says, because only with maturity have they escaped appalling circumstances or neuroses. Still, as we move toward celebration, we must keep always in mind those innumerable folk who find intolerable the prospect of joining Cornaro among the eighty-year-olds.

American popular culture four centuries later is full of Cornaro's kind of shaky comfort:

Darling, I am growing old,
Silver threads among the gold
Shine upon my brow to-day;
Life is fading fast away. . . .

But, my darling, you will be, will be,
Always young and fair to me.
Yes, my darling, you will be, will be,
Always young and fair to me.

Here in the cooling light of this collection, it is hard to believe that anybody ever took a claim like that as anything but tosh, whether in song or in life. Always young and fair? Always? Of course the claim is only that it will seem that way "to me." Nevertheless, the speaker—in my experience of this one it has always been a *singer*—surely knows very well that if he (could the song work if sung by a woman?) and his faithful love stay together, one of them will face a time when the other one is no longer even in the wildest effort of the imagination young and fair. On the other hand, singing in that earlier time when old age was less likely than death, the singer might better have echoed the old joke: Aging wife to aging husband, "If one of us ever dies, I think I'll move to California."

I want to be fair here. It would be absurd to wish that the deniers had not written at all. Indeed one might well pray for the guts and skill to write anything well into one's nineties, as Minnie Hodapp was when she wrote "Marbles."

With all that said, these admirable folks still present two problems. We know that they are probably hiding a lot from us: we can hardly believe that Minnie Hodapp as she wrote the poem had lost *none* of her marbles, whatever we may think the "marbles" are. Though wealthy and ostensibly healthy, even Cornaro must have had mornings when it was not as easy to get out of bed as it had been at thirty.

More important—at least for those of us who are looking for

stuff worth reading—such writers too often fail to embody, in their craft, literary analogues to the obstacles overcome in life. Everything is made just too easy. Even when, like Hodapp and Holmes, they take the trouble to create verse rather than simply blurting "All's well," it's as if they thought about the art of affirmation about the way Mark Twain's Emmeline Grangerford thought about the art of mourning. As Buck explains to Huck Finn,

> She could rattle off poetry like nothing. She didn't ever have to stop to think. He said she would slap down a line, and if she couldn't find anything to rhyme with it would just scratch it out and slap down another one, and go ahead. She waren't particular. She could write about anything you choose to give her to write about just so it was sadful.

Change the last word to "cheerful" and you will have described too many would-be comforters.

In contrast, when I read the following complex romp by James Merrill, I haven't a doubt that he is grappling honestly both with what he knows about aging and with the problems of constructing an original, intricately crafted poem. He indeed inspirits me, by requiring me to rise to my interpretative best to follow both his complex thought and his wonderfully subtle music.

LOSING THE MARBLES
for John Malcolm Brinnin

1
Morning spent looking for my calendar—
Ten whole months mislaid, name and address,
A groaning board swept clean . . .
And what were we talking about at lunch? Another
Marble gone. These latter years, Charmides,
Will see the mind eroded featureless.

Ah. We'd been imagining our "heaven"'s.
Mine was to be an acrobat in Athens
Back when the Parthenon—
Its looted nymphs and warriors pristine
By early light or noon light—dwelt
Upon the city like a philosopher,
Who now—well, you have seen.

Here in the gathering dusk one could no doubt
"Rage against the dying of the light."
But really—rage? (So like the Athens press,
Breathing fire to get the marbles back.)
These dreamy blinkings-out
Strike me as grace, if I may say so,
Capital punishment,
Yes, but of utmost clemency at work,
Whereby the human stuff, ready or not,
Tumbles, one last drum-roll, into thyme,
Out of time, with just the fossil quirk
At heart to prove—hold on, don't tell me . . . What?

2
Driving its silver car into the room,
The storm mapped a new country's dry and wet—
Oblivion's ink-blue rivulet.
Mascara running, worksheet to worksheet
Clings underfoot, exchanging the wrong words.
The right ones, we can only trust will somehow
Return to the tongue's tip,
Weary particular and straying theme,
Invigorated by their dip.

Invigorated! Gasping, shivering
Under our rough towels, never did they dream—!
Whom mouth-to-mouth resuscitation by
Even your *Golden Treasury* won't save,
They feel their claim
On *us* expiring: starved to macron, breve,
Those fleshless ribs, a beggar's frame . . .
From the brainstorm to this was one far cry.

Long work of knowing and hard play of wit
Take their toll like any virus.
Old timers, cured, wade ankle-deep in sky.

Meanwhile, come evening, to sit
Feverishly restoring the papyrus.

3

body, favorite
            gleaned,   at the
                        vital
            frenzy—

act and moonshaft, peaks
                        stiffening
            Unutter[able]
        the beloved's

                                slowly
            stained in the deep   fixed
                        summer nights
            or,

                scornful   Ch[arm]ides,
                        decrepitude
            Now, however, that
        figures also

                            body everywhere
                    plunders and
    what we cannot—from the hut's lintel
                flawed

                                white as
    sliced turnip   the field's brow.
            our old
        wanderings

home   palace, temple,
    having   of those blue foothills
        no further   clear
                fancy[.]

4

Seven ages make a crazy quilt
Out of the famous web. Yet should milk spilt
(As when in Rhetoric one's paragraph
Was passed around and each time cut in half,
From eighty words to forty, twenty, ten,
Before imploding in a puff of Zen)
White out the sense and mutilate the phrase,
My text is Mind no less than Mallarmé's.
My illustration? The Cézanne oil sketch
Whose tracts of raw, uncharted canvas fetch
As much per square inch as the fruit our cloyed
Taste prizes for its bearing on the void.
Besides, Art furnishes a counterfeit
Heaven wherein ideas escape the fate
Their loyal adherents—brainwashed, so to speak,
By acid rain—more diatribes in Greek—
Conspicuously don't. We diehard few
Embark for London on the QE2.
Here mornings can be spent considering ours
Of long ago, removed and mute, like stars
(*Un*like vociferous Melina, once
A star herself, now Minister of Stunts).
Removed a further stage, viewed from this high wire
Between the elegiac and the haywire,
They even so raise questions. Does the will-
To-structural-elaboration still
Flute up, from shifting dregs of would-be rock,
Glints of a future colonnade and frieze?
Do higher brows unknit within the block,
And eyes whose Phidias and Pericles
Are eons hence make out through crystal skeins
Wind-loosened tresses and the twitch of reins?
Ah, not for long will marble school the blood
Against the warbling sirens of the flood.
All stone once dressed asks to be worn. The foam-

Pale seaside temple, like a palindrome,
Had quietly laid its plans for stealing back.
What are the Seven Wonders now? A pile
Of wave-washed pebbles. Topless women smile,
Picking the smoothest, rose-flawed white or black,
Which taste of sunlight on moon-rusted swords,
To use as men upon their checkerboards.

5
The body, favorite trope of our youthful poets . . .
    With it they gleaned, as at the sibyl's tripod,
        insight too prompt and vital for words.
            Her sleepless frenzy—

cataract and moonshaft, peaks of sheer fire at dawn,
    dung-dusted violets, the stiffening dew—
        said it best. Unutterable too
            was the beloved's

save through the index of refraction a fair, slowly
    turned head sustained in the deep look that fixed him.
        From then on veining summer nights with
            flickering ichor,

he had joined an elite scornful—as were, Charmides,
    your first, chiseled verses—of decrepitude
        in any form. Now, however, that
            their figures also

begin to slip the mind—while the body everywhere
    with peasant shrewdness plunders and puts to use
        what we cannot—from the hut's lintel
            gleams one flawed image;

another, cast up by frost or earthquake, shines white as
    sliced turnip from a furrow on the field's brow.
        Humbly our old poets knew to make
            wanderings into

homecomings of a sort—harbor, palace, temple, all
   having been quarried out of those blue foothills
      no further off, these last clear autumn
         days, than infancy.

6
Who gazed into the wrack till
Inspiration glowed,
Deducing from one dactyl
The handmaiden, the ode?

Or when aphasia skewered
The world upon a word,
Who was the friend, the steward,
Who bent his head, inferred

Then filled the sorry spaces
With pattern and intent,
A syntax of lit faces
From the impediment?

               No matter, these belated
Few at least are back. And thanks
To their little adventure, never so
Brimming with jokes and schemes,
Fussed over, fêted
By all but their fellow saltimbanques—
Though, truth to tell,
Who by now doesn't flip
Hourly from someone's upper story
("That writer . . . no, on shipboard . . . wait . . . Charmides?")
And come to, clinging to the net?
And yet, and yet
Here in the afterglow
It almost seems
Death has forgotten us
—As the old lady said to Fontenelle.

And he,

A cautionary finger to his lip:
"Shh!"

7

After the endless jokes, this balmy winter
Around the pool, about the missing marbles,
What was more natural than for my birthday
To get—from the friend whose kiss that morning woke me—
A pregnantly clicking pouch of targets and strikers,
Aggies and rainbows, the opaque chalk-red ones,
Clear ones with DNA-like wisps inside,
Others like polar tempests vitrified . . .
These I've embedded at random in the deck-slats
Around the pool. (The pool!—compact, blue, dancing,
Lit-from-beneath oubliette.) By night their sparkle
Repeats the garden lights, or moon- or starlight,
Tinily underfoot, as though the very
Here and now were becoming a kind of heaven
To sit in, talking, largely mindless of
The risen, cloudy brilliances above.

—James Merrill

I go about the world showing Merrill's poem to other people.
I read it aloud, again and again. My own mildly increasing "mar-
ble-loss" is illuminated by it—and even made to seem funny. He
thus becomes a boon companion, by revealing no denial whatever
and by being so skillful. This suggests once again that the most
fully realized curses and laments of Part I almost deserve to be here
in Part II, so consoling is it to see folks dancing their dirges so
delightfully.

Still, we must say on behalf of even the least adroit of verbal
deniers that, unlike some of the lamenters, they are *trying* to make
things better, not worse. At the very least they must be helpful for
many readers as narcotics; if they were not, our libraries wouldn't

be full of them. Should we reject poetic substitutes for alcohol or Prozac, aspirin or Advil, Valium or Seconal? Can we afford to give up a resource that to any degree will narcotize painful losses—and with no harmful side-effects?

If you chant as mantra "Every day I get younger, not older" or "It only matters how old you feel" (or even "how old you *look*," as in the Bloomingdale's ad) or "To be old is delicious, golden, the best thing that ever happened to me," you may come to moments when you and your body will actually believe it. We have lots of evidence by now that many illnesses retreat when threatened by an aggressively cheerful and resistant soul. There's good evidence that affirmers live longer than deniers. But even if that's so, it's too late in this book to practice simple denial. Only those who have skipped or repressed our lamenting and cursing in Part I can now pretend that old age is uniformly golden and glorious.

If we reject denial, what can we say about those who think of old age as some kind of disease and offer us cures?

There is in fact only one possibility for complete cure: death. This side of that cure-which-is-not-a-cure, we can only hope, if we're a certain kind of hoper, that medical research has found or will find some cure for this or that *symptom* of age, postponing the ultimate decline.

During the years I've been assembling this collection, doctors have announced, almost daily, this or that new cure for this or that curse of old age. If they keep it up, we can reasonably hope that somebody will soon discover how to cure our diverticulosis, our prostatitis, our frequent common colds, our wrinkles, our aching joints. The morning paper tells me, quite regularly, that this or that operation or medicine will—how shall I put it?—"set me up —for life"? Why should I resist it? At the very worst it could only cure me by killing me. But if I took the cure, would it give me any real help in my effort to feel right about my aging? Maybe, for a day or two. But then . . .

Or I could join the crazy worshippers of cryonics: get myself frozen, so that "I" can wait for a couple of centuries and awake to find cures for *all* my ills. Such a choice requires a lot more faith in biological progress than I can muster. More and more people seem to manage such faith, hoping for a kind of physical immortality, absurdly ignoring the powerful claims of satirists like Swift that physical immortality would be the worst imaginable curse (pages 32–33).

What remains, in the way of cure? Well, there is always suicide: Join the Hemlock Society and, like Bruno Bettelheim, buy yourself some pills and a plastic bag. One such "cure" or another is easily available, if one doesn't delay the choice too far into one's dotage. But for our purposes here, it is curious that there seem to be few good poems—at least in our culture—that seriously contemplate this path, let alone recommend it. Could John Berryman be said to recommend suicide in "No," written not long before he jumped to his death, not yet sixty?

No

She says: *Seek help!* Ha-ha Ha-ha & Christ.
Gall in every direction, putrid olives,
stench of the Jersey flats, the greasy clasp
crones in black doorways afford their violent clients.

A physicist's lovely wife grinned to me in Cambridge
she only liked, apart from getting gamblers hot
& stalk out on them, a wino for the night
in a room off Scollay Square, a bottle, his efforts

Dust in my sore mouth, this deafening wind,
frightful spaces down from all sides, I'm pale
I faint for some soft & solid & sudden way out
as quiet as hemlock in that Attic prose

with comprehending friends attending—
a certain reluctance but desire here too,
the sweet cold numbing upward from my burning feet,
a last & calm request, which will be granted.

What we mainly have are a few prosy arguments that under certain extreme circumstances suicide is the way to go.

Obviously the best arguments against suicide as a cure for aging will be the consolations and celebrations we turn to now. One of those will be humor, so let's buck up our spirits with a bit of it—a famous response to the temptation to end it all:

RÉSUMÉ

Razors pain you;
Rivers are damp;
Acids stain you;
And drugs cause cramp.
Guns aren't lawful;
Nooses give;
Gas smells awful;
You might as well live.

—Dorothy Parker

Langston Hughes plays with the same ironies in his late forties:

LIFE IS FINE

I went down to the river,
I set down on the bank.
I tried to think but couldn't.
So I jumped in and sank.

I came up once and hollered!
I came up twice and cried!
If that water hadn't a-been so cold
I might've sunk and died.

But it was
Cold in that water
It was cold!

I took the elevator
Sixteen floors above the ground.
I thought about my baby
And thought I would jump down.

I stood there and I hollered!
I stood there and I cried!
If it hadn't been so high
I might've jumped and died.

But it was
High up there!
It was high!

So since I'm still here livin',
I guess I will live on.
I could've died for love—
But for livin' I was born.

Though you may hear me holler,
And you may see me cry—
I'll be dogged, sweet baby,
If you gonna see me die.

Life is fine!
Fine as wine!
Life is fine!

—Langston Hughes

Perhaps a majority of those who tell us that aging need not be taken lying down say something like this: "You can cure your condition if you just stop thinking about it and embrace some attitude or action that in itself demonstrates the value of your life." Just about every piece from here on could be described as an exhortation, sometimes blatant and preachy, sometimes so subtle as to be hard to figure out: "If you want to cope with aging, here is what you must do: think *this* way or take up *this* activity." As Beauvoir puts it in *The Coming of Age,*

> There is only one solution if old age is not to be an absurd parody of our former life, and that is to go on pursuing ends that give our existence a meaning—devotion to individuals, to groups or to causes, social, political, and to intellectual or creative work. . . . One's life has value so long as one attributes value to the life of others, by means of friendship, indignation, compassion.

Let's look at the action folks first, those who in effect say, "Pull up your socks! Get out into the world and *do* something with your life. And don't wait: do it now! Stop wasting your time lamenting: in some form of action lies your salvation, and you'll be surprised to find that in many domains you can act now more effectively than you could twenty years ago."

Here's B. F. Skinner, with a "self-management" program offered in his book *Enjoy Old Age:*

> If you cannot find the kind of work you have done in the past, try something new. It need not be something that appeals to you at first sight. . . . Look for something you *can* do; the chances are, you will begin to enjoy it as soon as you do it well. If frustration or failure bothers you, start slowly. . . . You may be surprised at how easily you move on to longer hours and harder work.

We'll look more closely at "harder work" in a moment. For now the point is the more general one: "Do something, anything other than just bemoaning your condition." Almost two hundred years before Skinner, that great wise sufferer Samuel Johnson wrote in his early sixties to his long-time friend John Taylor in pretty much the same "behaviorist" terms:

> I am sorry to find . . . that your health is in a state so different from what might be wished. The Langleys impute a great part of your complaints to a mind unsettled and discontented. I know that you have disorders, though I hope not very formidable, independent of the mind, and that your complaints do not arise from the mere habit of complaining. Yet there is no distemper, not in the highest degree acute, on which the mind has not some influence, and which is not better resisted by a cheerful than a gloomy temper. I know that you do not much [two words obscured; my editorial guess is that they were *"enjoy reading"*], yet I would have you read when you can settle your attention but that perhaps will be not so often as is necessary to encrease the general cheerfulness of Life. If you could get a little apparatus for chimestry or experimental philosophy it would offer you some diversion, or if you made some little purchase at a small distance, or took some petty farm into your own hands, it would break your thoughts when they become tyrannous and troublesome, and supply you at once with exercise and amusement.

Such exhorters sometimes weaken their point by implying, as Marya Mannes does in *More in Anger,* that it may just be too late. "The process of maturing is an art to be learned, an effort to be sustained. By the age of fifty you have made yourself what you are, and if it is good, it is better than your youth." Well, yes, but what if my past was a poor one, and the character I became as I lived it weak and—when viewed honestly now—even contemptible? What if I have botched things right up until today, when I woke to my first realization that I'm getting older? Many an adviser ignores the question, echoing Cicero's claim that the best preparation for old age is a productive, prudent, even wise youth —early decades that build the right kind of character.

LAELIUS. Now, Cato, if you don't mind: you have reached, so to speak, the end of a long journey which we too must make. We should like to see what sort of place it is that you have come to.

CATO. I'll do the best I can, Laelius. Again and again I have been in the company of men of my age (you know the old saying about "birds of a feather!") and have heard them complaining—Salinator, for example, and Albinus, men who had held the consulship and were as old as I. They were always weeping and wailing, first, because they had been cut off from the pleasures of life—and what, they thought, is life without its pleasures?—and, second, because the people who used to seek out their company were now avoiding them. It always seemed to me that they were finding fault with the wrong thing. Why! If old age were to blame for their unhappiness, then I would be having the same experiences, and so would all other older people. Yet I have known many men who, in their later years, never uttered a word of complaint. They were not at all disturbed at being released, as they put it, from the chains of lust, and they didn't think that people were avoiding them, either. No, no! In every case when men complain like that, the fault is one of character, not of years. Old men who exercise self-discipline, who are not peevish or insensitive, find old age quite bearable; but peevishness and insensitivity are a blight to any man, no matter what his age.

Cicero goes on:

You must remember, to be sure, that in all my discourse I have been praising an old age that is firmly based on a foundation laid in the earlier years. [It is a] sorry old age that had to make speeches in its own defense. Gray hair and wrinkles do not without further ado proclaim a man influential; no, influence is rather the end-product of a lifetime honorably spent.

No doubt about it. Maybe we don't even have to insist on the "honorably"—just make it "shrewdly," or "wisely." Is that the point of Robert Frost's warning, published at the age of sixty?

PROVIDE, PROVIDE

The witch that came (the withered hag)
To wash the steps with pail and rag,
Was once the beauty Abishag,

The picture pride of Hollywood.
Too many fall from great and good
For you to doubt the likelihood.

Die early and avoid the fate.
Or if predestined to die late,
Make up your mind to die in state.

Make the whole stock exchange your own!
If need be occupy a throne,
Where nobody can call *you* crone.

Some have relied on what they knew;
Others on being simply true.
What worked for them might work for you.

No memory of having starred
Atones for later disregard,
Or keeps the end from being hard.

Better to go down dignified
With boughten friendship at your side
Than none at all. Provide, provide!

—Robert Frost

COPYRIGHT KARSH.

Robert Frost

Yes, yes, of course we should provide. But just what we should provide, or what we should have provided long ago, varies from adviser to adviser. For Frost the advice seems—to use his own word—rather "hard": unless you have the unlikely fortune to be contented with your own knowledge and integrity, you'd better start accumulating money and power—and "boughten friendship" —now.

A. E. Housman is equally gloomy, and seemingly even surer, at sixty-three, that the best preparation for age is an un-illusioned or even disillusioned youth.

> I to my perils
>   Of cheat and charmer
>   Came clad in armour
>   By stars benign.
> Hope lies to mortals
>   And most believe her,
>   But man's deceiver
>   Was never mine.
>
> The thoughts of others
>   Were light and fleeting,
>   Of lovers' meeting
>   Or luck or fame.
> Mine were of trouble,
>   And mine were steady,
>   So I was ready
>   When trouble came.

Thomas Hardy said it, too, at eighty-six!

He Never Expected Much
A Consideration on My Eighty-sixth Birthday

Well, World, you have kept faith with me,
        Kept faith with me;
Upon the whole you have proved to be
        Much as you said you were.
Since as a child I used to lie
Upon the leaze and watch the sky,
Never, I own, expected I
        That life would all be fair.

'Twas then you said, and since have said,
        Times since have said,
In that mysterious voice you shed
        From clouds and hills around:
"Many have loved me desperately,
Many with smooth serenity,
While some have shown contempt of me
        Till they dropped underground.

"I do not promise overmuch,
        Child; overmuch;
Just neutral-tinted haps and such,"
        You said to minds like mine.
Wise warning for your credit's sake!
Which I for one failed not to take,
And hence could stem such strain and ache
        As each year might assign.

                    —Thomas Hardy

The truth is that if you want to exhort me to do something about my old age now, you'd better concentrate on what I *can* do, not on what I should have done. And that's the move made by the comforters who to me are most convincing. Here is how Ronald Blythe talks about it in his sensitive book *The View in Winter*.

Perhaps, with full-span lives the norm, people may need to learn how to be aged as they once had to learn to be adult. It may soon be necessary and legitimate to criticise the long years of vapidity in which a healthy elderly person does little more than eat and play bingo. . . . To fall into purposelessness is to fall out of all real consideration. Many old people reduce life to such trifling routines that they cause the rest of us to turn away in revulsion.

The magazine *Modern Maturity* is full of such sensible advice, often no more specific than that. B. F. Skinner recommends specific daily tasks that will postpone or compensate for the losses. Even the title of his book is worded as a command. Chant it— *Enjoy Old Age, Enjoy Old Age*—and before you can say "principles of behavior modification," you'll feel euphoric. Skinner does not offer prose poems about how aging feels, but he does offer excellent advice about how to combat the stereotyped roles assigned to the elderly and how to avoid lapsing into self-pity.

All the world's a stage, and you are not the first to play the part of Old Person. The audience has seen the play thousands of times and knows your lines better than you do. The role you are expected to play is not flattering. The Old Persons who have walked the boards before you have been crotchety, stingy, boastful, boring, demanding, and arrogant. They have complained of their illnesses and many other things. You may be surprised at how easy it is to play the part that way. . . . And just as an audience will laugh at everything a great co-median says, so it will interpret your slightest gesture as the skillful portrayal of a familiar, and usually unpleasant, character.

It would be wrong to conclude that the role you play must represent the real you. If the traits of stinginess, boastfulness, and so on are inborn, not much can be done about them; if their frequent presence can be traced to special features of the world of old people, the problem is easier to solve. If you are not displaying your character, but are merely being a good character actor, you may play a different role as convincingly under different circumstances.

Skinner then offers specific commonplace but useful advice about how to change the circumstances that elicit stinginess, boring long-windedness, moralizing, and so on.

The famous list of "don'ts" by Jonathan Swift, a behaviorist before his time, also suggests that the best way to deal with one's problems is not to inflict them on others.

RESOLUTIONS WHEN I COME TO BE OLD

Not to marry a young Woman.

Not to keep young Company, unless they really desire it.

Not to be peevish, or morose, or suspicious.

Not to scorn present Ways, or Wits, or Fashions, or Men, or War, &c.

Not to be fond of children.

Not to tell the same Story over and over to the same People.

Not to be covetous.

Not to neglect decency, or cleanliness, for fear of falling into Nastiness.

Not to be over severe with young People, but give Allowances for their youthful follyes, and Weaknesses.

Not to be influenced by, or give ear to knavish tattling servants, or others.

Not to be too free of advice, nor trouble any but those that desire it.

To desire some good Friends to inform me which of these Resolutions I break, or neglect, & wherein; and reform accordingly.

Not to talk much, nor of myself.

Not to boast of my former beauty, or strength, or favour with ladyes, &c.

Not to hearken to Flatteries, nor conceive I can be beloved by a young woman; *et eos qui haereditatem captant, odisse ac vitare.*

Not to be positive or opinionative.

Not to sett up for observing all these Rules, for fear I should observe none.

—Jonathan Swift

Once we think about the range of useful advice, it is clear that almost any human activity that could be recommended honestly to a twenty-year-old *could* prove profitable to even the sourest old-ster. Of course there are limits. I wouldn't recommend high diving, weight lifting, discus throwing, or aspiring to become the world champion chess player, though I do hear of amazing marathon runners and mountain climbers far beyond seventy. But aside from these, once we accept the notion that the answer is to get up off that couch and *act,* the main limits on our advisers are literary: Can you turn your advice into something worth reading, something that will provide moments that in themselves amount to a cure, even if the advice is not followed? I can preach the advice implicit throughout this book—read good poetry!—until I am blue in the face and it will do you no good. But if I can show you a poem or meditation that you find good, you will not, at the moment of reading, *feel* old.

Some of the specific recommended paths are fairly obvious. We are often told, for example, that we should keep our curiosity alive—precisely the advice that I would give any college student who threatened to deal with academic boredom by dropping out. Robertson Davies, that splendid novelist now producing furiously as he pushes eighty, puts the case for curiosity with characteristic vigor. Not all old people are totally standardized boring types, he says, though too many of them fit the description.

I have grown old myself, and have opinions about it, and about my coevals. What ails most of them, and what has ailed them all their lives, is that they lack curiosity. They have never engaged themselves strongly in anything. The waters of life have washed over them without anything soaking in. They are not interesting when old because they were never interesting when young. . . .

Curiosity . . . is the great preservative and the supreme emollient. Not, of course, curiosity about theater history alone or at all, but curiosity about *something*. Enthusiasm. Zest. That is what makes old age (forgive me, I must leave my typewriter to throw up, for I have just heard someone use that nauseating expression, "the twilight years"—ah, that feels better) a delight. One has seen so much, and one is eager to see more. One has reached a few conclusions. The twilight years (!) are a glorious sundown. . . .

[As Jung says], we spend the first half of our span of years . . . finding our place in the world, finding our sexual orientation, finding our appointed work, finding what things can serve us and what we must avoid or abjure. But by the age of 40 or so we take a change of direction, and henceforth seek knowledge of the world and of mankind, and above all knowledge of ourselves. In the theological phrase, we "make up our souls"; this is the great achievement that makes death the completion of something that has become a unity, with a quality of accomplishment and significance for ourselves and those around us. This is what makes age not a burden and a defeat, but marvelously enjoyable in spite of the limitations of the aging body.

COPYRIGHT KARSH.

Robertson Davies

Davies hints that the rewards of curiosity can grow richer with age, as year by year we discover just how little we know compared with what would be worth knowing. The sour version of this discovery can turn into helpless nihilism, an exaggeratedly solemn version of Socrates' claim that he was the only man in Athens who knew that he knew nothing. The liberating version is a grand opened passageway into a reborn curiosity.

The word "curiosity" may not cover the full ground of what our best advisers have in mind here. "Old men ought to be explorers," says T. S. Eliot. Obviously the great anguished prober was not thinking of ordinary learning but of the kind of spiritual exploration that his later poetry provides. Thus the pursuit of curiosity can lead quickly to the more generalized advice, implied here by E. M. Forster, in near despair at eighty-two, to find something, *anything,* that will "take one out of oneself."

Going to Bits. This phrase describes me today and is indeed the one I have been looking for; not tragic, not mortal disintegration; only a central weakness which prevents me from concentrating or settling down. I have so wanted to write and write ahead. The phrase "obligatory creation" has haunted me. I have so wanted to get out of my morning bath promptly: have decided to do so beforehand, and have then lain in it as usual and watched myself not getting out. It looks as if there is a physical as well as a moral break in the orders I send out. I have plenty of interesting thoughts but keep losing them like the post cards I have written, or like my cap. I can't clear anything up yet interrupt a "good read" in order to clear up. I hope tomorrow to copy out a piece of someone else's prose: it is the best device known to me for taking one out of oneself. Plunge into another's minutiae.

The profound, healing truth underlying all this advice about *doing something* is that even the most ordinary down-to-earth tasks and problems of life can be transformed from curse to cure, or even to celebration, simply by learning how to think and talk about

Gertrude Stein
Courtesy of the Department of Special Collections, University Research
Library, UCLA.

them—how to turn them into "poetry." I wouldn't have pre-
dicted, for example, that an exhortation to diet, to remain slim,
could be made into fine poetry. But look what fun Kay Boyle
manages to make out of it in her early eighties by exploring its full
metaphoric possibilities.

POETS

Poets, minor or major, should arrange to remain slender,
Cling to their skeletons, not batten
On provender, not fatten the lean spirit
In its isolated cell, its solitary chains.
The taut paunch ballooning in its network of veins
Explodes from the cumberbund. The hardening artery of neck
Cannot be masked by turtle-throated cashmere or foulard of
  mottled silk.

Poets, poets, use rags instead; use rags and consider
That Poe did not lie in the morgue swathed
Beyond recognition in fat. Consider on this late March
Afternoon, with violet and crocus outside, fragile as glass,
That the music of Marianne Moore's small polished bones
Was not muffled, the score not lost between thighs as thick as
  bass-fiddles
Or cat-gut muted by dropsy. Baudelaire did not throttle on
  corpulence,
Rimbaud not strangle on his own grease. In the unleafed trees,
  as I write,
Birds flicker, lighter than lace. They are the lean spirit,
Beaks asking for crumbs, their voices like reeds.

William Carlos Williams sat close, close to the table
  always, always,
Close to the typewriter keys, his body not held at bay by a
  drawbridge of flesh

Under his doctor's dress, no gangway to lower, letting the
    sauces,
The starches, the strong liquor, enter and exit
With bugles blowing. Over and over he was struck thin
By the mallet of beauty, the switchblade of sorrow, died slim as a
    gondola,
Died curved like the fine neck of a swan.

These were not gagged, strangled, outdone by the presence
Of banquet selves. They knew words make their way through
    navel and pore,
Move weightless as thistle, as dandelion drift, unencumbered.
Death happens to fatten on poets' glutted hearts. ("Dylan!"
Death calls, and the poet scrambles drunk and alone to what were
    once swift, bony feet,
Casting a monstrous shadow of gargantuan flesh before he
    crashes.)

Poets, remember your skeletons. In youth or dotage,
    remain as light as ashes.

—Kay Boyle

    No doubt a poet as clever as Boyle could manage equally rich
metaphoric transformations of any quotidian practice. Study cook-
books, O poet. Get your daily exercise. Take up macramé, take up
golf. Where is the Kay Boyle who could make such meanings out
of working for charity, say, or of hard physical labor, of scholar-
ship, of dictionary making, of chess or crossword puzzles, of knit-
ting, of practicing the thumb position on the cello, of skillful
gossip, of coin collecting, of politics in all its varieties, including
demonstrations for or against abortion, vivisection, or nuclear
waste dumps—you name it and I'll warrant that somebody will
have beat us to it, maybe not with a really good poem but at least
with a letter in Ann Landers' column recommending the activity
as a way of feeling good about life as life slips by. No doubt I'll
now receive many an irritated note: "How could you possibly

© JERRY BAUER.

Samuel Beckett

overlook Frost's 'After Apple Picking,' or Robert Burns's playful hymn to yarn making, 'The Cardin o't, the Spinnin o't,' or the marvelous sonnet by X or Y?"

You have an inclination to return to politics? Most older people would tell you not to be so foolish: they have seen their political dreams collapse, again and again. But if you still have a dream, note how Kay Boyle (yes, I'm still browsing in her works) can make poetry out of that dream, taking up, in her early sixties, a cause embraced by her students in *the* sixties:

A Poem About Black Power

Let us grow old with modesty,
See with our rheumy, failing eyes
That prophets wear cloaks of fire now
(As then). Let us not pound our canes
On the boards for order as we limp across
The blazing stage we knew must blaze.
"Where, where is the red glow spelling 'Exit'?"
Panic cries out; "where, where the asbestos curtain that must fall
Between us and the footlights of our rage?"
Sweethearts, the script has changed (or perhaps not changed),
And with it the stage directions which advise
Lowered voices, genteel asides,
And the white hand slowly turning the dark page.

Let us grow old admitting we saw the fire, the savage betrayed
    eyes,
Heard the screaming terror of their deaths, and wrote a letter,
Nicely phrased, to someone else, and slept then,
As the old sleep, nodding, remembering. *Remembering what?*
That four little black girls died in a church?
Are we quite certain that we heard their cries?

When they cite Gandhi to you please recall
That he built fires hot enough and tall
Enough to light the whole of India. I was a child then
And, troubled by their flames, each evening knelt and asked my
    mother
What he burned. "Clothing and rice," she answered,
"Clothing and rice in time of want and famine. Clothing and rice
England had sent in charity to change the look of history,
And did not change it, for Gandhi turned that bribery to flame."

Those fires consumed the debris of my youth,
Burned steadily, burn still, and now I see the lone immortal bird
That wings up from their ash, so clear, so plain,
That the old tremble and tremble and tremble, and cannot say its
    name.

—Kay Boyle

I assume that you've been impatient through all this, wonder-
ing when I would get around to poems about sex as palliative.
We've already seen perhaps more than enough, in Part I, about
how loss of attractiveness and sexual drive, or interest, or success
can plague old age. But what about sex as *cure* for the losses,
whether or not it borders on love?

As every reader knows, I could easily fill the rest of this book
with poems recommending as the best way to seize the day the
simple sexual embrace. You know the famous ones already—at
least I hope you know the best one of all, by Andrew Marvell.

To His Coy Mistress

Had we but world enough, and time,
This coyness, lady, were no crime.
We would sit down, and think which way
To walk, and pass our long love's day.
Thou by the Indian Ganges' side
Shoudst rubies find; I by the tide
Of Humber would complain. I would
Love you ten years before the flood,
And you should, if you please, refuse
Till the conversion of the Jews.
My vegetable love should grow
Vaster than empires and more slow;
An hundred years should go to praise
Thine eyes, and on thy forehead gaze;
Two hundred to adore each breast,
But thirty thousand to the rest;
An age at least to every part,
And the last age should show your heart.
For, lady, you deserve this state,
Nor would I love at lower rate.
　　But at my back I always hear
Time's wingéd chariot hurrying near;
And yonder all before us lie
Deserts of vast eternity.
Thy beauty shall no more be found;
Nor, in thy marble vault, shall sound
My echoing song; then worms shall try
That long-preserved virginity,
And your quaint honor turn to dust,
And into ashes all my lust:
The grave's a fine and private place,
But none, I think, do there embrace.
　　Now therefore, while the youthful hue
Sits on thy skin like morning glow,

And while thy willing soul transpires
At every pore with instant fires,
Now let us sport us while we may,
And now, like amorous birds of prey,
Rather at once our time devour
Than languish in his slow-chapped power.
Let us roll all our strength and all
Our sweetness up into one ball,
And tear our pleasures with rough strife
Thorough the iron gates of life:
Thus, though we cannot make our sun
Stand still, yet we will make him run.

—Andrew Marvell

When I first fell under the spell of this poem, in a required literature course long ago, I thought of the poet as a young man courting a slightly younger woman. I later learned from scholars that Marvell was sixty when he first published it, in 1681; he started his composing in 1646 (or perhaps, as some say, seven years later), still just as I had pictured him, a dashing, confident pursuer somewhere between his mid twenties and early thirties. But everyone agrees that he went on revising the poem decade after decade, and I now prefer to think of him as finishing it off, one gray morning in his late fifties, after his much younger friend had told him, the night before, that because he was as old as her father she intended to go on being "coy" indefinitely. But at *his* back he could always hear, "Time's wingéd chariot hurrying near," and *he* knew what it felt like to see ahead of him "deserts of vast eternity." Sex —we simply cannot tell whether with or without love—was his proposed remedy.

Here's a less famous passage along the same lines, tucked away in a largely unread great classic, Edmund Spenser's *The Faerie Queene.*

> So passeth, in the passing of a day,
> Of mortal life the leaf, the bud, the flower,
> No more doth flourish after first decay,
> That erst was sought to deck both bed and bower,
> Of many a Lady, and many a Paramour:
> Gather therefore the Rose, whilst yet is prime,
> For soon comes age, that will her pride deflower:
> Gather the Rose of love, whilst yet is time,
> Whilst loving thou mayst loved be with equal crime.
>
> —Edmund Spenser

Oscar Wilde, who knew at thirty-three that he was already aging, is more aggressive: he has his Lady Windermere say, "An inordinate passion for pleasure is the secret of remaining young." André Gide at eighty felt that his most important task was to do all that he could to keep his sex life alive.

I remain extremely sensitive to the spectacle of adolescence. Moreover, I have taken care not to allow my desires to fall asleep. In this I have listened to the advice of Montaigne, who proved particularly wise in this matter; he knew, and I know, that wisdom is not to be found in renunciation or abstinence, and he took care not to let that secret source dry up, even going so far as to "encourage" himself toward pleasure, if I understand him correctly.

Montaigne is indeed quite explicit in his repudiation of those philosophers (whom we'll come to) who claimed that the loss of sexual desire is a blessing.

I hate this incidental repentance that age brings with it. That man who once said he was grateful to the years for having taken sensual delights away from him had an opinion quite unlike mine: I could never thank impotence for the kindness it does me. . . . In old age our appetites are rare, and afterwards deep satiety comes upon us; here I see nothing of conscience at work. Affliction and weakness impart a rheumy, faint-hearted virtue.

—Michel de Montaigne

I'll be much surprised if you already know the next one, though at one time every schoolboy—or so I'm told—would have read Anacreon in the original Greek.

DEFIANCE OF AGE

The women tell me every day
That all my bloom has passed away.
"Behold," the pretty wantons cry,
"Behold this mirror with a sigh;
The locks upon thy brow are few,
And, like the rest, they're withering too!"
Whether decline has thinned my hair
I'm sure I neither know nor care;
But this I know, and this I feel,
As onward to the tomb I steal,
That still, as death approaches nearer,
The joys of life are sweeter, dearer;
And had I but an hour to live,
That little hour to bliss I'd give!

As everybody over forty knows, there's a slight hitch in Anacreon's pursuit of that little hour of bliss, that pursuit (as I read the poem) of sexual pleasure until the last possible moment: unfortunately it is the young who are most desirable, and they generally do not desire *us*. Indeed it is more likely that we disgust them. They—those delicious young creatures—are likely to look on us as Prince Hal looks on Falstaff:

Do you set down your name in the scroll of youth, that are written down old with all the characters of age? Have you not a moist eye, a dry hand, a yellow cheek, a white beard, a decreasing leg, an increasing belly? Is not your voice broken, your wind short, your chin double, your wit single, and every part of you blasted with antiquity? And will you yet call yourself young? Fie, fie, fie, Sir John!

As John Cowper Powys sums up this nasty problem:

How well old people come to know that peculiar look of suppressed disgust which their obstinate concentration on some restricted sensual pleasure excites in the feverish idealism of the young and in the impatient pragmatism of the middle-aged! What is their wisest method of mental defence against the shameful discomfort caused by this look?

Perhaps the most frequently recommended kind of action, beyond sheer busyness, is work, work in the sense of self-motivated, sustained labor. The elderly weakening Matisse writes letter after letter explaining why work is the only thing that redeems his life —or complaining because he cannot do more of it. Bernard Berenson at eighty-four confides to his diary, "If only I don't get too invalid, keep my head and a certain capacity for work!"

When we were younger, if we were lucky we felt that life justified itself whenever we were plunged deeply into satisfying work. When we are older, the same kind of plunge can produce the same effect. Our advisers, most of them in this matter not poets but gerontologists or memoirists, tell us to get moving on a piece of work that is not just keeping us busy but is producing something we care about. The more sophisticated advisers know that they are themselves "working" within a splendid Aristotelian tradition which says you will not find happiness, well-being, by seeking it directly; you may find it only by *performing* it. That is to say, "happiness" is our word for how we feel when we are exercising some capacity or power or gift. In this view just plain work, when it is performed on tasks that the worker respects, is about the best cure for aging there is.

For reasons I don't quite understand, I have found almost no beautifully written paeans to work, except for the work of making "works" of art. You just do not find hymns to work-in-general in anthologies of finer poetry. Where they are found, in superabundance, is in Protestant hymnals (prose versions fill the books of advice written by gerontologists). The hymns go like this:

Today, while the sun shines,
Work with a will;
Today all your duties with patience fulfill.
Today, while the birds sing, harbor no care;
Call life a good gift; call the world fair.

Today, today, work with a will;
Today, today, your duties fulfill.
Today, today, work while you may,
There is no tomorrow, but only today.

The work that such works-celebrating-work-of-any-kind perform in the world by cheering people up is not to be sneezed at, but that's the only one of them that will make the grade into this collection—and it achieves that happy fate by the sheer historical accident of having occupied too much of my childhood. If we're looking for quality, and that is indeed what we are doing, we have to turn to poems that celebrate the artist's labors, the making of poems or the reveling in others' makings. Most of these do not even mention aging, though we've already seen a fair number, in Part I, lamenting the loss of the artist's working powers. This scarcity makes all the more precious the late poems by Yeats—those in which the specific cure for aging is found in works of art, "monuments of unageing intellect." Though "Sailing to Byzantium," perhaps his most famous statement, speaks explicitly only of turning to the works made by others, one can read it as his celebration of the glorious labor that making such a poem requires.

SAILING TO BYZANTIUM

I

That is no country for old men. The young
In one another's arms, birds in the trees
—Those dying generations—at their song,
The salmon-falls, the mackerel-crowded seas,
Fish, flesh, or fowl, commend all summer long
Whatever is begotten, born, and dies.
Caught in that sensual music all neglect
Monuments of unageing intellect.

II

An aged man is but a paltry thing,
A tattered coat upon a stick, unless
Soul clap its hands and sing, and louder sing
For every tatter in its mortal dress,
Nor is there singing school but studying
Monuments of its own magnificence;
And therefore I have sailed the seas and come
To the holy city of Byzantium.

III

O sages standing in God's holy fire
As in the gold mosaic of a wall,
Come from the holy fire, perne in a gyre,
And be the singing-masters of my soul.
Consume my heart away; sick with desire
And fastened to a dying animal
It knows not what it is; and gather me
Into the artifice of eternity.

IV

Once out of nature I shall never take
My bodily form from any natural thing,
But such a form as Grecian goldsmiths make
Of hammered gold and gold enamelling
To keep a drowsy Emperor awake;
Or set upon a golden bough to sing
To lords and ladies of Byzantium
Of what is past, or passing, or to come.

—W. B. Yeats

The bliss of working oneself into the *work* of art, whether one's own or the gift of another artist, is precisely the consolation I have hoped this anthology would offer. The other consolations I can only talk about or show others talking about, but this one is here before your eyes, and mine. We live the consolation as we read, just as I assume Thomas Hart Benton and Georgia O'Keeffe did as they went on producing into their last years. (See pages 156–57.)

We cannot share here the special joy that artists themselves experience at the moment when the whole endeavor comes right —the joy that only those who actually work at making art can know. Occasionally we find testimonials to the utter bliss of placing the precise brush stroke at the precise spot, or the precise word in the precise position. A favorite example was created by Virginia Woolf when she was already "getting on," at forty-five, writing the final scene of *To the Lighthouse*. Ten years before that final scene, Lily Briscoe had tried unsuccessfully to complete a landscape painting. Now, plagued by the passage of time and the deaths it has brought, she seeks consolation.

> Suddenly she remembered. . . . There had been a problem about a foreground of a picture. Move the tree to the middle, she had said. She had never finished that picture. She would paint that picture now. It had been knocking about in her mind all these years.

© THOMAS H. BENTON AND RITA P. BENTON TESTAMENTARY TRUST/VAGA, NEW YORK 1992. LITHOGRAPH CIRCULATED BY ASSOCIATED AMERICAN ARTISTS.

Thomas Hart Benton, *Self-Portrait.*

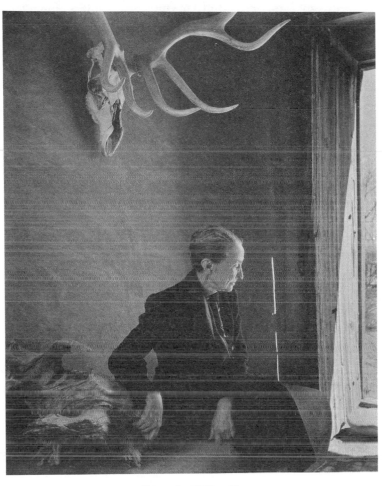

COPYRIGHT KARSH.

Georgia O'Keeffe

Lily goes on struggling to find her compositional center through the rest of the novel, though her struggle is by no means a simple center for Virginia Woolf's own compositional problem —at least until the very end. Then finally everything—including "the weakness and suffering of mankind"—comes into focus.

> Quickly . . . she turned to her canvas. There it was—her picture. Yes, with all its greens and blues, its lines running up and across, its attempt at something. It would be hung in the attic, she thought; it would be destroyed. But what did that matter? she asked herself, taking up her brush again. She looked . . . at her canvas; it was blurred. With a sudden intensity, as if she saw it clear for a second, she drew a line there, in the centre. It was done; it was finished. Yes, she thought, laying down her brush in extreme fatigue. I have had my vision.

And Virginia Woolf—growing older—has had hers.

As Thoreau says, "The art of life, of a poet's life, is, not having anything to do, to do something"—that is, get down to work and write sentences like that. We'll come to more of these consolations of art later on. Meanwhile I can only plead with the poets to create some good poems about the joys of other kinds of work besides the making of art. Surely the celebrations of manual labor, for example, need not be as empty of literary interest as were most of those devoutly leftwing novels of the thirties?

Advice is actually more often about attitudes than actions. Much of the best poetry amounts to a twist on Rilke's famous admonition, "You must change your life"—change your stance toward it. We all like to advise one another about attitudes, and though most modern poets work hard not to *sound* didactic, many of their best poems, like many of the best poems of earlier poets, are best read as hard-worked advice from schoolmasters-of-the-soul.

Perhaps the favorite advice, from ancient days till now, has been to take courage, and we find plenty of evidence that aging brings to some a freedom to exercise new kinds of courage. When Dr. Benjamin Spock, at eighty, was asked why he risked imprisonment to protest the Vietnam War he said, "At my age, why should I be afraid to make public protests along with [young] Stokely Carmichael?" As Simone de Beauvoir says, reporting this incident,

> With men who have taken risks all their lives, it often happens that their boldness shines out with particular brilliance in their last years. [Bertrand] Russell was always brave and determined, but he never showed it in so striking a manner as in 1961, when he was eighty-nine. At this time he was a member of the Committee of a Hundred against nuclear weapons: he called upon the public to join in a non-violent manifestation, and in spite of the police prohibition he sat down on the ground among the others. His age and his name gave his act such importance that there was no possibility of its being overlooked, and in fact he spent a week in prison.

Sursum corda—lift up your hearts, then, and defy aging to do its worst. If you can't find anything good about your condition, at least you can be courageous about it: face it like a . . . woman, I would say, since women are on the whole more courageous about suffering and loss than men are. Is that why they live longer?

It's not easy to exhort to courage without seeming to protest too much, as we might accuse Emily Brontë of doing in her hymn to the "God within my breast/ Almighty ever-present Deity"— we might accuse her, that is, if we did not know that it was her last poem, written not long before her death at age thirty.

> No coward soul is mine
> No trembler in the world's storm-troubled sphere
> I see Heaven's glories shine
> And Faith shines equal arming me from Fear.

And thus on for six stanzas. Here's another of her odes to courage, written (imitating the voice of a stoic) when she clearly felt already old—at twenty-three!

THE OLD STOIC

Riches I hold in light esteem
And Love I laugh to scorn
And lust of Fame was but a dream
That vanished with the morn—

And if I pray, the only prayer
That moves my lips for me
Is—"Leave the heart that now I bear
And give me liberty."

Yes, as my swift days near their goal
'Tis all that I implore—
Through life and death, a chainless soul
With courage to endure!

As Edna St. Vincent Millay worried about aging in her early sixties, she longed for the courage her mother had.

[THE COURAGE THAT MY MOTHER HAD]

The courage that my mother had
Went with her, and is with her still:
Rock from New England quarried;
Now granite in a granite hill.

The golden brooch my mother wore
She left behind for me to wear;
I have no thing I treasure more:
Yet, it is something I could spare.

COPYRIGHT KARSH.

George Bernard Shaw

Or, if instead she'd left to me
The thing she took into the grave!—
That courage like a rock, which she
Has no more need of, and I have.

—Edna St. Vincent Millay

Elinor Wylie in her late thirties found it essential to profess a courage and sense of wry humor that put her above the battle.

LET NO CHARITABLE HOPE

Now let no charitable hope
Confuse my mind with images
Of eagle and of antelope:
I am in nature none of these.

I was, being human, born alone;
I am, being woman, hard beset;
I live by squeezing from a stone
The little nourishment I get.

In masks outrageous and austere
The years go by in single file;
But none has merited my fear,
And none has quite escaped my smile.

NADIR

If we must cheat ourselves with any dream,
Then let it be a dream of nobleness:
Since it is necessary to express
Gall from black grapes—to sew an endless seam
With a rusty needle—chase a spurious gleam
Narrowing to the nothing through the less—
Since life's no better than a bitter guess,
And love's a stranger—let us change the theme.

Let us at least pretend—it may be true—
That we can close our lips on poisonous
Dark wine diluted by the Stygean wave;
And let me dream sublimity in you,
And courage, liberal for the two of us:
Let us at least pretend we can be brave.

—Elinor Wylie

The exhortation to courage can be extremely muted, as if to say no more than simply "we mustn't complain, because everyone goes through this." That seems to be what William James is saying, sadly, not far from death at age sixty-eight.

To Henry P. Bowditch

Bad-Nauheim, *June* 4, 1910.

Dearest Heinrich,

. . . The baths may or may not arrest for a while the downward tendency which has been so marked in the past year—but at any rate it is a comfort to know that my sufferings have a respectable organic basis, and are not, as so many of my friends tell me, due to pure "nervousness." Dear Henry, you see that you are not the only pebble on the beach, or toad in the puddle, of senile degeneration! I admit that the form of your tragedy beats that of most of us; but youth's a stuff that won't endure, in any one, and to have had it, as you and I have had it, is a good deal gained anyhow, while to see the daylight still under *any* conditions is perhaps also better than nothing, and meanwhile the good months are sure to bring the final relief after which, "when you and I behind the veil are passed, Oh, but the long, long time the world shall last!" etc., etc. Rather gloomy moralizing, this, to end an affectionate

Thomas Hart Benton, *Aaron*.

© THOMAS H. BENTON AND RITA P. BENTON TESTAMENTARY TRUST/VAGA, NEW YORK 1992. LITHOGRAPH CIRCULATED BY ASSOCIATED AMERICAN ARTISTS.

family letter with; but the circumstances seem to justify it, and I know that you won't take it amiss. . . .

Believe me, ever your affectionately sympathetic old friend,

Wm. James.

Am I right in hearing something of the same tone in a journal "Entry" by Wu Yü-pi, in his early sixties, about four and a half centuries earlier?

Today I have been thinking how to reach the principle of "being at ease in all circumstances": "As long as there is any breath remaining, a person must not tolerate the least bit of negligence with respect to his effort of will." How can I use the excuse of old age to feel wearied by events!

Most men, when they enter vigorously into the courageous act, seem to try harder to *sound* courageous than do women. To read Cicero on old age you'd think he never had a moment when he doubted his capacity to see it all through. William Ernest Henley's "Invictus," with its stance of total courage against total awfulness, sounds like a bid to appear at this precise spot in this collection—though it perhaps belongs more properly among the deniers:

> Out of the night that covers me,
> Black as the Pit from pole to pole,
> I thank whatever gods may be,
> For my unconquerable . . .

But I refuse to go on with it. If you heard "Invictus" sung as often as I did in childhood, you will understand why. And even if you have never heard it, you can fill in the right rhyme in the final slot. It happens to be a word I'd like to see rehabilitated, but not by anyone who thinks his soul is an unconquerable stronghold against everything.

In contrast, Dylan Thomas's famous poem addressed as to his father in his final illness survives the passage of time very well, in part no doubt because Thomas had the courage to call his destroying night "good." And I hope that *that* choice did not depend on his being well under forty when he wrote the poem.

Do Not Go Gentle into That Good Night

Do not go gentle into that good night,
Old age should burn and rave at close of day;
Rage, rage against the dying of the light.

Though wise men at their end know dark is right,
Because their words had forked no lightning they
Do not go gentle into that good night.

Good men, the last wave by, crying how bright
Their frail deeds might have danced in a green bay,
Rage, rage against the dying of the light.

Wild men who caught and sang the sun in flight,
And learn, too late, they grieved it on its way,
Do not go gentle into that good night.

Grave men, near death, who see with blinding sight
Blind eyes could blaze like meteors and be gay,
Rage, rage against the dying of the light.

And you, my father, there on the sad height,
Curse, bless, me now with your fierce tears, I pray.
Do not go gentle into that good night.
Rage, rage against the dying of the light.

—Dylan Thomas

Pierre Auguste Renoir, *Self-Portrait,* 1897. Oil on canvas. Sterling and Francine Clark Art Institute, Williamstown, Massachusetts.

Thomas knew, as he says in other famous poems, that the same force "that through the green fuse drives the flower / Drives my green age," that even when he was young "Time held me green and dying" (See "Fern Hill," pages 278–80). Unlike Henley, he knew that when he "sang in my chains, like the sea," he could not boast a totally unconquerable soul, any more than he could claim that the night that covered him, and was about to cover his father, was totally black: it was *good* night. Time holds us all *"green"* while dying, and Thomas helps us see that, with a courage more honest than Henley's, we can sing a better song about our fate.

The statements of courage tend to be more muted as the writers move from young age to old age. Henry James, near death at seventy-two, wrote in his diary:

29 August 1915 Sunday
Unwell, dismally unwell and helpless, for many past days; almost, or quite, unprecedented and illuminated, or at least illuminating, stomachic and digestive crisis; with, suddenly, gout as climax.

12 September 1915 Sunday
Very big, quite dreadful, panting night. Very bad a.m. hours —foodless; but more and more convinced, of vital, life-saving necessity of getting able to walk again and recovering precious help from it that has again and again so affirmed its value in the long and ravaged past! Such a consecrated confidence!

Confidence in what? There's no easy boast here about a soul that is unconquerable. But to me the very act of addressing the journal is an expression of courage: I am still determined to make something, however meager, out of my "helpless," "ravaged" days and nights. For me the advice to take courage works best when it is expressed in the kind of lovely metaphor created by Theodore Roethke and Kay Boyle in these two pieces:

THE DECISION

1

What shakes the eye but the invisible?
Running from God's the longest race of all.
A bird kept haunting me when I was young—
The phoebe's slow retreating from its song,
Nor could I put that sound out of my mind,
The sleepy sound of leaves in a light wind.

2

Rising or falling's all one discipline!
The line of my horizon's growing thin!
Which is the way? I cry to the dread black,
The shifting shade, the cinders at my back.
Which is the way? I ask, and turn to go,
As a man turns to face on-coming snow.

—Theodore Roethke

ADVICE TO THE OLD
(including myself)

Do not speak of yourself (for God's sake) even when asked.
Do not dwell on other times as different from the time
Whose air we breathe; or recall books with broken spines
Whose titles died with the old dreams. Do not resort to
An alphabet of gnarled pain, but speak of the lark's wing
Unbroken, still fluent as the tongue. Call out the names of stars
Until their metal clangs in the enormous dark. Yodel your way
Through fields where the dew weeps, but not you, not you.
Have no communion with despair; and, at the end,
Take the old fury in your empty arms, sever its veins,
And bear it fiercely, fiercely to the wild beast's lair.

—Kay Boyle

We could go on indefinitely to other recommended actions or stances. Almost every virtue has been offered, by poets, philosophers, and barroom sages, as the one best way to fight old age. In turning now to more muted "answers," I don't mean to suggest that we should feel the least bit superior to the exhorters. Who am I—working hard and of course courageously, full of curiosity, laboring day by day at the task of putting this book together, much of the time forgetting that in less than ten years I'll be eighty— who am I to pretend that I'd be better off if I gave up this practical activity and spent my days following the *implied* advice of those we turn to now? Should I just burn the mottled manuscript and spend my hours meditating on newfound wisdom, or simply re-reading poems of celebration? Instead, I slave away here following the exhorters' advice—have you thought about how much drudgery is involved in trying to get all the data here more or less straight? The result? For hours at a time I simply forget the plain fact that even as I collect these fine words, and try to add to them, I am—growing older.

When our authors exhort us to be courageous or to get out there and *do something,* they imply that age is something like a disease—something to be overcome by trying to revert to a more desirable condition: youth. Indeed, whatever consolations we've seen so far could all be described, on a bad morning, as simply shrunken versions of rewards that were available to us in delicious plenitude when we were young. A cynic could even claim that we have so far said little more than "stay young as long as you can"— not quite the empty message of Bloomingdale's ad but perilously close to it.

Fortunately, we could now more than fill another book with celebrations of rewards reserved exclusively for those who find themselves, almost always to their surprise, growing old: *new* pleasures and discoveries, not just compensations for what aging inevitably subtracts. Our aging friends tell us, in astonishing numbers, that *here are new rewards.* And some of them even say, persuasively, that in some respects "what I have now is better than what I had when young."

So we are now embarked not on some gloomy salvage operation—an effort to clean up the beach after the oil spill—but rather a voyage of exploration: life this far along has its own interests and pleasures that are quite inaccessible to youth; we can become a new kind of "explorer" (obeying T. S. Eliot)! In short, these subtle advisers seem to say, "You needn't necessarily *do* anything different; all you need do is think about where you really are and what resources of feeling are already within you—just by virtue of being older."

At its most relaxed, this tone sounds something like John Selden's in his *Table Talk,* where he leaves no doubt that *in spite of all its ills,* old age offers its own rewards. "Old friends are best. King James used to call for his old shoes; they were easiest for his feet." Sometimes such claims are so muted that they might seem to belong among the denials, like this report by a woman interviewed by Ronald Blythe:

> Every morning I wake up in pain. I wiggle my toes. Good. They still obey. I open my eyes. Good. I can see. Everything hurts but I get dressed. I walk down to the ocean. Good. It's still there. Now my day can start. About tomorrow I never know. After all, I'm eighty-nine. I can't live forever.

Blythe collects many such calm assertions in *The View in Winter.* There is the "shepherd's widow" who, when asked, "What does it *feel* like to be nearly a hundred years old?" answered, "Well, you wake up in the morning, you say to yourself, 'What, still here?' And then you make tea."

Or the same Florida Scott-Maxwell we met on page 21: "When a new disability arrives I look about to see if death has come, and I call quietly, 'Death, is that you? Are you there?' So far the disability has answered, 'Don't be silly, it's me.' "

Adrienne Rich, writing in her early fifties but imagining the coming "winter," articulates more fully this plea to love "the time we have," rather than lamenting the time we have lost:

28.

This high summer we love will pour its light
the fields grown rich and ragged in one strong moment
then before we're ready will crash into autumn
with a violence we can't accept
a bounty we can't forgive
Night frost will strike when the noons are warm
the pumpkins wildly glowing   the green tomatoes
straining huge on the vines
queen anne and blackeyed susan will straggle rusty
as the milkweed stakes her claim
she who will stand at last   dark sticks barely rising
up through the snow   her testament of continuation
We'll dream of a longer summer
but this is the one we have:
I lay my sunburnt hand
on your table: this is the time we have

—Adrienne Rich

Am I right in hearing the same kind of loving resignation in Sappho, through the dense fog of translation from more than twenty-five hundred years ago?

AGE AND LIGHT

Here are fine gifts, children.
O friend, singer on the clear tortoise lyre,

all my flesh is wrinkled with age,
my black hair has faded to white,

my legs can no longer carry me,
once nimble like a fawn's,

but what can I do?
It cannot be undone,

no more than can pink-armed Dawn
not end in darkness on earth,

or keep her love for Tithonos,
who must waste away;

yet I love refinement, and beauty and light
are for me the same as desire for the sun.

—Sappho

These women do not say outright anything as absurd as "Old age is in every way better than youth." But they imply, by their way of accepting the small blessings of each moment, that they have *learned something by becoming old.* A pessimist might claim that they are simply clinging to illusory remnants, like the tragic/comic character Winnie in Beckett's *Happy Days.* Buried act by act in deeper piles of sand, she keeps on saying, even when only her head remains visible, "Oh this *is* a happy day, this will have been another happy day!" They could be accused of resembling my old confreres who mutter, when I ask them how they are, "Pretty good, *considering.*" But it takes no blind optimist to hear in the women's voices something they could not have expressed when young: "I now know—and am grateful for knowing—just what is important."

I hear that same point behind the sharp slap that Pauline Kael, at an age that she keeps as a secret, throws at the movie director Federico Fellini: he shouldn't be "so upset about ageing," she says.

It isn't as if he had never lived. As Ovid said, time devours everything. So why be cranky about it? While time is devouring everything we have some good moments.

When Clemenceau was asked in his old age "What will you do now?" he didn't snarl, "Old age is a shipwreck," but rather said, "I am going to live till I die." E. M. Forster, in his late seventies, reports Clemenceau's reply toward the end of his *Commonplace Book,* and comments, "I like this answer." Earlier, in his mid-seventies, he indirectly lets us know why he would like such a muted, and perhaps equivocal, affirmation.

How peaceful it was here this quiet afternoon with a crescent moon thickening, and terrors and duties rushing close to me and failing to perturb, with my diarrhoea likely to improve under treatment. . . . I thought of the imperfect but tear-drawing poems of Yeats . . . And I thought of the Rubens which has come to spend its last days in our chapel . . . *It* is not dishonest, it does not (like Yeats occasionally) try to take us in when its inspiration flags; but it is an inadequate mystery compared to the one surrounding us, and our pretty blunt sickle of a moon! . . .

My calm, idleness and good temper may irritate my colleagues shortly, especially when they find I never do or say anything helpful. I believe that the game is up, and the top shelf of the cupboard labelled Dangerous is being rifled now that the children's arms have grown longer. I know of nothing I can do . . .

How peaceful it is here, with the West Hackhurst clock still ticking, the Rooksnest fire irons still warm in the hearth, and Little Master [his dog], his feet on Rob's rug, nodding towards the end of a successful career.

Such uncomplaining resignation about the miseries, such quiet whole-hearted acceptance of the simple blessing of *being alive,* floods the literature of aging. Though it may not quite qualify as the wisdom that we'll come to further on, it obviously can be spoken only by someone who has touched that wisdom. Not surprisingly, it resembles closely what many philosophers, especially

Stoics like Seneca, have recommended as the best attitude toward life at any age.

> Old age is full of enjoyment if you know how to use it. . . .
> Life is most delightful when it is on the down slope but not at
> the edge yet. Even when it trembles on the eaves it still has its
> pleasures, I opine, or else [the lost] pleasures are compensated
> by freedom from the need for them

No doubt most of us will want to modify Seneca's claim: "Lost pleasures are *partially* compensated by freedom from the need for them." We can assume that there were days when the philosopher would have hit that "partially" rather strongly. Even after qualification, however, one must be impressed by the number of older authors who have found a new pleasure in being freed from the need to cope, in simply relinquishing—I'm resigned now to the end, and I accept what pleasures remain: "How peaceful it is here."

We find something like the same tone in many of Walter Savage Landor's late poems. At seventy-eight he published a volume with the forlorn title *The Last Fruit Off an Old Tree,* including many poems like this.

> Leaf after leaf drops off, flower after flower,
> Some in the chill, some in the warmer hour:
> Alike they flourish and alike they fall,
> And Earth who nourisht them receives them all.
> Should we, her wiser sons, be less content
> To sink into her lap when life is spent?

When such resignation gets touched with pain or grief, the words naturally shift their emphasis slightly and begin to sound like the exhortations to courage that we heard above. Or they can come uncomfortably close to the flat denial by Henley that I expressed suspicion about earlier. The following "Epigram" by Landor, published in his early seventies (he lived to be eighty-nine, pouring out poems most of the way), is usually taken "straight," as expressing Landor's own true courage.

> Death stands above me, whispering low
>   I know not what into my ear:
> Of his strange language all I know
>   Is, there is not a word of fear.

But I wonder. Are not Landor's mixed feelings revealed in the confusing grammar here? Just whose language is it that shows not a word of fear, the poet's or death's?

The most famous of all his many poems addressed to age and death reveals a different kind of ambiguous resignation.

DYING SPEECH OF AN OLD PHILOSOPHER

> I strove with none, for none was worth my strife:
>   Nature I loved, and, next to Nature, Art:
> I warm'd both hands before the fire of Life;
>   It sinks; and I am ready to depart.

The joker here is that Landor was famous for his contentiousness; he was frequently "striving," in litigation and public quarrels, right on through the time in which this poem was written, in his early seventies (published 1849). What he has given us is not, then, his own fully realized resignation but a kind of ideal: it is the imagined *philosopher,* not the old quarreler, who claims a peaceful life and—in a giveaway?—boasts that all potential enemies were not worth bothering about.

At its most elaborate—and for some, most depressing—the effort to relinquish becomes an energetic claim that your pain doesn't matter, because in the great scheme of things—or non-scheme—you are a cipher. Who are you, aspiring Job that you are, to complain? Most authors who talk this way are not deniers; they just want to insist that you and your aging and its attendant pains do not matter much.

The bland comfort of not mattering can result from trying to see yourself in the eyes of God: your soul matters, but your accidental pains and losses in this world do not. Or it can come from seeing your fate philosophically in the light of the universe's immensities, as Forster attempted to do as he approached eighty. The plan he writes for his new *Commonplace Book* sounds like an effort to develop an agnostic's equivalent to Pascal's religious response to the "immensities." It begins like this:

> It is wrong to think one has to say something. It may be wrong to think one has something to say. An old author who is beginning his last book, as here I am, is depressed by the little effect his opinions have had—he might as well have never expressed them—and he is tempted to a last-minute emphasis or to a filling up of gaps, which will make his purpose clearer. Vain effort . . . It is not to extend my influence that I am writing now, or even to help. It is an attempt to be more honest with myself than I yet have [been]. . . . I think of death as a permanent anaesthetic—to be reached amidst pain or fear if my luck is bad, and under perfect hospital conditions if the luck's good. In either case it finishes me off as a memoirist or an observer. My great extension is not through time to eternity, but through space to infinity: here: now: and one of my complaints against modern conditions is that they prevent one from seeing the stars.

Looking steadily at the stars while contemplating Forster's "infinity" seems to me first cousin to claiming that one should—

especially when old—learn to live in the soul rather than the body, the view that we saw Montaigne rejecting on page 150. Sometimes such sublimation is involuntary, as when men (it is usually men here) discover their loss of sexual capacity; they often then express relief that they no longer are plagued by desire. The relief can even turn to celebration, as it does in what is perhaps the most famous expression of this kind, at the beginning of Plato's *Republic*—no doubt the very passage Montaigne was dubious about. Socrates is conversing with a rich, cheerful old man. "To tell the truth," he says to Cephalus,

> I enjoy talking with very old people. They have gone before us on a road by which we too may have to travel, and I think we do well to learn from them what it is like, easy or difficult, rough or smooth. And now that you have reached an age when your foot, as the poets say, is on the threshold, I should like to hear what report you can give and whether you find it a painful time of life.
>
> I will tell you by all means [Cephalus replies] what it seems like to me, Socrates. Some of us old men often meet, true to the old saying that people of the same age like to be together. Most of our company are very sorry for themselves, looking back with regret to the pleasures of their young days, all the delights connected with love affairs and merry-making. They are vexed at being deprived of what seems to them so important; life was good in those days, they think, and now they have no life at all. Some complain that their families have no respect for their years, and make that a reason for harping on all the miseries old age has brought. But to my mind, Socrates, they are laying the blame on the wrong shoulders. If the fault were in old age, so far as that goes, I and all who have ever reached my time of life would have the same experience; but in point of fact, I have met many who felt quite differently. For instance, I remember someone asking Sophocles, the poet, whether he was still capable of enjoying awoman. "Don't talk in that way," he answered. "I am

only too glad to be free of all that; it is like escaping from bondage to a raging madman." I thought that a good answer at the time, and I still think so; for certainly a great peace comes when age sets us free from passions of that sort. When they weaken and relax their hold, most certainly it means, as Sophocles said, a release from servitude to many forms of madness. All these troubles, Socrates, including the complaints about not being respected, have only one cause; and that is not old age, but a man's character. If you have a contented mind at peace with itself, age is no intolerable burden; without that, Socrates, age and youth will be equally painful.

Like Plato, many a philosopher has extended Cephalus's point to make the even stronger claim that the pleasures of the soul are superior to those of the body.

Among the poets, Yeats is perhaps the best known for his attempt to show how soul can triumph over body. As we saw in "Sailing to Byzantium," we are doomed *"unless / Soul clap its hands and sing, and louder sing / For every tatter in its mortal dress."* That *"unless"* is important for him always, and he often seems unsure about whether the soul can really do that required clapping and singing. He understandably goes up and down in his confidence about defeating the losses. In "From 'Oedipus at Colonus' " in *The Tower,* he echoes the more gloomy words of Sophocles' chorus.

Endure what life God gives and ask no longer span;
Cease to remember the delights of youth, travel-wearied aged man;
Delight becomes death-longing if all longing else be vain . . .
In the long echoing street the laughing dancers throng,
The bride is carried to the bridegroom's chamber through torchlight and tumultuous song;
I celebrate the silent kiss that ends short life or long.

Never to have lived is best, ancient writers say;
Never to have drawn the breath of life, never to have looked into
    the eye of day;
The second best's a gay goodnight and quickly turn away.

                                            —W. B. Yeats

    Yet in the title poem of that same volume, "The Tower," the
"sixty-year-old smiling public man" can answer the question he
raised for us on page 30—

        What shall I do with this absurdity
        O heart, O troubled heart—this caricature,
        Decrepit age that has been tied to me
        As to a dog's tail?

—as if the soul really could master all problems:

            Now shall I make my soul,
            Compelling it to study
            In a learned school
            Till the wreck of body,
            Slow decay of blood,
            Testy delirium
            Or dull decrepitude,
            Or what worse evil come—
            The death of friends, or death
            Of every brilliant eye
            That made a catch in the breath—
            Seem but the clouds of the sky
            When the horizon fades;
            Or a bird's sleepy cry
            Among the deepening shades.

Perhaps such "answers" must always prove precarious; Yeats seems even here to imagine the "wreck" and "slow decay" more vividly than the abstract "learned school." How is the poet to dramatize the soul's triumphs? One solution is to turn the soul into a wounded—and healed—body.

THE RESTORED

In a hand like a bowl
Danced my own soul,
Small as an elf,
All by itself.

When she thought I thought
She dropped as if shot.
"I've only one wing," she said,
"The other's gone dead,"

"I'm maimed; I can't fly;
I'm like to die,"
Cried the soul
From my hand like a bowl.

When I raged, when I wailed,
And my reason failed,
That delicate thing
Grew back a new wing,

And danced, at high noon,
On a hot, dusty stone,
In the still point of light
Of my last midnight.

—Theodore Roethke

Beyond such liberations, what positive additions can we boast of, to answer the condescensions of the young? Ironically enough, one of the most important is found in the very point about which the young seem to condescend most: memory. "I've already told you that twice, and you keep forgetting." Well, of course I do! Why should I bother to remember the trivia you offer now, when my mind, unlike your half-empty one, is crammed with important memories of a lifetime? At seventy-four, Edith Wharton made the point in a letter to a friend.

> I wish I knew what people mean when they say they find "emptiness" in this wonderful adventure of living, which seems to me to pile up its glories like an horizon-wide sunset as the light declines. I'm afraid I'm an incorrigible life-lover & life-wonderer & adventurer.

Life by its nature accumulates memories—until memory fails. Does it finally fail partly because of overload? Physiologists don't seem to have any convincing theories about the holding capacity of this mysterious memory-tank of ours. Obviously anyone who is "older" has poured in so much more than anyone who is "younger" that we shouldn't be surprised when the tank registers "Sorry, full."

There is an African proverb that can be interpreted either as a lament about ultimate loss or as a celebration: "When an old man dies, a library burns down." Whether our "libraries" consist of books or simply of daily experience, we all have this one possession that we lacked when young: an accumulation of experience, stored in memory, reshuffled, re-evaluated, reshaped in dreams and day-dreams, and all the while steeped in feeling. Even as we notice a "losing of the marbles"—that home telephone number, the name of the medicine prescribed by the doctor yesterday—our memories of the ever-lengthening years remain as vivid as ever, the pleasant ones still pleasant and, if we work at it, the painful ones turned to the pleasures of humor or revenge. Here's a seventy-nine-year-old "Crossing-Keepers Son," interviewed by Ronald Blythe.

This is the happiest time of my life—that is, and I tell you straight! I wish there was twenty-four hours in the day. Wuk hours, awake hours. Yew can keep y' sleep; plenty of time for that later on. I niver thowt I'd come to this. . . . Time's a funny thing, you know, a very funny thing. I'll tell y' somethen—that don't fare to be no time at all since I was a little ol' boy. That all seem to be some time yisterday. I come out with tales and sich-like about that time to Mother [his wife] and she say, "Why don't you write a book?" I could, tew! But that would be tellin'!

As Charles Nodier, the French romantic author, puts it, "The kindest privilege that nature grants the aging man is that of recovering the impressions of his childhood with an extraordinary ease." Unfortunately for our purposes, Nodier didn't live even to sixty-five. Perhaps more impressive is the report of the eighty-six-year-old woman who told Simone de Beauvoir "that as soon as she went to bed at night she would tell herself about things that had happened in her early childhood; she would tell them over and over again, and they gave her inexhaustible joy."

Here once again we encounter the frustrating advisers like Cicero and Mannes (pages 130 and 131) who tell us that we should have lived right when young, in order to provide good memories for the downslope. More useful, though still hard to emulate, are those rare ones who have mastered the art of elevating painful memories into gripping anecdote, or even into humor. How one longs, at any age, to be like those who can pass through gross misfortune and come out on the other end hale and hearty.

I had another aunt, Aunt Relva, who had suffered more hardship and sorrow than anyone else I know, and who in her eighties filled our time at her hospital bedside with lively and often comic remembrances of things past. She would often say, "Just remember the good things." When my eighteen-year-old son died, she advised, "Talk about it, keep talking about *him*—until you can relive the laughing times." I believe that she really possessed the gift of forgetting or forgiving the wrongs she had endured.

How different that is from Beauvoir's way of talking about what we forget. For her, led as she was by a philosophy that almost requires a daily dose of angst, our ability to forget the past is a source of anguish. Just think, she moans in *The Coming of Age,* of how much raw wonderful experience your memory has simply scrapped.

> "A very old man's memories are like ants whose ant-hill has been destroyed," says Mauriac. "One's eyes cannot follow any single one of them for long." And Hermann Broch: "Memories rise up, then sink down, often vanishing altogether. How timid they are! . . . Oh, what chasms of forgetfulness underlie our life; from what a great way off we must recall a memory that is scarcely a memory any more." . . .
>
> A friend said to me, "I find very old people touching because of the long past they have behind them." Unfortunately this is just what they do not have. The past is not a peaceful landscape lying there behind me, a country in which I can stroll wherever I please, and which will gradually show me all its secret hills and dales. As I was moving forward, so it was crumbling. Most of the wreckage that can still be seen is colourless, distorted, frozen: its meaning escapes me. Here and there, I see occasional pieces whose melancholy beauty enchants me. They do not suffice to populate this emptiness that Chateaubriand calls "the desert of the past."

If the joys of a well-stocked memory seem blasted by awareness of how much has been lost, one can always do an about-face and look to the future, either the future of one's country or world, or the more personal future implied by a good look at one's posterity, either biological or cultural. Just take a real look at that four-year-old grandchild and think of what she is now and what she may become. How fine it is to see that student one struggled to rescue, when he was seventeen and you were almost sixty, now flourishing at twenty-eight, when you are seventy-one.

This turn can easily be corrupted by assuming that the value of *now* depends on what *now* will lead to. To look to posterity is to risk losing the very equanimity that mastering the past can bring. My present, at any age, can be spoiled by a self-destructive futurism that worries about how I may look or feel if I reach ninety, or about whether my progeny, biological or cultural, will turn out as I would like.

It's easier these days to find good poems exulting in grandchildren than good poems imagining some glorious future for our country or our world. Hope for society, or even praise for how things are now, is generally muted, when it is not positively repudiated either by environmentalists or fundamentalists waiting for Armageddon. Everyone seems to be rediscovering that ancient truth about the world: It *is* contingent. As most religious traditions have it, this world was never *intended* to be permanent. Time will devour everything, sooner or later—except of course for whatever we can, with our thinking, with our poetry, rescue into the timeless. Buddhists, Muslims, Jews, and Christians all agree that something is radically wrong with the creation as it now stands, and it must somehow be redeemed or transcended or outgrown or repudiated.

Meanwhile, for the time being, let us dwell on the second kind of "future," the kind embodied *now* in those lively lithe lovelies, those children whom time holds green, as Dylan Thomas puts it, (and oh, yes, dying), as they sing in their chains like the sea.

Many a poet these days is taking comfort from the sheer existence of descendants—whether or not they are the poet's literal kin. Though some few disillusioned folks seem to view their progeny as total losses, many of us view our grandchildren as godlike creatures come to save the world.

About fifty years ago a poem appeared in *The New Yorker* (I think) that went like this (I think):

> Though styles in art may come and go
> The golden sunlight still contrives
> To make a Currier and Ives
> Of children playing in the snow.

Don't ask me who wrote it. As I've already told you too many times, I'm seventy-one; I can't remember, and I don't want to look it up for fear I've mutilated it in memory. But what I *can* remember —was I only twenty?—is feeling something like, "Now *there* is where the permanence lies. If, as has not yet happened, I should lose my faith in God, at least I will have *that.*"

Here is Ruth Pitter, in her late sixties, imagining how such comfort might work in a life that by most standards has been relatively comfortless:

YORKSHIRE WIFE'S SAGA

War was her life, with want and the wild air;
Not for life only; she was out to win.
Houses and ground were cheap, out on the bare
Moor, and the land not bad; they could begin,
Now that the seven sons were mostly men.

Two acres and a sow, on hard-saved brass;
Men down the mine, and mother did the rest.
Pity, with all those sons, they had no lass;
No help, no talk, no mutual interest,
Made fourteen slaving hours empty at best.

Fierce winter mornings, up at three or four;
Men bawl, pigs shriek against the raving beck.
Off go the eight across the mile of moor,
With well-filled dinner-pail and sweat-ragged neck;
But pigs still shriek, and wind blows door off sneck.

Of course they made it; what on earth could stop
People like that? Marrying one by one,
This got a farm, the other got a shop;
Now she was left with but the youngest son,
But she could look about and feel she'd won.

Doctor had told her she was clean worn out.
All pulled to bits, and nowt that he could do.
But plenty get that way, or die, without
Having a ruddy ten-quid note to show.
She'd got seven thriving sons all in a row.

And grandchildren. She liked going by bus
Or train, to stay a bit in those snug homes.
They were her colonies, fair glorious.
"Sit by the fire, ma, till the dinner comes.
Sit by the fire and cuddle little lass."

—Ruth Pitter

Maxine Kumin, in her mid-fifties, thinks of the "chain letter"
from mothers through daughters as an answer to Heideggerian
angst.

The Envelope

It is true, Martin Heidegger, as you have written,
I *fear to cease,* even knowing that at the hour
of my death my daughters will absorb me, even
knowing they will carry me about forever
inside them, an arrested fetus, even as I carry
the ghost of my mother under my navel, a nervy
little androgynous person, a miracle
folded in lotus position.

Like those old pear-shaped Russian dolls that open
at the middle to reveal another and another, down
to the pea-sized, irreducible minim,
may we carry our mothers forth in our bellies.
May we, borne onward by our daughters, ride
in the Envelope of Almost-Infinity,
that chain letter good for the next twenty-five
thousand days of their lives.

—Maxine Kumin

Perhaps the most thoroughgoing celebration of how a blossoming child can transform the old and disillusioned is Victor Hugo's *The Art of Being a Grandfather*, published when he was seventy. Addressed ostensibly to his two grandchildren, Georges and Jeanne, it seems really addressed to adults as forlorn advice on how, in a world full of despicable people, one might hope for better examples in the next generation. (For those who know French, and for any who would like, as I would, to improve on the only translation I can find, I give the original in the notes.)

The Contented Exile

What is this earth of ours? A storm of souls,
In this gloom where we wandering pilots reach
No shore but rocks, mistaking them for ports;
Amid the tempest of desires, of cries . . .
The fleeting kisses of those prostitutes
We call ambition, fortune and success;
Before the suffering Job's: "What do I know?"
The trembling Pascal's: "What then do I think?" . . .
In this corroding nothingness, and false
And lying chaos, what at last man sees Clearly is this:
. . . Above our sorrows . . . the reign of innocence,
And sovereignty of innocent things and pure. . . .
In truth, 'tis salutary for the mind . . . to contemplate
. . . a peace
Deep and profound and made of shining stars;
It is of this God thought, what time He placed
The poets near the cradles made for sleep.

Hugo's effort here to place all hope on his still innocent progeny may seem excessive, but to me the intensity with which he goes on and on about it carries the point home.

GEORGES AND JEANNE

I, whom a little child makes far from wise,
Have two,—sweet Georges and Jeanne; in this one's eyes
My sunlight dwells, by this one's hand I'm led;
Jeanne's but ten months, o'er Georges two years have sped.
Divinely subtle are their baby-ways,
And from their trembling utterance love essays
To catch the birth-star song ere it take flight;
While I—like evening darkening into night,
Whose destiny hath lost the light of day—
Take heart to sing: "What dawn so fair as they!" . . .
Georges dreams of cakes, perchance, of playthings fine,
Dog, cock, or cat; Jeanne chats with friends divine;
Then their eyes open wide, and make the whole world shine.
Their dawn, alas! marks growth of our decline.

—Victor Hugo

Though this seems in part an echo of Wordsworth's claim that children at birth "trail clouds of glory," coming directly, in all innocence, "from God who is their home," the claim here is much different from Wordsworth's: it is one's own progeny, as representative innocents, who carry the sole compensation for a despairing old age.

Shakespeare is surprisingly insistent in his earlier sonnets on what we might call redemption through one's literal descendants. At least he surprises me. Though I had read all his sonnets at one time or another, and had reread many of them again and again, I had never until recently fully attended to those we turn to now.

SONNET 3

Look in thy glass, and tell the face thou viewest
Now is the time that face should form another,
Whose fresh repair if now thou not renewest
Thou dost beguile the world, unbless some mother.
For where is she so fair whose uneared womb
Disdains the tillage of thy husbandry?
Or who is he so fond will be the tomb
Of his self-love, to stop posterity?
Thou art thy mother's glass, and she in thee
Calls back the lovely April of her prime;
So thou through windows of thine age shalt see,
Despite of wrinkles, this thy golden time.
   But if thou live remembered not to be,
     Die single, and thine image dies with thee.

SONNET 4

Unthrifty loveliness, why dost thou spend
Upon thyself thy beauty's legacy?
Nature's bequest gives nothing, but doth lend,
And being frank she lends to those are free.
Then, beauteous niggard, why dost thou abuse
The bounteous largess given thee to give?
Profitless usurer, why dost thou use
So great a sum of sums, yet canst not live?
For having traffic with thyself alone,
Thou of thyself thy sweet self dost deceive.
Then how, when Nature calls thee to be gone,
What acceptable audit canst thou leave?
   Thy unused beauty must be tombed with thee,
     Which, usèd, lives th' executor to be.

SONNET 6

Then let not winter's ragged hand deface
In thee thy summer ere thou be distilled.
Make sweet some vial; treasure thou some place
With beauty's treasure ere it be self-killed.
That use is not forbidden usury
Which happies those that pay the willing loan;
That's for thyself to breed another thee,
Or ten times happier, be it ten for one.
Ten times thyself were happier than thou art,
If ten of thine ten times refigured thee;
Then what could death do, if thou shouldst depart,
Leaving thee living in posterity?
  Be not self-willed, for thou art much too fair
  To be death's conquest and make worms thine heir.

SONNET 7

Lo, in the orient when the gracious light
Lifts up his burning head, each under eye
Doth homage to his new-appearing sight,
Serving with looks his sacred majesty;
And having climbed the steep-up heavenly hill,
Resembling strong youth in his middle age,
Yet mortal looks adore his beauty still,
Attending on his golden pilgrimage;
But when from highmost pitch, with weary car,
Like feeble age, he reeleth from the day,
The eyes, 'fore duteous, now converted are
From his low tract and look another way.
  So thou, thyself outgoing in thy noon,
  Unlooked on diest, unless thou get a son.

—William Shakespeare

Such testimony may seem crudely conventional when compared with much of Shakespeare's later work. His better-known sonnets concentrate on the quite different—though equally self-centered—hope: *"someday* I'll get the fame I deserve." All of these imply that if only the poet's descendants will have a close look at how he has described the losses, they can be turned to gains.

Sonnets like the next one are usually read, quite appropriately, as efforts to stave off Time's attacks on the "beauty" and "worth" of Shakespeare's true love. But they can be seen just as well as a claim that by composing his "black lines," he reverses the losses entailed in his own aging by projecting his own soul into the future (see also, for example, Sonnets 60 and 81).

SONNET 63

Against my love shall be, as I am now,
With Time's injurious hand crushed and o'erworn;
When hours have drained his blood and filled his brow
With lines and wrinkles; when his youthful morn
Hath traveled on to age's steepy night,
And all those beauties whereof now he's king
Are vanishing or vanished out of sight,
Stealing away the treasure of his spring;
For such a time do I now fortify
Against confounding age's cruel knife,
That he shall never cut from memory
My sweet love's beauty, though my lover's life.
　His beauty shall in these black lines be seen,
　And they shall live, and he in them still green.

For consolation or mitigation we can, then, look either to memory or hope. But neither memories of the past nor hopes for the future can be readily consoling unless somehow the present can be redeemed. To echo T. S. Eliot's *Four Quartets* one last time:

what might have been, what has been, and what will be all "Point to one end, which is always present." Memories of the past are not past but present, and as we have seen, if they are good, the present is good. Hopes are not future but present, and if they are good, the present feels good. When they center on grandchildren, a beautiful and relatively innocent future seems present before our eyes.

Present thoughts about either past or future, however, can seem like second-class substitutes, mere mitigations and no real comforts—unless our active present provides a life sufficiently self-justifying to validate those memories and hopes. As the greatest of philosophers and religious prophets have said, the place to look for happiness, or salvation, or celebration of "eternal life" is here and now.

Every recommended activity or attitude we've met so far here can be turned, at the right moment and in the right intensity, into such celebration. But it is found most convincingly, for most of our authors, in the topics we turn to here at last: ripened friendship and deepening love, a laughter that depends on a mature vision, a sense of freedom from the ills and limitations of youth, and a deepened capacity for religious contemplation and prayer.

Lifetime friendships can be destroyed by any oldster who falls into cynicism, self-absorption, and self-pity. They are certain to be shattered by death, as was Burke's lifetime friendship with his wife, "Shorty" (page 77). But they can, for the time being, move toward a unique kind of sharing, as if to say, *We* know what we know, you and I, and we value each other more because of what we know.

Henry James was often penetrating on the subject, in his novels as in his correspondence, and as he is in these lines written to Hugh Walpole:

. . . Cultivate with me, darlingest Hugh, the natural affections, so far as you are lucky enough to have matter for them.
I mean don't wait till you are eighty to do so—though indeed

I haven't waited, but have made the most of them from far back. I like exceedingly to hear that your work has got so bravely on, and envy you that sovereign consciousness. When it's finished—well, when it's finished let some of those sweet young people the *bons amis* (yours) come to me for the small change of remark that I gathered from you the other day (you were adorable about it) they have more than once chinked in your ear as from my poor old pocket, and they will see, *you* will see, in what coin I shall have paid them. I too am working with a certain shrunken regularity—when not made to lapse and stumble by circumstances (damnably physical) beyond my control. These circumstances tend to come, on the whole (thanks to a great power of patience in my ancient organism), rather *more* within my management than for a good while back; but to live with a bad and chronic anginal demon prey- ing on one's vitals takes a great deal of doing. However, I didn't mean to write you of that side of the picture (save that it's a large part of that same), and only glance that way to make sure of your tenderness even when I may seem to you backward and blank. It isn't to exploit your compassion—it's only to be able to feel that I am not without your fond under- standing: so far as your blooming youth (*there's* the crack in the fiddle-case!) *can* fondly understand my so otherwise-con- ditioned age. However, there's always understanding enough when there's affection enough, and you touch me almost to tears when you tell me how I touched the springs of yours that last time in London. . . .

And here is Kenneth Burke again, writing at seventy-three to Malcolm Cowley to thank him for one of the most impressively sustained modern friendships on record.

I miss our walks greatly . . . I knew, every minute of the time, how happy I was to be with youenz. We move on—yes, we move on. But there was a kind of lovely poignancy in our aging friendship there. It's not the sort of thing that could be reclaimed. If we tried it again, it would probably be as Marx says about the difference between tragedy and farce. It's gone beyond recovery (except that, in my memory, I recover it again and again).

I am so grateful, not just to youenz, but to the nature of things, that I can carry away with me the sense of our truly humane relationship in that interim. . . . Thanks. K.B.

Such friendships are in fact indistinguishable from love—that is, love without sex. Deep friendship, like sex itself, frequently slides into love. Is Shakespeare writing of a lover or a friend in Sonnet 30?

SONNET 30

When to the sessions of sweet silent thought
I summon up remembrance of things past,
I sigh the lack of many a thing I sought,
And with old woes new wail my dear time's waste.
Then can I drown an eye, unused to flow,
For precious friends hid in death's dateless night,
And weep afresh love's long since canceled woe,
And moan th' expense of many a vanished sight.
Then can I grieve at grievances foregone,
And heavily from woe to woe tell o'er
The sad account of fore-bemoanèd moan,
Which I new pay as if not paid before.
    But if the while I think on thee, dear friend,
    All losses are restored and sorrows end.

The answer seems clear enough in Sonnet 31—the words "love" and "friendship" become interchangeable.

SONNET 31

Thy bosom is endearèd with all hearts,
Which I by lacking have supposèd dead,
And there reigns love and all love's loving parts,
And all those friends which I thought burièd.
How many a holy and obsequious tear
Hath dear religious love stol'n from mine eye
As interest of the dead, which now appear
But things removed that hidden in thee lie!
Thou art the grave where buried love doth live,
Hung with the trophies of my lovers gone,
Who all their parts of me to thee did give;
That due of many now is thine alone.
   Their images I loved I view in thee,
   And thou, all they, hast all the all of me.

—William Shakespeare

The speaker here expresses a kind of love that no very young person could experience to the full: I love you because you embody the many loves we both have lost. Nobody knows exactly how old Shakespeare was when he wrote these sonnets—they were published when he was about forty-five, an age which in his time meant that both he and the addressed friend had long since shared the loss of more friends to death than most seventy-year-olds have experienced today. Like today's people with AIDS and early cancer, he knew what it was to lose friend after friend, and he knew just how precious it is to have at least one friend who can share those losses.

He also knew how much intensity is added to such love by the thought of how fragile it is:

SONNET 73

That time of year thou mayst in me behold
When yellow leaves, or none, or few, do hang
Upon those boughs which shake against the cold,
Bare ruined choirs, where late the sweet birds sang.
In me thou seest the twilight of such day
As after sunset fadeth in the west,
Which by and by black night doth take away,
Death's second self, that seals up all in rest.
In me thou seest the glowing of such fire
That on the ashes of his youth doth lie,
As the deathbed whereon it must expire,
Consumed with that which it was nourished by.
   This thou perceiv'st, which makes thy love more strong,
   To love that well which thou must leave ere long.

—William Shakespeare

Matthew Arnold was also in his mid-forties when he wrote "Dover Beach," a poem not ostensibly about aging at all but about the world as nothing but a "darkling plain" where "ignorant armies clash by night." Is it only my own preoccupation with aging these days that leads me to hear, in the conclusion to this portrait of universal decay, the voice of the same "old man" who at thirty had seen himself as "three parts iced over"? The difference is that now that voice has found love: sustained love is the last refuge of the disillusioned—and thus presumably of the old?

Dover Beach

The sea is calm to-night.
The tide is full, the moon lies fair
Upon the straits; on the French coast the light
Gleams and is gone; the cliffs of England stand,
Glimmering and vast, out in the tranquil bay.
Come to the window, sweet is the night-air!
Only, from the long line of spray
Where the sea meets the moon-blanch'd land,
Listen! you hear the grating roar
Of pebbles which the waves draw back, and fling,
At their return, up the high strand,
Begin, and cease, and then again begin,
With tremulous cadence slow, and bring
The eternal note of sadness in.

Sophocles long ago
Heard it on the Aegean, and it brought
Into his mind the turbid ebb and flow
Of human misery; we
Find also in the sound a thought,
Hearing it by this distant northern sea.

The Sea of Faith
Was once, too, at the full, and round earth's shore
Lay like the folds of a bright girdle furl'd.
But now I only hear
Its melancholy, long, withdrawing roar,
Retreating, to the breath
Of the night-wind, down the vast edges drear
And naked shingles of the world.

Ah, love, let us be true
To one another! for the world, which seems
To lie before us like a land of dreams,
So various, so beautiful, so new,
Hath really neither joy, nor love, nor light,

Nor certitude, nor peace, nor help for pain;
And we are here as on a darkling plain
Swept with confused alarms of struggle and flight,
Where ignorant armies clash by night.

—Matthew Arnold

Because such thoughts touch everyone's experience, they have bred thousands of poems, before and after Arnold. Most of the assertions that love is the sole or main consolation for aging seem to me as shallow as the worst of the deniers. Henry Chudakoff collects a lot of these in *How Old Are You?*

When you and I were young. Maggie . . . etc., etc.

And now we are aged and gray, Maggie,
The trials of life nearly done.
Let's sing of the days that are gone, Maggie . . .

We are old folks, now, my darling
Our beards are growing grey,
But taking the year, all around, my dear,
You will always find a May.

Obviously a whole anthology could easily be built out of popular songs and poems on this one consolation alone. Though most of it would be conventional, much of it could be as conventionally lovely as one of Robert Burns's most famous songs.

JOHN ANDERSON MY JO

John Anderson my jo, John,
    When we were first acquent;
Your locks were like the raven,
    Your bony brow was brent;

But now your brow is beld, John,
    Your locks are like the snaw;
But blessings on your frosty pow,
    John Anderson my Jo.

John Anderson my jo, John,
    We clamb the hill the gither;
And mony a canty day, John,
    We've had wi' ane anither:

Now we maun totter down, John,
    And hand in hand we'll go;
And sleep the gither at the foot,
    John Anderson my Jo.

                —Robert Burns

Or it can be as forlorn as Theodore Roethke's "prayer," at fifty-six, for his "young wife,"

WISH FOR A YOUNG WIFE

My lizard, my lively writher,
May your limbs never wither,
May the eyes in your face
Survive the green ice
Of envy's mean gaze;
May you live out your life
Without hate, without grief,
And your hair ever blaze,
In the sun, in the sun,
When I am undone,
When I am no one.

Or we could fill this book with love poems as full of an implicit fear of aging and death as Elizabeth Barrett Browning's famous sonnet, written at age forty-four, with the decades racing past.

43

How do I love thee? Let me count the ways.
I love thee to the depth and breadth and height
My soul can reach, when feeling out of sight
For the ends of Being and ideal Grace.
I love thee to the level of everyday's
Most quiet need, by sun and candlelight.
I love thee freely, as men strive for Right;
I love thee purely, as they turn from Praise.
I love thee with the passion put to use

In my old griefs, and with my childhood's faith.
I love thee with a love I seemed to lose
With my lost saints,—I love thee with the breath,
Smiles, tears, of all my life!—and, if God choose,
I shall but love thee better after death.

—Elizabeth Barrett Browning

With friends dying at a great rate all around them, it is no wonder that writers in previous centuries often turned to those more enduring friends, the ever-faithful authors on their shelves. If you want lasting comfort in your old age, comfort from friends who will *never* let you down, turn to reading as your supreme consolation. (What, never? Well, *almost* never.) Listen to Machiavelli on the subject:

> When evening has arrived, I return home, and go into my study. . . . I pass into the antique courts of ancient men, where, welcomed lovingly by them, I feed upon the food which is my own, and for which I was born. Here, I can speak with them without show, and can ask of them the motives of their actions; and they respond to me by virtue of their humanity. For hours together, the miseries of life no longer annoy me; I forget every vexation; I do not fear poverty; and death itself does not dismay me, for I have altogether transferred myself to those with whom I hold converse.

To me one of the most powerful healing gifts of friendship with those authors on our shelves is the one my Aunt Relva recommended: laughter. Though they may be hundreds of years old, they find it easier to look at life and laugh at it wholeheartedly than do most of our aging flesh-and-blood friends coping with their woes. Purged of all signs of the pettinesses they no doubt plagued their real-life friends with, they can play humorous games with us to the very end.

It's true that most of what we have met so far here has been rather solemn, but that's only because I've saved most of the humor for this moment. Many of the authors I've quoted frequently offer, if not belly laughs, at least what George Meredith calls the "smile of the mind." Even Victor Hugo, along with the totally solemn, not to say gloomy self-portrait in most of his grandfather-poems, shows a sense of humor about the grandchildren's wild behavior. But the fact is that authors who can make genuinely amusing hay out of the dry straws of Part 1 are rare—and their very rarity makes them all the more precious.

Most of what I find is a bit feeble, like this well-meant joshing by Frank C. Laubach:

LIFE BEGINS AT 80

I have good news for you. The first 80 years are the hardest. The second 80 are a succession of birthday parties.

Once you reach 80, everyone wants to carry your baggage and help you up the steps. If you forget your name or anybody else's name, or an appointment, or your own telephone number, or promise to be three places at the same time, or can't remember how many grandchildren you have, you need only explain that you are 80.

Being 80 is a lot better than being 70. At 70 people are mad at you for everything. At 80 you have a perfect excuse no matter what you do. If you act foolishly, it's your second childhood. Everybody is looking for symptoms of softening of the brain.

Being 70 is no fun at all. At that age they expect you to retire to a house in Florida and complain about your arthritis (they used to call it lumbago) and you ask everybody to stop mumbling because you can't understand them. (Actually your hearing is about 50 percent gone.)

If you survive until you are 80, everybody is surprised that you are still alive. They treat you with respect just for having lived so long. Actually they seem surprised that you can walk and talk sensibly.

So please, folks, try to make it to 80. It's the best time of life. People forgive you for anything. If you ask me, life begins at 80.

—Frank C. Laubach

Considerably better to me, for comfort on a bad day, is Walter Savage Landor's twisting of the old advice, "Just seize time by the forelock."

The burden of an ancient rhyme
Is, "By the forelock seize on Time."
Time in some corner heard it said;
Pricking his ears, away he fled;
And, seeing me upon the road,
A hearty curse on me bestow'd.
"What if I do the same by thee?
How wouldst thou like it?" thunder'd he,
And, without answer thereupon,
Seizing *my* forelock—it was gone.

Like humor about anything else, humor about aging can't be achieved just by trying, or by proclaiming, "I've gotta funny story for ya." Perhaps that is why so many exhorters and comforters just ignore it. But when it works it works dramatically, not just on the mind but on our physical ills themselves. Norman Cousins some years ago was told by his doctors, when he went to them suffering intense pain, that he was dying. Desperate, he turned to laughter, and he was able to prove to those who would listen that laughter was a better analgesic than aspirin. Lying on what was said to be his deathbed, he experimented with watching comic movies and made a "joyous discovery":

. . . that ten minutes of genuine belly laughter had an anesthetic effect and would give me at least two hours of pain-free sleep. When the pain-killing effect of the laughter wore off, we would switch on the motion-picture projector again, and, not infrequently, it would lead to another pain-free sleep interval.

—Norman Cousins

Then he turned to reading—just what the doctor is ordering throughout this book—and found that anthologies of American humor produced the same effects as the movies. They not only relieved the pain; they cured his illness.

Of course he did not confine himself to humor about illness, any more than oldsters should confine themselves to humor about old age. But there is something especially toughening about laughter at your own condition—at least when the jesting does not cut too close to the decaying bone.

Why is humor about aging so effective—when it works—and so exasperating—at least to the elderly—most of the time? No doubt because effective comedy preserves the losses while transcending them, while too many attempts at humor simply fall into denials—like the passage from Ann Landers.

Here is James Ball Naylor, preserving the full sense of loss of sexual prowess, while having his fun:

DAVID AND SOLOMON

King David and King Solomon
    Led merry, merry lives,
With many, many lady friends
    And many, many wives;
But when old age crept over them,
    With many, many qualms,
King Solomon wrote the Proverbs
    And King David wrote the Psalms.

Though we may not write many funny poems about aging, we do joke about our fears a lot. Older friends have told me four or five times, and started to tell me many more times, the story about the elderly golfer whose eyesight is so bad he can't see where his ball lands, and he runs into another old duffer, with perfect eyesight, who agrees to be his seeing eye, and he tees off with a wonderful long drive, and his partner says, "What a wonderful drive," and he asks, "Where'd it go, where'd it go?" and his partner says—stop me if you've heard it—his partner says, "I can't remember."

I've not heard young people tell that joke, or many others like it, only oldtimers, Alzheimer's to Alzheimer's. Reminds me—the subject of humor leads us always into the anecdotal style—reminds me of a song my daddy used to sing me, back in 'bout '26:

> Good mornin', Mr. Zip, Zip, Zip,
> With yore hair cut jes as short-as mine.
> Good mornin', Mr. Zip, Zip, Zip,
> Yore shorely lookin' fine.
> Ashes to ashes, and dust to dust,
> If Camels don't kill ya then Fatimas must.
> Good mornin', Mr. Zip, Zip, Zip,
> With your hair cut jes as short-as,
> Yore hair cut jes as short-as,
> Yore hair cut jes as short-as mi-ine.

I'm not sure about the spelling or source of "Fatimas." I've always assumed they were another kind of cigarette. I could look it up, but I prefer not to.

Anyway, it seems to me—no doubt because my Daddy sang it—to represent about the best of folk humor, not belly laughs but *humor* about our woes. Of course it's not about aging, exactly, but it comes close: How do you relate a life full of zip to what we know about universal death—to say nothing about the ravages of nicotine? (Oh, yes, cigarettes were called coffin nails at least as early as 1926, unless my memory is playing tricks again.)

"Ashes to ashes, and dust to dust, / If Alzheimer's don't kill ya then Parkinson's must . . ."

The morning paper is full of joking about the woes of age. In the comic strip Cathy, the heroine's boyfriend, dressed in a party hat, looks worried as he says, "The aging man has a one-in-five chance of having a heart attack . . . one-in-five chance of kidney stones . . . three-in-five chance of prostate trouble. . . . . and a 99.9 percent chance of weaker muscles, poorer vision, stiffer joints, reduced hearing, lower sex drive, and. . . ." Cathy, bored silly, replies, "Irving, you're young, healthy and strong! Why are you thinking like this??" And the age-hypochondriac shrieks, *"Aack! My brain has already started to shrink!!"*

Autobiographers play with it, though not as often as I wish they would: "A year ago," writes Bruce Bliven, "when I was only eighty-two, I wrote somebody that 'I don't feel like an old man, I feel like a young man' who has something the matter with him.' I have now found what it is: it is the approach of middle age, and I don't care for it." Try these:

The Last Laugh

I made hay while the sun shone.
  My work sold.
Now, if the harvest is over
  And the world cold,
Give me the bonus of laughter
  As I lose hold.

—John Betjeman

Of late I appear
To have reached that stage
When people look old
Who are only my age.

—Richard Armour

Do not mock at the old; God takes it ill;
For old as they are, He is older still.

—Elder Olson

Mark Twain all his life knew that life is funny. He is popularly thought to have become seriouser and seriouser as he aged; his books become downright nasty toward the end. When he was put on public display, though, asked to respond to a toast at his seventieth birthday banquet, he knew how to make something of it.

MARK TWAIN'S SEVENTIETH BIRTHDAY DINNER, DELMONICO'S, NEW YORK, DECEMBER 5, 1905

I have had a great many birthdays in my time. I remember the first one very well, and I always think of it with indignation; everything was so crude, unesthetic, primeval. Nothing like this at all. No proper appreciative preparation made; nothing really ready. Now, for a person born with high and delicate instincts—why, even the cradle wasn't whitewashed—nothing ready at all. I hadn't any hair, I hadn't any teeth, I hadn't any clothes, I had to go to my first banquet just like that. Well, everybody came swarming in. It was the merest little bit of a village—hardly that, just a little hamlet, in the backwoods of Missouri, where nothing ever happened, and the people were all interested, and they all came; they looked me over to see if there was anything fresh in my line. Why, nothing ever happened in that village—I—why, I was the only thing that had really happened there for months and months and months; and although I say it myself that shouldn't, I came the nearest to being a real event that had happened in that village in more than two years. Well, those people came, they came with that curiosity which is so provincial, with that frankness which also is so provincial, and they examined me all around and gave their opinion. Nobody asked them, and I shouldn't have minded if anybody had paid me a compliment, but nobody did. Their opinions were all just green with prejudice, and I feel those opinions to this day. Well, I stood that as long as—well, you know I was born courteous, and I stood it to the limit. I stood it an hour, and then the worm turned. I was the worm; it was my turn to turn, and I turned. I knew very well the strength of my position; I knew that I was the only spotlessly pure and innocent person in that whole town, and I came out and said so. And they could not say a word. It was so true. They blushed; they were embarrassed. Well, that was the first after-dinner speech I ever made. I think it was after dinner.

It's a long stretch between that first birthday speech and this one. That was my cradle song, and this is my swan song, I suppose. I am used to swan songs, I have sung them several times.

This is my seventieth birthday, and I wonder if you all rise to the size of that proposition, realizing all the significance of that phrase, seventieth birthday.

The seventieth birthday! It is the time of life when you arrive at a new and awful dignity; when you may throw aside the decent reserves which have oppressed you for a generation and stand unafraid and unabashed upon your seven-terraced summit and look down and teach—unrebuked. You can tell the world how you got there. It is what they all do. You shall never get tired of telling by what delicate arts and deep moralities you climbed up to that great place. You will explain the process and dwell on the particulars with senile rapture. I have been anxious to explain my own system this long time, and now at last I have the right.

I have achieved my seventy years in the usual way: by sticking strictly to a scheme of life which would kill anybody else. It sounds like an exaggeration, but that is really the common rule for attaining to old age. When we examine the program of any of these garrulous old people we always find that the habits which have preserved them would have decayed us; that the way of life which enabled them to live upon the property of their heirs so long, as Mr. Choate says, would have put us out of commission ahead of time. I will offer here, as a sound maxim, this: That we can't reach old age by another man's road.

I will now teach, offering my way of life to whomsoever desires to commit suicide by the scheme which has enabled me to beat the doctor and the hangman for seventy years. Some of the details may sound untrue, but they are not. I am not here to deceive; I am here to teach.

We have no permanent habits until we are forty. Then they begin to harden, presently they petrify, then business begins. Since forty I have been regular about going to bed and getting up—and that is one of the main things. I have made it a rule to go to bed when there wasn't anybody left to sit up with; and I have made it a rule to get up when I had to. This has resulted in an unswerving regularity of irregularity. It has saved me sound, but it would injure another person.

In the matter of diet—which is another main thing—I have been persistently strict in sticking to the things which didn't agree with me until one or the other of us got the best of it. Until lately I got the best of it myself. But last spring I stopped frolicking with mince pie after midnight; up to then I had always believed it wasn't loaded. For thirty years I have taken coffee and bread at eight in the morning, and no bite nor sup until seven-thirty in the evening. Eleven hours. That is all right for me, and is wholesome, because I have never had a headache in my life, but headachy people would not reach seventy comfortably by that road, and they would be foolish to try it. And I wish to urge upon you this—which I think is wisdom—that if you find you can't make seventy by any but an uncomfortable road, don't you go. When they take off the Pullman and retire you to the rancid smoker, put on your things, count your checks, and get out at the first way station where there's a cemetery.

I have made it a rule never to smoke more than one cigar at a time. I have no other restriction as regards smoking. I do not know just when I began to smoke, I only know that it was in my father's lifetime, and that I was discreet. He passed from this life early in 1847, when I was a shade past eleven; ever since then I have smoked publicly. As an example to others, and not that I care for moderation myself, it has always been my rule never to smoke when asleep, and never to refrain when awake. It is a good rule I mean, for me; but some of you know quite well that it wouldn't answer for everybody that's trying to get to be seventy.

I smoke in bed until I have to go to sleep; I wake up in the night, sometimes once, sometimes twice, sometimes three times, and I never waste any of these opportunities to smoke. This habit is so old and dear and precious to me that I would feel as you, sir, would feel if you should lose the only moral you've got—meaning the chairman—if you've got one; I am making no charges. I will grant, here, that I have stopped smoking now and then, for a few months at a time, but it was not on principle, it was only to show off; it was to pulverize those critics who said I was a slave to my habits and couldn't break my bonds.

Today it is all of sixty years since I began to smoke the limit. I have never bought cigars with life belts around them. I early found that those were too expensive for me. I have always bought cheap cigars—reasonably cheap, at any rate. Sixty years ago they cost me four dollars a barrel, but my taste has improved, latterly, and I pay seven now. Six or seven. Seven, I think. Yes, it's seven. But that includes the barrel. I often have smoking parties at my house; but the people that come have always just taken the pledge. I wonder why that is?

As for drinking, I have no rule about that. When the others drink I like to help; otherwise I remain dry, by habit and preference. This dryness does not hurt me, but it could easily hurt you, because you are different. You let it alone.

Since I was seven years old I have seldom taken a dose of medicine, and have still seldomer needed one. But up to seven I lived exclusively on allopathic medicines. Not that I needed them, for I don't think I did; it was for economy; my father took a drug store for a debt, and it made cod liver oil cheaper than other breakfast foods. We had nine barrels of it, and it lasted me seven years. Then I was weaned. The rest of the family had to get along with rhubarb and ipecac and such things, because I was the pet. I was the first Standard Oil Trust. I had it all. By the time the drug store was exhausted my health was established and there has never been much the matter with me since. But you know very well it would be foolish for the average child to start for seventy on that basis. It happened to be just the thing for me, but that was merely an accident; it couldn't happen again in a century.

I have never taken any exercise, except sleeping and resting, and I never intend to take any. Exercise is loathsome. And it cannot be any benefit when you are tired; and I was always tired. But let another person try my way, and see where he will come out.

I desire now to repeat and emphasize that maxim: We can't reach old age by another man's road. My habits protect my life but they would assassinate you.

I have lived a severely moral life. But it would be a mistake for other people to try that, or for me to recommend it. Very few would succeed: you have to have a perfectly colossal stock of morals; and you can't get them on a margin; you have to have the whole thing, and put them in your box. Morals are an acquirement—like music, like a foreign language, like piety, poker, paralysis—no man is born with them. I wasn't myself, I started poor. I hadn't a single moral. There is hardly a man in this house that is poorer than I was then. Yes, I started like that—the world before me, not a moral in the slot. Not even an insurance moral. I can remember the first one I ever got. I can remember the landscape, the weather, the—I can remember how everything looked. It was an old moral, an old secondhand moral, all out of repair, and didn't fit, anyway. But if you are careful with a thing like that, and keep it in a dry place, and save it for processions, and chautauquas, and World's Fairs, and so on, and disinfect it now and then, and give it a fresh coat of whitewash once in a while, you will be surprised to see how well she will last and how long she will keep sweet, or at least inoffensive. When I got that mouldy old moral, she had stopped growing, because she hadn't any exercise; but I worked her hard, I worked her Sundays and all. Under this cultivation she waxed in might and stature beyond belief, and served me well and was my pride and joy for sixty-three years; then she got to associating with insurance presidents, and lost flesh and character, and was a sorrow to look at and no longer competent for business. She was a great loss to me. Yet not all loss. I sold her—ah, pathetic skeleton, as she was—I sold her to Leopold, the pirate King of Belgium; he sold her to our Metropolitan Museum, and it was very glad to get her, for, without a rag on, she stands fifty-seven feet long and sixteen feet high, and they think she's a brontosaur. Well, she looks it. They believe it will take nineteen geological periods to breed her match.

Morals are of inestimable value, for every man is born crammed with sin microbes, and the only thing that can extirpate these sin microbes is morals. Now you take a sterilized Christian—I mean, you take *the* sterilized Christian, for there's only one. Dear sir, I wish you wouldn't look at me like that.

Threescore years and ten!

It is the Scriptural statute of limitations. After that, you owe no active duties; for you the strenuous life is over. You are a time-expired man, to use Kipling's military phrase. You have served your term, well or less well, and you are mustered out. You are become an honorary member of the republic, you are emancipated, compulsions are not for you, nor any bugle call but "lights out." You pay the timeworn duty bills if you choose, or decline if you prefer—and without prejudice—for they are not legally collectible.

The previous engagement plea, which in forty years has cost you so many twinges, you can lay aside forever; on this side of the grave you will never need it again. If you shrink at thought of night, and winter, and the late homecoming from the banquet and the lights and the laughter through the deserted streets—a desolation which would not remind you now, as for a generation it did, that your friends are sleeping, and you must creep in a-tiptoe and not disturb them, but would only remind you that you need not tiptoe, you can never disturb them more—if you shrink at thought of these things, you need only reply, "Your invitation honors me, and pleases me because you still keep me in your remembrance, but I am seventy; seventy, and would nestle in the chimney corner, and smoke my pipe, and read my book, and take my rest, wishing you well in all affection, and that when you in your turn shall arrive at pier No. 70 you may step aboard your waiting ship with a reconciled spirit, and lay your course toward the sinking sun with a contented heart."

—Mark Twain

Here are some other efforts I've found to turn the losses to humorous profit. For once, here you will not find attributions in the notes at the back. I don't even know the source of some of these, and I am a bit suspicious of some of the attributions. Can anyone, by the way, explain to me why the collections I've raided here have yielded only one *mot* by a woman—the first one—and even it perhaps vaguely sexist?

If God had to give a woman wrinkles, He might at least have put them on the soles of her feet.

—Ninon (Anne) de Lenclos

I have discovered the secret formula for a carefree Old Age: ICR = FI—"If You Can't Recall It, Forget It."

—Goodman Ace

I am in the prime of senility.

—Joel Chandler Harris

I'll never make the mistake of bein' seventy again!

—Casey Stengel

If I'd known I was going to live so long, I'd have taken better care of myself.

—Eubie Blake (also attributed to León Eldred and others, and perhaps traceable to the pre-Socratics)

I'm sixty-five and I guess that puts me in with the geriatrics, but if there were fifteen months in every year, I'd only be forty-eight.

—James Thurber

I'm saving the rocker for the day when I feel as old as I really am.

—Dwight D. Eisenhower

Old age is when you know all the answers but nobody asks you the questions.

—Lawrence J. Peter (from whom I borrow some of these bits)

Life is a jest; and all things show it.
I thought so once; but now I know it.

—John Gay, "My Own Epitaph"

CROSSING THE BORDER

Senescence begins
And middle age ends
The day your descendants
Outnumber your friends.

—Ogden Nash

The painful truth, for any older person who thinks about the humor of aging, is that too much of it is cruel: it is written by those who are, or like to think they are, young. Edward Lear was in his mid-thirties when he penned the following bits of "nonsense." Would he have written anything like them forty-two years later just before he died, at seventy-six? Were old gentlemen funny then?

THERE WAS AN OLD MAN WITH A BEARD

There was an Old Man with a beard,
Who said, "It is just as I feared!—
Two Owls and a Hen,
Four Larks and a Wren,
Have all built their nests in my beard!"

There Was an Old Man Who Supposed

There was an Old Man who supposed,
That the street door was partially closed;
But some very large rats
Ate his coats and his hats,
While that futile old gentleman dozed.

—Edward Lear

Approaching forty, Lewis Carrol thought—rightly in my view—that parodic nonsense about old, old men could be great fun.

Advice from a Caterpillar

"You are old, Father William," the young man said,
    "And your hair has become very white;
And yet you incessantly stand on your head—
    Do you think, at your age, it is right?"

"In my youth," Father William replied to his son,
    "I feared it might injure the brain;
But, now that I'm perfectly sure I have none,
    Why, I do it again and again."

"You are old," said the youth, "as I mentioned before,
    And have grown most uncommonly fat;
Yet you turned a back-somersault in at the door—
    Pray, what is the reason of that?"

"In my youth," said the sage, as he shook his grey locks,
    "I kept all my limbs very supple
By the use of this ointment—one shilling the box—
    Allow me to sell you a couple?"

"You are old," said the youth, "and your jaws are too weak
    For anything tougher than suet;
Yet you finished the goose, with the bones and the beak—
    Pray, how did you manage to do it?"

"In my youth," said his father, "I took to the law,
    And argued each case with my wife;
And the muscular strength, which it gave to my jaw
    Has lasted the rest of my life."

"You are old," said the youth, "one would hardly suppose
    That your eye was as steady as ever;
Yet you balanced an eel on the end of your nose—
    What makes you so awfully clever?"

"I have answered three questions, and that is enough,"
    Said his father. "Don't give yourself airs!
Do you think I can listen all day to such stuff?
    Be off, or I'll kick you down-stairs!"

—Lewis Carroll

Ben Jonson was in his early thirties—in his time that was already "getting on"—when he wrote Volpone's marvelous tirade against one kind of oldster:

So many cares, so many maladies,
So many fears attending on old age,
Yea, death so often called on, as no wish
Can be more frequent with 'em, their limbs faint,
Their senses dull, their seeing, hearing, going,
All dead before them; yea, their very teeth,
Their instruments of eating, failing them;
Yet this is reckoned life! Nay, here was one,
Is now gone home, that wishes to live longer!
Feels not his gout, nor palsy; feigns himself
Younger by scores of years, flatters his age

With confident belying it, hopes he may
With charms, like Aeson, have his youth restored;
And with these thoughts so battens, as if fate
Would be as easily cheated on as he,
And all turns air!

—Ben Jonson

Should we be surprised that we find nothing anywhere near as bouncy in what Jonson wrote during the nine years between his stroke, in his mid-fifties, and his death, in his mid-sixties?

You can see why my thoughts here lead naturally to the so-called black humor of modern literature. It has often been criticized by moral critics as degrading life. It does that, of course, on its surface, just as Volpone's tirade "degrades" old age. But to the degree that it gets us laughing it is no longer totally degrading. At that moment of laughter we can feel redeemed. By deflecting the specific woes of age from tragedy to absurdity, authors like Samuel Beckett make life worth living, during the moments we spend with them, even as the surface texts tell us, as in this passage from Watt, that we are doomed.

After a short time Watt returned to the music-room, with a tray, of refreshments.

Not Mr. Gall Senior, but Mr. Gall Junior, was tuning the piano, to Watt's great surprise. Mr. Gall Senior was standing in the middle of the room, perhaps listening. Watt did not take this to mean that Mr. Gall Junior was the true piano-tuner, and Mr. Gall Senior simply a poor blind old man, hired for the occasion, no. But he took it rather to mean that Mr. Gall Senior, feeling his end at hand, and anxious that his son should follow in his footsteps, was putting the finishing touches to a hasty instruction, before it was too late.

While Watt looked round, for a place to set down his tray, Mr. Gall Junior brought his work to a close. He reassembled the piano case, put back his tools in their bag, and stood up.

The mice have returned, he said.

The elder said nothing. Watt wondered if he had heard.

Nine dampers remain, said the younger, and an equal number of hammers.

Not corresponding, I hope, said the elder.

In one case, said the younger.

The elder had nothing to say to this.

The strings are in flitters, said the younger.

The elder had nothing to say to this either.

The piano is doomed, in my opinion, said the younger.

The piano-tuner also, said the elder.

The pianist also, said the younger.

—Samuel Beckett

A wonderful story about Beckett in his old age—probably apocryphal—has him attending the annual British cricket matches on a beautiful June day.

"Isn't this a wonderful day?" he says to his companion.

"Yes, just the sort of day that makes life worth living."

A thoughtful pause.

"Oh, I wouldn't go that far," says the master of Nada, the author of *Happy Days*. His works never explicitly even hint that life might be worth the living. But like that June day, they are worth experiencing for the sheer fun of it.

We should remember, though, that Beckett was relatively young (in his forties and early fifties) when he published his funniest stuff. As he grew older, solemnity set in, making his bleak portraits sadder and sadder. Some of them dwell on despair at such length, and with so little redeeming wit, that I get off Charon's boat.

Short of that point almost any human emotion or experience, if viewed slightly askance, can yield as much or more fun when we are old as when young. Hatred, envy, humiliation, egotistical triumph—even the desire for revenge can be transformed by a mind ready to turn on itself. Here is Kenneth Burke (who seems to be rivaling Yeats as hero of this volume) enjoying at just my age the *fun of making fun* of his need for revenge.

Thank God, I have enough enemies to keep me living. Otherwise the self-kill would be all about me. One must watch everywhere one turns. For instance, a publisher writes, saying that a certain thing of one's is "gorgeous." And one wakes up just in time to catch the mail, with one's answer to him *on a postcard.* . . . those bastard shits, the Phartisan [*Partisan Review*] Crowd and sech, I wanna hold out as long as I can, against those poops.

Obviously Burke could write that way only because he felt free to, and he felt free to both because he was writing privately and because he was old enough not to worry about exposing a revengeful vein. Was it such freedom that allowed the usually solemn Walter Savage Landor to play with revenge like this, as he approached eighty? When young he never abandoned, so far as I can discover, the literary pose of a generous-spirited genius far above the battle (see page 176).

Epigram XXVI

Alas! 'tis very sad to hear,
Your and your Muse's end draws near:
I only wish, if this be true,
To lie a little way from you.
The grave is cold enough for me
Without you and your poetry.

Such freedom to laugh openly about one's less admirable emotions and irritations can take almost any direction. Here is a "lament" by Auden that playfully summarizes almost the whole range of losses that we saw in Part I, only to conclude with a stanza that goes beyond scoffing to a serious, and certainly in this poem unearned, claim to be in touch with Reality with a capital R.

DOGGEREL BY A SENIOR CITIZEN
for Robert Lederer

Our earth in 1969
Is not the planet I call mine,
The world, I mean, that gives me strength
To hold off chaos at arm's length.

My Eden landscapes and their climes
Are constructs from Edwardian times,
When bath-rooms took up lots of space,
And, before eating, one said Grace.

The automobile, the aeroplane,
Are useful gadgets, but profane:
The enginry of which I dream
Is moved by water or by stream.

Reason requires that I approve
The light-bulb which I cannot love:
To me more reverence-commanding
A fish-tail burner on the landing.

My family ghosts I fought and routed,
Their values, though, I never doubted:
I thought their Protestant Work-Ethic
Both practical and sympathetic.

When couples played or sang duets,
It was immoral to have debts:
I shall continue till I die
To pay in cash for what I buy.

The Book of Common Prayer we knew
Was that of 1662:
Though with-it sermons may be well,
Liturgical reforms are hell.

Sex was, of course—it always is—
The most enticing of mysteries,
But news-stands did not yet supply
Manichaean pornography.

Then Speech was mannerly, an Art,
Like learning not to belch or fart:
I cannot settle which is worse,
The Anti-Novel or Free Verse.

Nor are those Ph.D's my kith,
Who dig the symbol and the myth:
I count myself a man of letters
Who writes, or hopes to, for his betters.

Dare any call Permissiveness
An educational success?
Saner those class-rooms which I sat in,
Compelled to study Greek and Latin.

Though I suspect the term is crap,
If there *is* a Generation Gap,
Who is to blame? Those, old or young,
Who will not learn their Mother-Tongue.

But Love, at least, is not a state
Either *en vogue* or out-of-date,
And I've true friends, I will allow,
To talk and eat with here and now.

Me alienated? Bosh! It's just
As a sworn citizen who must
Skirmish with it that I feel
Most at home with what is Real.

—W. H. Auden

CECIL BEATON PHOTOGRAPH COURTESY OF SOTHEBY'S LONDON.

W. H. Auden

To make Auden's claim, however lightly, is to move far beyond mere consolation and introduce again one of the major causes for celebration of age: its capacity to liberate us to say and do what we think we *really*—Really?—ought to do or want to do instead of merely what convention asks of us. Confucius speaks for dozens I have found saying something of this kind:

The Master said, "At fifteen, I had my mind bent on learning. At thirty, I stood firm. At forty, I had no doubts. At fifty, I knew the decrees of Heaven. At sixty, my ear was an obedient organ for the reception of truth. At seventy, I could follow what my heart desired, without transgressing what was right."

Though I can't pretend to know what Confucius really meant by that, I like to imagine it was something like, "I could follow what my heart desired, without having to worry about what other people thought was right, because by that time I had my own strong sense of what was right, imbibed, no doubt, largely from others, but still by that time *my own*."

You like his shorter version better? So do I.

E. M. Forster quotes Bacon about a slightly different source of freedom, with implied approval—or maybe not Bacon; neither Forster nor I have been able to find the quotation.

And this dear freedom hath begotten me this peace, that I mourn not that end which must be, nor spend one wish to have one minute added to the uncertain date of my years.

Sometimes the freedom found with age can sound very much like the turn from body to soul that we saw above, in expressions of resignation or relinquishing. Here is Arthur Schopenhauer (not, I confess, my favorite among the philosophers; for one thing, some of his comments on women are among the worst in the whole sexist philosophical tradition):

Towards the close of life, much the same thing happens as at the end of a *bal masque*—the masks are taken off. Then you can see who the people really are, with whom you have come into contact in your passage through the world. For by the end of life characters have come out in their true light, actions have borne fruit, achievements have been rightly appreciated, and all shams have fallen to pieces. For this, Time was in every case requisite.

But the most curious fact is that it is also only towards the close of life that a man really recognizes and understands his own true self, the aims and objects he has followed in life, more especially the kind of relation in which he has stood to other people and to the world. It will often happen that as a result of this knowledge, a man will have to assign himself a lower place than he formerly thought was his due. But there are exceptions to this rule, and it will occasionally be the case that he will take a higher position than he had before. This will be owing to the fact that he had no adequate notion of the *baseness* of the world, and that he set up a higher aim for himself than was followed by the rest of mankind.

The progress of life shows a man the stuff of which he is made.

It is customary to call youth the happy, and age the sad part of life. This would be true if it were the passions that made a man happy. Youth is swayed to and fro by them, and they give a great deal of pain and little pleasure. In age the passions cool and leave a man at rest, and then forthwith his mind takes a contemplative tone; the intellect is set free and attains the upper hand. And since, in itself, intellect is beyond the range of pain, a man feels happy just in so far as his intellect is the predominating part of him.

Beauvoir, despite her fashionably melancholy tone about almost everything, does manage in her early sixties to see how such liberation can serve as a genuine new gift of life. "On the intellectual plane," she says, "old age may also bring liberation: it sets one free from false notions." It is true that "the clarity of mind that comes with it is accompanied by an often bitter disillusionment."

> [But once] illusions have been swept away, [age can bring] a questioning, challenging state of mind. Doing, while at the same time "placing one's activity into a parenthesis," means achieving authenticity; it is harder to adopt than falsehood, but, once reached, it cannot but bring happiness. This sweeping away of fetishes and illusions is the truest, most worthwhile of all the contributions brought by age.

Beauvoir tells us that François Mauriac, for example, suddenly felt freed, in what he called his "waning years," to engage in a kind of aggressive political action that he had previously been afraid of (though when he became really old he discontinued even that).

The sense of moving into a new and freer territory can lead to many fresh discoveries—to a new kind of carefree laughter. Or—as we've already observed in many authors—it can lead to a new appreciation for just plain everyday *living* in the world of physical sensation, the kind of bliss John Updike records here.

> Like my late Unitarian father-in-law am I now in my amazed, insistent appreciation of the physical world, of this planet with its scenery and weather—that pathetic discovery which the old make that every day and season has its beauty and its uses, that even a walk to the mailbox is a precious experience, that all species of tree and weed have their signature and style and the sky is a pageant of clouds. Aging calls us outdoors, after the adult indoors of work and love-life and keeping stylish, into the lowly simplicities that we thought we had outgrown as children. We come again to love the plain world, its stone and wood, its air and water. "What a glorious view!" my father-in-law would announce as we smirked in the back seat of the car he was inattentively driving. But in truth all views have something glorious about them. The act of seeing is itself glorious, and of hearing, and feeling, and tasting. One of my

dead golf partners, Ted Lucas, said once within my hearing to another dear departed fellow golfer, John Conley, "Life is bliss." . . . Ted also, on another occasion, while we were floundering around in the sunshine on a little friendly nine-hole course called Cape Ann, suddenly exclaimed, "Ah, to be alive, on a June day, in Ipswich, Massachusetts!"

We could turn here once again to art as a prime solace; indeed, it would not be hard to fill the remainder of this book with testimonials to the ways in which music, painting, sculpture, dance, and various other arts and crafts can celebrate age in ways not available to youth.

Of these, the celebration that means most to me—at times even more than the best poetry—is music. And it is the most frustrating to me as collector, because obviously I cannot illustrate what the great composers—most of whom seem to go on creating longer than do most poets—accomplish with musical meanings. It is impossible, for example, to talk adequately about, let alone demonstrate, what Beethoven achieves in his final quartet when he asks, with a musical interrogative labeled "Muss es sein?" (Must it be?), in F minor, and then answers aggressively with what he calls the "schwer gefasste Entschluss" (the "hard-reached conclusion," or "resolution"), a melody in F major that he also labels with words, as if worried that we'll miss the point: It *must* be! (See next page.) The very cumbersomeness of that last sentence illustrates my point: Musical illustration of how to cope with growing older can be found only in listening to the music.

Forster, when ill in his early eighties, received a letter from a friend and copied a fine sentence, as we have seen him do before, into his *Commonplace Book:*

The days potter by here much the same; sometimes the sad sound of their ticking feet gets into my ears as they disappear into history, carrying nothing in their delicate hands but a yawn.

IV

Der schwer gefasste Entschluss.

Last movement of Beethoven's final quartet (#16, op. 135).

To which Forster comments: "Can any day that produced such a sentence be lost?"

That comment could take us back to "Sailing to Byzantium" or indeed to any one piece that you have found especially felicitous: Can any week or month or year that produced the best poems here be lost? Many a poet, like e. e. cummings in his "62," openly declares that the losses are in some sense canceled if the soul can rise "and sing." (See next page.)

Turning at last to "wisdom," the celebration that is perhaps the most difficult to discuss without sounding pretentious or banal, we must tread lightly. Is wisdom in any sense separated from the various liberations we have seen already? Further, if wisdom is a special preserve of old folks, why are so few old folks visibly wise?

The truth is that more authors have fun scoffing at the foolishness of the elderly than praising them for wisdom. As H. L. Mencken put it, making fun not just of others but of himself, "The older I grow the more I distrust the familiar doctrine that age brings wisdom." Lin Yutang reports a Chinese proverb: "Wisdom does not depend on age; a man of a hundred may be full of empty talk."

Do the old people you know seem on average any wiser than their juniors? All my life I've noticed that most of the world's folly has been committed by people older than I—an observation especially compelling when I was in my late teens and two friends and I were the only wise people I knew. We shared daily comments on what a mess the oldsters had made of things. There are days when I say the same thing even now, even though many of the "oldsters" are, after all, younger than I am. Perhaps we should just close up shop, then, and retreat to Part I with the nineteenth-century French literary critic and historian Charles Augustin Sainte-Beuve: "We harden in some places and rot in others: we never ripen."

Yet I cling—don't we all cling?—to the intuition that the changed way we look at the world, even when that way includes disillusionment, is a gain. That we have something that "they"—those youngsters—do not yet have. What is it, this wisdom that

62

now does our world descend
the path to nothingness
(cruel now cancels kind;
friends turn to enemies)
therefore lament, my dream
and don a doer's doom

create is now contrive;
imagined, merely know
(freedom: what makes a slave)
therefore, my life, lie down
and more by most endure
all that you never were

hide, poor dishonoured mind
who thought yourself so wise;
and much could understand
concerning no and yes:
if they've become the same
it's time you unbecame

where climbing was and bright
is darkness and to fall
(now wrong's the only right
since brave are cowards all)
therefore despair, my heart
and die into the dirt

but from this endless end
of briefer each our bliss—
where seeing eyes go blind
(where lips forget to kiss)
where everything's nothing
—arise, my soul; and sing

—e. e. cummings

aging *sometimes* yields, the wisdom that no youngster could even suspect?

Simone de Beauvoir gives one fine description of it in her praise for the way Montaigne grew wiser as he aged. Seeing Montaigne as the only writer in the sixteenth century who could write about aging without falling into cliché, she traces his path to wisdom in a way that may protect us from cliché here.

Using his own experience, he examined old age as though no one before him had ever spoken of it; and here, in this direct, hard look at a reality that most people did their best to disguise, is the secret of his profundity. The ancient world caricatured old men while at the same time it praised old age. Montaigne refused either to make fun of it or to glorify it. He wanted to disentangle the truth. For himself, he thought that age had not enriched him. He brought forward his own evidence in opposition to Plato's and Cicero's moralizing optimism and in opposition to the claim of the old to wisdom. He was a little over thirty-five when he looked back at the period of his life before thirty and wrote, "For my part, I think it certain that since that age both my mind and my body have rather lessened than grown and rather gone back than forward. It may be that with those who use time well knowledge and experience increase with life; but liveliness, firmness, quickness and other qualities far more part of ourselves, more important and essential, fade and grow weaker."

Again, "Since then I have grown older for a great length of time, but not an inch wiser am I, I am sure. Myself at this moment and myself then are certainly two different beings; but which the better? I cannot tell. Being old would be very well if we moved on only towards improvement. But it is with a drunkard's step that we advance, staggering, giddy, with no set direction; or like straws that the wind turns according to its own mere motion."

In the later third book, Montaigne still preferred his youth

to the period that he already looked upon as old age. He felt
that he had only moved backwards, that he had not advanced.

"In any event, I hate this incidental repentance that age
brings with it. That man who once said he was grateful to the
years for having taken sensual delights away from him had an
opinion quite unlike mine: I could never thank impotence for
the kindness it does me. . . . In old age our appetites are rare,
and afterwards deep satiety comes upon us; here I see nothing
of conscience at work. Affliction and weakness impart a
rheumy, faint-hearted virtue. I who stir my reason briskly and
attentively, find that it is the very same that I had in my more
licentious days, except perhaps in so far as it has weakened
and deteriorated in growing older. I think it none the braver,
just because I see it unable to fight. I do not find it considers
anything now that it did not consider then; nor has it any new
lights.
    ". . . I should be grudging and ashamed if the wretched-
ness and misfortune of my decrepitude were rightly to set
itself above my good, healthy, eager, vigorous years, and if
men were to judge me not by where I have been but by where
I am no longer. . . . In the same way, my wisdom may well
be of the same size in both the one time and the other; but it
was far prompter to do, more supple, green, gay, natural than
it is at present, stale, sullen, painful . . .
    "Our humours are hard to please; present things disgust us;
and this we call wisdom. But the truth is that we do not so
much leave our vices as change them; and in my opinion for
the worse. . . . Never a soul is to be seen, or very few, who in
growing old does not take on a sour and mouldy smell. A man
moves towards his full and his decline as an entity, a whole."
    I find it wonderful that Montaigne, tossing traditional and
comforting clichés overboard, refuses to accept any kind of
mutilation as an advance, or to look upon the mere accumulation of years as an enrichment. But in Montaigne there is a
curious paradox that may have escaped him but that is strik-

ingly obvious to the reader: the *Essais* become richer and richer, more and more intimate, original and profound as the author of the book advances in age. He would never have been capable of writing these fine, biting, disillusioned pages upon old age when he was thirty. It was when he felt that his powers had declined that he was at his greatest. But no doubt he would never have attained this greatness but for the severity with which he treated himself. All self-satisfaction dulls: the ageing Montaigne was able to preserve himself from it. The reason why he advanced is that his attitude towards the world and towards himself became more and more critical; and the reader is in the difficult position of agreeing with the criticism while at the same time he observes the advance.

—Simone de Beauvoir

Does Beauvoir fall here, in spite of her abhorrence of cliché, into a modernist cliché of her own: wisdom is found by becoming "more and more critical," sloughing off illusion after illusion? Wisdom = Full Disillusionment—which is what age alone can yield?

If we define illusion simply as falsehood, the formula of course works fine: the fewer untruths we fall for, the better. But one oldster's "illusion" can be another one's profound truth.

Sometimes the claim to wisdom is no more than a cynical retreat from hope: You're "wise" if you're smart enough to know that most plans don't work out. Sometimes it's no more than collecting enough experience to teach you that on the whole, strangers can't be totally trusted, especially when they offer political, social, or monetary panaceas. That can be a gain, in a time when everyone seems to be competing for the Gullibility Blue Ribbon. (But apparently it's not a gain shared by the majority of our older brothers and sisters—not if we judge by the annual statistics reporting the elderly victims of con artists.)

For Walter Savage Landor, approaching eighty, the wisdom-of-disillusionment yields a triumph over Fear and Hope, a triumph that makes him sound perhaps just a bit too confident about the next years.

To Age

Welcome, old friend! These many years
    Have we lived door by door:
The Fates have laid aside their shears
    Perhaps for some few more.

I was indocil at an age
    When better boys were taught,
But thou at length hast made me sage,
    If I am sage in aught.

Little I know from other men,
    Too little they from me,
But thou hast pointed well the pen
    That writes these lines to thee.

Thanks for expelling Fear and Hope,
    One vile, the other vain;
One's scourge, the other's telescope,
    I shall not see again:

Rather what lies before my feet
    My notice shall engage—
He who hath braved Youth's dizzy heat
    Dreads not the frost of Age.

           —Walter Savage Landor

I have no doubt that Landor wants us to see him here as wise, his wisdom a result of age. Like most of us some of the time, but none of us all of the time, he clearly would hesitate, at least until the full blows of senility struck, to trade his present life for the tensions and battles of dizzying hot anguished Youth. But if we are to talk of genuine wisdom, we must not forget what we learned in "Losses." Whatever wisdom poets claim, they must somehow face the question of how they will talk when cancer strikes. How does the wisdom work then? Can it be anything more than something longed for?

Lord, what is man, that Thou hast regard for him?
Or the son of man, that Thou takest account of him?

Man is like a breath,
His days are as a fleeting shadow.

In the morning he flourishes and grows up like grass,
In the evening he is cut down and withers.

So teach us to number our days,
That we may get us a heart of wisdom.

—Adapted from Psalms 144 and 90.

While hoping, even praying, for wisdom, there's no escaping the fact that the final months, or even years, will for many of us be pretty awful—and we really cannot predict which ones they will be. Once the brain is hit, we are no longer ourselves and we can't be responsible for how we feel or think. Our quest is for a wisdom that will not just get us through the years before that final stroke, that final infarction, but that will turn those years into a flowering. I am quite willing to follow Diogenes Laertius's advice,

Let no one be slow to seek wisdom when he is young nor weary of the search thereof when he is grown old. For no age is too early or too late for the health of the soul. And to say that the season for studying philosophy has not yet come, or that it is past and gone, is like saying that the season for happiness is not yet or that it is now no more. Therefore both young and old ought to seek wisdom, the former in order that, as age comes over him, he may be young in good things because of the grace of what has been, and the latter in order that, while he is young, he may at the same time be old, because he has no fear of the things which are to come.

Unfortunately, that advice is so general that I don't know how to apply it. Just where, seeking something more specific, should I look?

Each of the four cardinal virtues has had its advocates: Courage (as we have seen), Temperance, Justice, Prudence. T. S. Eliot, like many a Christian adviser, elects humility: "The only wisdom we can hope to acquire/Is the wisdom of humility: humility is endless." And he tells us that the place to look is—just as we've been implying all along—in the works of the greatest authors: for him, Dante, Shakespeare, Goethe. Did he have in mind, I wonder, something like the humility shown by the formerly arrogant King Lear when he regains his sanity and expresses his humble dream to Cordelia?

> Come, let's away to prison.
> We two alone will sing like birds i' the cage.
> When thou dost ask me blessing, I'll kneel down
> And ask of thee forgiveness. So we'll live,
> And pray, and sing, and tell old tales, and laugh
> At gilded butterflies, and hear poor rogues
> Talk of court news . . .
> And take upon 's the mystery of things,
> As if we were God's spies; and we'll wear out
> In a walled prison, packs and sects of great ones,
> That ebb and flow by the moon.

George Santayana changes Eliot's list of Greatest Counselors of Wisdom, in *Three Philosophical Poets,* substituting Lucretius for Shakespeare. As a Spanish philosopher, could he have missed the grandeur of *our* Greatest's celebration of humility? Much as I admire the books of that Grandee Santayana, I doubt that humility was even on his list to be crossed off. Perhaps he would have embraced Bertrand Russell's quite different line—not "I have learned humility" but "I have learned how, in spite of many defeats, not to feel defeated." Beneath my "load of failure," Russell says,

> . . . I am still conscious of something that I feel to be victory. I may have conceived theoretical truth wrongly, but I was not wrong in thinking that there is such a thing, and that it deserves our allegiance [note the almost-religious terminology of this "atheist"]. I may have thought the road to a world of free and happy human beings shorter than it is proving to be, but I was not wrong in thinking that such a world is possible, and that it is worth while to live with a view to bringing it nearer. I have lived in the pursuit of a vision, both personal and social. Personal: to care for what is noble, for what is beautiful, for what is gentle; to allow moments of insight to give wisdom at more mundane times. Social: to see in imagination the society that is to be created, where individuals grow freely, and where hate and greed and envy die because there is nothing to nourish them. These things I believe, and the world, for all its horrors, has left me unshaken.

As Walt Whitman tries to express the coming of wisdom with age, he adds some names to the list of wise counselors:

To Get the Final Lilt of Songs

To get the final lilt of songs,
To penetrate the inmost lore of poets—to know the mighty ones,
Job, Homer, Eschylus, Dante, Shakspere, Tennyson, Emerson;
To diagnose the shifting—delicate tints of love and pride and
    doubt—
                to truly understand,
To encompass these, the last keen faculty and entrance-price,
Old age, and what it brings from all its past experiences.

(You may want to say about such a poem that it is closer to plain prose than some of the prose passages I have quoted. Indeed I hope that in reading some of them you've seen how easily they could be lined out as poems. We might, for example, play with Russell, from page 238:

> To care for what is noble,
> For what is beautiful,
> For what is gentle,
> To allow moment of insight
> To give wisdom

Or Forster, from page 177:

> My great extension
> Is not through time
> To eternity
> But through space
> To Infinity:
> Here
> Now . . .
> Seeing the stars.

Not great poems, those two transformations: as abstract as Whitman's but no more "prosaic." The point of this self-indulgent parenthesis is to bring to the surface, as one subtext of this whole collection, two ancient and forgotten points about poetry: it's not confined to verse, and there's more of it bursting forth every day than we ordinarily credit.)

Having spent years as a critic touting the ethical powers of long fictions, I am distressed to find none of the great novelists on these lists of gurus. My own list would include a fair number of nineteenth-century novels that enmesh us in characters' sustained quests for wisdom—not just the coming-of-age kind, *Erziehungs-romane* like Goethe's *Wilhelm Meister's Apprenticeship,* but novellas like Tolstoy's *The Death of Ivan Ilych* and many of his monumental blockbusters (some of which Henry James faults as "great fluid puddings"): *Anna Karenina*, George Eliot's *Middlemarch*, Jane Austen's *Emma*, James's own *The Ambassadors*, and so on. The frustrating fact for me as collector is that the wisdom of such works cannot be discovered in bits and pieces: full immersion in their depths is required, and one always comes up from the depths with only muddy reports on what one has seen.

Short of such massive fictional "demonstrations," such "showings forth" of the wisdom of implied authors so much wiser than their flesh-and-blood makers could ever have been, is there any persuasive wisdom to be had in shorter statements of the kind we're looking at here? In a sense they are all doomed to fall short of such ambitious fulfilment, but let us try a few.

Here is M. F. K. Fisher, concluding her *Sister Age,* written when she was "well into" her seventies:

> By now, several years after I turned my back on all this, I think that I know a few things more clearly than I did when I was young, long before Ursula helped pull my fumblings into focus.
>
> I know, for instance, that I like old people, when they have aged well. And old houses with an accumulation of sweet honest living in them are good. And the timelessness that only the passing of Time itself can give to objects both inside and outside the spirit is a continuing reassurance.
>
> I have formed a strong theory that there is no such thing as "turning into" a Nasty Old Man or an Old Witch. I believe that such people, and of course they are legion, were born nasty and witch-like, and that by the time they were about five years old they had hidden their rotten bitchiness and lived fairly decent lives until they no longer had to conform to rules of social behavior, and could revert to their original horrid natures.
>
> This theory is hard to prove, because by the time a person begins to show his true-born nature, most of the people who

knew him when he was little have either died or gone into more immediate shadows. I still believe that it is probable, however. I have lived long enough to keep a sharp eye on a few of my peers, and they bear out almost frighteningly the sad natures they first promised us to end with.

On the other hand, there are a lot of people who seem to be born merry or serene or very lively. They are happy vital little babies and children, whether they live in ghettos or in suburban villas surrounded by electronic security systems. They need only one thing in life besides food and shelter, and that is warm open love from some person or animal or thing in their surroundings. They often live until they are very old, through the same delights and sadnesses that everyone else does, but after all the years of social subterfuge and conniving they emerge as bright souls . . . not nasty, not bitchy, just *good*.

If I could choose, I would like that to happen to me, because in our culture it is difficult to be old, and still live with younger fellowmen, and it helps to be tolerably acceptable instead of boring or obnoxious. So far, myself, I think I am in luck, because I was a lively, healthy child who wanted and got a great share of affection. I notice that as I get rid of the protective covering of the middle years, I am more openly amused and incautious and less careful socially, and that all this makes for increasingly pleasant contacts with the world. (It also compensates for some of the plain annoyances of decrepitude, the gradual slowing down of physical things like muscles, eyes, bowels. In other words, old age is more bearable if it can be helped by an early acceptance of being loved and of loving.)

The physical hindrances are of course important, no matter how little an old person manages to admit their dominance. As I write this I am well into my seventies, and I think that I have aged faster than I meant to, whatever that means! (It means, for one thing, that I resent being stiff and full of creaks and twinges.) I did not plan to be the way I am, although I

probably knew more than most of my peers about the inevit-
abilities of disintegration. Fortunately, though, because I met
Sister Age so long ago, I can watch my own aging with a
detachment she has taught me. I know about the dismays and
delights of my condition, and wish that all of us could prepare
ourselves for them as instinctively and with as much outside
help as we do those of puberty, adolescence, pregnancy, men-
opausal and climacteric changes. . . .

The Aging Process is a part of most of our lives, and it
remains one we try to ignore until it seems to pounce upon us.
We evade all its signals. We stay blandly unprepared for some
of its obnoxious effects, even though we have coped with the
cracked voices and puzzling glands of our emerging natures,
and have been guided no matter how clumsily through bud-
ding love-pains, morning-sickness, and hot flashes. We do
what our mentors teach us to do, but few of us acknowledge
that the last years of our lives, if we can survive to live them
out, are as physically predictable as infancy's or those of our
full flowering. This seems impossible, but it is true.

We are helped by wise parents and teachers and doctors to
live through our first couple of decades, and then to behave
more or less like creative, productive social creatures, and then
to withdraw from the fray, if possible on our various kinds of
laurels. And then what?

We are unprepared for the years that may come as our last
ones. We are repelled and frightened by our physical changes,
some of them hindering and boring, and we feel puzzled and
cheated.

Plainly, I think that this clumsy modern pattern is a wrong
one, an ignorant one, and I regret it and wish I could do more
to change it. Ours is not a society that can accept with patience
the presence of clumsy or inept or slow-spoken human beings,
and just as untrained puzzled young people drift aimlessly
through our slums, untrained puzzled old men and women
wait to die in rest-homes everywhere. The statistics of a Beauvoir tome are as monotonous as the outcries of sensational

journalism: there is no room, right now in our society, for the useless.

That does not mean, though, that some of us who seem meant to survive *need* do it blindly. I think we must use what wits we have, to admit things like the fact that it is harder to get up off the floor at seventy than at forty . . . or even fourteen. We must accept and agree with and then attend to with dispassion such things as arthritis, moles that may be cancerous, constipation that may lead to polyps and hernias, all the boring physical symptoms of our ultimate disintegration. (Old clocks tick more slowly than they did when young.)

What is important, though, is that our dispassionate acceptance of attrition be matched by a full use of everything that has ever happened in all the long wonderful-ghastly years to free a person's mind from his body . . . to use the experience, both great and evil, so that physical annoyances are surmountable in an alert and even mirthful appreciation of life itself.

This sounds mawkish and banal as I try to write it, but I believe it. I am glad that I have been able to live as long as I have, so that I can understand why Ursula von Ott did not weep as she stood by the funeral urn of her son, surrounded by all the vivid signs of his short silly life . . . the fat cupids, the fatter Venuses whose satiny knees he lolled against. She did not smile, but behind her deep monkey-eyes she surely felt a reassuring warmth of amusement, along with her pity that he never had tried to feel it too.

Parts of the Aging Process are scary, of course, but the more we know about them, the less they need be. That is why I wish we were more deliberately taught, in early years, to prepare for this condition. It would leave a lot of us freed to enjoy the obvious rewards of being old, when the sound of a child's laugh, or the catch of sunlight on a flower petal is as poignant as ever was a girl's voice to an adolescent ear, or the tap of a golf-ball into its cup to a balding banker's.

When I was about twelve, my grandmother died and we

all relaxed, especially at table. She was puritanical by nature, and did not believe in the indulgences of the flesh, so that sitting lazily after a good meal was not our privilege until she left us. Then we were like mice, with the cat gone. One day, after a long Sunday lunch, my younger sister and I stayed at table with our parents in the cool dining room. We were quiet, full of sponge-cake and peace. Mother murmured toward the end of the table where her husband sat. They sipped glasses of port from the decanter that usually stood untouched on the sideboard. Mother said idly something about Old Mrs. Tolbert, the organist at church. "I do wish she would stop scratching herself," she said. Father said, just as lazily and with as little malice, "Maybe she doesn't take enough baths." His wife protested gently, with a soft shrug and a little grimace. I said, with some boldness because although Anne and I were invited to stay on at the table now and then, we still spoke only when spoken to, as in Grandmother's recent days, "No. It's because she itches."

My parents put down their glasses. Anne looked daringly at me, although with correct politeness because of where we were.

"No," I said again. "She is old, and old people itch."

"Ah?" Mother asked, and Father went on, "Is that so? What do you think you mean?"

I said, "Well, I think the skin gets drier when people start to wither. You can see old women's arms. And when the skin gets withery, it itches. And anyway, they don't know they are scratching. They aren't dirty. They may just need to be oiled."

Anne said, "Scratching is rude. It's disgusting."

"I think so too," Mother said. "Disgusting. Old Mrs. Tolbert is really . . ." She sipped the last of her wine, and Father tipped his glass back and stood up. "Now that we've had our little lesson in geriatrics," he said, "and know all about how we'll itch as we age, I suggest that our medical advisor and her sister clear the table and leave us to our own pursuits. I may rub a little lotion on my chin, or—"

Mother laughed and we all went our ways on that fine free Sunday afternoon. But I knew I was right about Mrs. Tolbert. I did not like her, because she had a strong smell, but it was plain that she could not help her scratching: she was drying up like an old shoe and needed to be waxed. She did not need soap and water. Anne and I went on talking about this, as we tidied the kitchen before the cook came back from her Sunday cavortings. We decided that baths are all right, even fun, but that old people need *oil* on their skins, just as new babies do . . . olive oil, or maybe Hinds' Honey and Almond Cream, our current dream of exotic ointments.

And I kept on thinking about old people, and writing notes about them, and readying my spirit to meet Ursula von Ott on that dank crooked street in Zurich. Then, for decades, I kept on clipping and writing some of the notes that are in this book, instead of in a weighty set of statistics on library reference shelves. In one way or another they are about *why* Ursula was not weeping as she held the notice of her son's brave death in her slack old hand, and perhaps of why Old Mrs. Tolbert would have been better off with oil instead of soap and water on her itchy skin.

The crux of it all, perhaps the real secret, is that there was nobody to rub the gentle oil into Mrs. Tolbert's itch. She was alone, and unprepared to be so. There are too many people like her, caught unready for their last days, unprepared to cope with the logistics of dignified acceptance. She forgot to bathe now and then, forgot that she was scratching herself in front of finicky observers . . . finally forgot to breathe. There was nobody in the world to help her.

Mrs. Tolbert possibly started me on my long ponderings about how hard it can be for lonely old people to stay sweet, much less give a small damn whether they are or not. And her common plight leads neatly into the saddest conclusion I have reached about the art of aging, which can and should be as graceful and generally beneficent a "condition" as any other in our lives.   —M. F. K. Fisher

What I especially like about Fisher's modest profession of wisdom about age is her honesty in facing just how hard it is to talk about "the obvious rewards of being old" without sounding "mawkish and banal." Our poets have all known about that obstacle, but none of them has talked much about it: talking about it is not likely in itself to make for poetry. The whole art of growing older is elusive, and the art of talking well about it is even more so. A first miracle comes when we discover a new species of flowers bursting out of our rotting soil. The second miracle comes, for some few among us, when they find words that do justice to those flowers. The word "miracle" is justified because finding those words requires the very poetic gifts that many poets see themselves as losing, along with other losses. The truth is that one could fill many an anthology with the abominable poems that garrulous old poets turned out, by habit, on their bad days; Wordsworth, Landor, Hardy—sometimes even Yeats—could count among their other losses the loss of discrimination. But that fact surely makes the good stuff they give us even more impressive.

It also helps explain why the best sustained prose discussions of aging are so full of ironic complexities that they risk downright inconsistency or incoherence. Discussions that avoid that risk—most essays by gerontologists advancing a thesis—leave me longing for more of what the great "personal essayists" of the past could offer, adopting a leisurely pace and playing with a delicate intricacy that would be acceptable to few editors these days.

To quote adequately from that tradition would make another book, but we can sample it now by turning to an essay that Robert Louis Stevenson wrote in the year of his death, as a prematurely wise old man of forty-four. Stevenson is now out of fashion, quite undeservedly as you will discover if you slow down now and read "Crabbed Age and Youth," from *Virginibus Puerisque,* with the kind of attention you will have given to our best poems.

> Old people have faults of their own; they tend to become cowardly, niggardly, and suspicious. Whether from the growth of experience or the decline of animal heat, I see that

age leads to these and certain other faults; and it follows, of course, that while in one sense I hope I am journeying towards the truth, in another I am indubitably posting towards these forms and sources of error.

As we go catching and catching at this or that corner of knowledge, now getting a foresight of generous possibilities, now chilled with a glimpse of prudence, we may compare the headlong course of our years to a swift torrent in which a man is carried away; now he is dashed against a boulder, now he grapples for a moment to a trailing spray; at the end, he is hurled out and overwhelmed in a dark and bottomless ocean. We have no more than glimpses and touches; we are torn away from our theories; we are spun round and round and shown this or the other view of life, until only fools or knaves can hold to their opinions. We take a sight at a condition in life, and say we have studied it; our most elaborate view is no more than an impression. If we had breathing space, we should take the occasion to modify and adjust; but at this breakneck hurry, we are no sooner boys than we are adult, no sooner in love than married or jilted, no sooner one age than we begin to be another, and no sooner in the fulness of our manhood than we begin to decline towards the grave. It is in vain to seek for consistency or expect clear and stable views in a medium so perturbed and fleeting. This is no cabinet science, in which things are tested to a scruple; we theorise with a pistol to our head; we are confronted with a new set of conditions on which we have not only to pass a judgment, but to take action, before the hour is at an end. And we cannot even regard ourselves as a constant; in this flux of things, our identity itself seems in a perpetual variation; and not infrequently we find our own disguise the strangest in the masquerade. In the course of time, we grow to love things we hated and hate things we loved. Milton is not so dull as he once was, nor perhaps Ainsworth so amusing. It is decidedly harder to climb trees, and not nearly so hard to sit still. There is no use pretending; even the thrice royal game of hide and seek has somehow lost in zest.

All our attributes are modified or changed; and it will be a poor account of us if our views do not modify and change in a proportion. To hold the same views at forty as we held at twenty is to have been stupefied for a score of years, and take rank, not as a prophet, but as an unteachable brat, well birched and none the wiser. It is as if a ship captain should sail to India from the Port of London; and having brought a chart of the Thames on deck at his first setting out, should obstinately use no other for the whole voyage.

And mark you, it would be no less foolish to begin at Gravesend with a chart of the Red Sea. *Si Jeunesse savait, si Vieillesse pouvait* [if only youth knew, if only age could] is a very pretty sentiment, but not necessarily right. In five cases out of ten, it is not so much that the young people do not know, as that they do not choose. There is something irreverent in the speculation, but perhaps the want of power has more to do with the wise resolutions of age than we are always willing to admit. It would be an instructive experiment to make an old man young again and leave him all his *savoir*. I scarcely think he would put his money in the Savings Bank after all; I doubt if he would be such an admirable son as we are led to expect; and as for his conduct in love, I believe firmly he would out-Herod Herod, and put the whole of his new compeers to the blush. Prudence is a wooden Juggernaut, before whom Benjamin Franklin walks with the portly air of a high priest, and after whom dances many a successful merchant in the character of Atys. But it is not a deity to cultivate in youth. If a man lives to any considerable age, it cannot be denied that he laments his imprudences, but I notice he often laments his youth a deal more bitterly and with a more genuine intonation.

It is customary to say that age should be considered, because it comes last. It seems just as much to the point, that youth comes first. And the scale fairly kicks the beam, if you go on to add that age, in a majority of cases, never comes at all. [Here Stevenson underlines a major point of my introduction.] Disease and accident make short work of even the most prosperous persons; death costs nothing, and the expense of a headstone is an inconsiderable trifle to the happy heir. To be suddenly snuffed out in the middle of ambitious schemes, is tragical enough at best; but when a man has been grudging himself his own life in the meanwhile, and saving up everything for the festival that was never to be, it becomes that hysterically moving sort of tragedy which lies on the confines of farce. The victim is dead—and he has cunningly overreached himself: a combination of calamities none the less absurd for being grim. To husband a favourite claret until the batch turns sour, is not at all an artful stroke of policy; and how much more with a whole cellar—a whole bodily existence! People may lay down their lives with cheerfulness in the sure expectation of a blessed immortality; but that is a different affair from giving up youth with all its admirable pleasures, in the hope of a better quality of gruel in a more than problematical, nay, more than improbable, old age. We should not compliment a hungry man, who should refuse a whole dinner and reserve all his appetite for the dessert, before he knew whether there was to be any dessert or not. If there be such a thing as imprudence in the world, we surely have it here. We sail in leaky bottoms and on great and perilous waters; and to take a cue from the dolorous old naval ballad, we have heard the mermaidens singing, and know that we shall never see dry land any more. Old and young, we are all on our last cruise. If there is a fill of tobacco among the crew, for God's sake pass it round, and let us have a pipe before we go!

Indeed, by the report of our elders, this nervous preparation for old age is only trouble thrown away. We fall on guard, and after all it is a friend who comes to meet us. After the sun is down and the west faded, the heavens begin to fill with shining stars. So, as we grow old, a sort of equable jogtrot of feeling is substituted for the violent ups and downs of passion and disgust; the same influence that restrains our hopes, quiets our apprehensions; if the pleasures are less intense, the troubles are milder and more tolerable; and in a word, this period for which we are asked to hoard up everything as for a time of famine, is, in its own right, the richest, easiest, and happiest of life. Nay, by managing its own work and following its own happy inspiration, youth is doing the best it can to endow the leisure of age. A full, busy youth is your only prelude to a self-contained and independent age; and the muff inevitably develops into the bore. There are not many Dr. Johnsons, to set forth upon their first romantic voyage at sixty-four. If we wish to scale Mont Blanc or visit a thieves' kitchen in the East End, to go down in a diving-dress or up in a balloon, we must be about it while we are still young. It will not do to delay until we are clogged with prudence and limping with rheumatism, and people begin to ask us: "What does Gravity out of bed?" Youth is the time to go flashing from one end of the world to the other both in mind and body; to try the manners of different nations; to hear the chimes at midnight; to see sunrise in town and country; to be converted at a revival; to circumnavigate the metaphysics, write halting verses, run a mile to see a fire, and wait all day long in the theatre to applaud *Hernani*. There is some meaning in the old theory about wild oats; and a man who has not had his green-sickness and got done with it for good, is as little to be depended on as an unvaccinated infant. "It is extraordinary," says Lord Beaconsfield, one of the brightest and best preserved of youths up to the date of his last novel, "it is extraordinary how hourly and how violently change the feelings of an inexperienced young man." And this mobility is a special talent entrusted to his care; a sort of indestructible virginity; a magic armour, with which he can pass unhurt through great dangers and come unbedaubed out of the miriest passages. Let him voyage, speculate, see all that he can, do all that he may; his soul has as many lives as a cat, he will live in all weathers, and never be a half-penny the worse. Those who go to the devil in youth, with anything like a fair chance, were probably little worth saving from the first; they must have been feeble fellows—creatures made of putty and pack-thread, without steel or fire, anger or true joyfulness, in their composition; we may sympathise with their parents but there is not much cause to go into mourning for themselves; for to be quite honest, the weak brother is the worst of mankind.

When the old man waggles his head and says, "Ah, so I thought when I was your age," he has proved the youth's case. Doubtless, whether from growth of experience or decline of animal heat, he thinks so no longer; but he thought so while he was young; and all men have thought so while they were young, since there was dew in the morning or hawthorn in May; and here is another young man adding his vote to those of previous generations and rivetting another link to the chain of testimony. It is as natural and as right for a young man to be imprudent and exaggerated, to live in swoops and circles, and beat about his cage like any other wild thing newly captured, as it is for old men to turn grey, or mothers to love their offspring, or heroes to die for something worthier than their lives.

By way of an apologue for the aged, when they feel more than usually tempted to offer their advice, let me recommend the following little tale. A child who had been remarkably fond of toys (and in particular of lead soldiers) found himself growing to the level of acknowledged boyhood without any abatement of this childish taste. He was thirteen; already he had been taunted for dallying overlong about the playbox; he had to blush if he was found among his lead soldiers; the shades of the prison-house were closing about him with a vengeance. There is nothing more difficult than to put the thoughts of children into the language of their elders; but this is the effect of his meditations at this juncture: "Plainly," he said, "I must give up my playthings, in the meanwhile, since I am not in a position to secure myself against idle jeers. At the same time, I am sure that playthings are the very pick of life; all people give them up out of the same pusillanimous respect for those who are a little older; and if they do not return to them as soon as they can, it is only because they grow stupid and forget. I shall be wiser; I shall conform for a little to the ways of their foolish world; but so soon as I have made enough money, I shall retire and shut myself up among my playthings until the day I die." Nay, as he was passing in the train along the Esterel mountains between Cannes and Fréjus, he remarked a pretty house in an orange garden at the angle of a bay, and decided that this should be his Happy Valley. Astrea Redux; childhood was to come again! The idea has an air of simple nobility to me, not unworthy of Cincinnatus. And yet, as the reader has probably anticipated, it is never likely to be carried into effect. There was a worm in the bud, a fatal error in the premises. Childhood must pass away, and then youth, as surely as age approaches. The true wisdom is to be always seasonable, and to change with a good grace in changing circumstances. To love playthings well as a child, to lead an adventurous and honourable youth, and to settle, when the time arrives, into a green and smiling age, is to be a good artist in life and deserve well of yourself and your neighbour.

You need repent none of your youthful vagaries. They may have been over the score on one side, just as those of age are probably over the score on the other. But they had a point; they not only befitted your age and expressed its attitude and passions, but they had a relation to what was outside of you, and implied criticisms on the existing state of things, which you need not allow to have been undeserved, because you now see that they were partial. All error, not merely verbal, is a strong way of stating that the current truth is incomplete. The follies of youth have a basis in sound reason, just as much as the embarrassing questions put by babes and sucklings. Their most antisocial acts indicate the defects of our society. When the torrent sweeps the man against a boulder, you must expect him to scream, and you need not be surprised if the scream is sometimes a theory. Shelley, chafing at the Church of England, discovered the cure of all evils in universal atheism. Generous lads, irritated at the injustices of society, see nothing for it but the abolishment of everything and Kingdom Come of anarchy. Shelley was a young fool; so are these cock-sparrow revolutionaries. But it is better to be a fool than to be dead. It is better to emit a scream in the shape of a theory than to be entirely insensible to the jars and incongruities of life and take everything as it comes in a forlorn stupidity. Some people swallow the universe like a pill; they travel on through the world, like smiling images pushed from behind. For God's sake give me the young man who has brains enough to make a fool of himself! As for the others, the irony of facts shall take it out of their hands, and make fools of them in downright earnest, ere the farce be over. There shall be such a mopping and a mowing at the last day, and such blushing and confusion of countenance for all those who have been wise in their own esteem, and have not learnt the rough lessons that youth hands on to age. If we are indeed here to perfect and complete our own natures, and grow larger, stronger, and more sympathetic against some nobler career in the future, we had all best bestir ourselves to the utmost while we have the time. To equip a dull, respectable person with wings would be but to make a parody of an angel.

In short, if youth is not quite right in its opinions, there is a strong probability that age is not much more so. Undying hope is co-ruler of the human bosom with infallible credulity. A man finds he has been wrong at every preceding stage of his career, only to deduce the astonishing conclusion that he is at last entirely right. Mankind, after centuries of failure, are still upon the eve of a thoroughly constitutional millennium. Since we have explored the maze so long without result, it follows, for poor human reason, that we cannot have to explore much longer; close by must be the centre, with a champagne luncheon and a piece of ornamental water. How if there were no centre at all, but just one alley after another, and the whole world a labyrinth without end or issue?

I overheard the other day a scrap of conversation, which I take the liberty to reproduce. "What I advance is true," said one. "But not the whole truth," answered the other. "Sir," returned the first (and it seemed to me there was a smack of Dr. Johnson in the speech), "Sir, there is no such thing as the whole truth!" Indeed, there is nothing so evident in life as that there are two sides to a question. History is one long illustration. The forces of nature are engaged, day by day, in cudgelling it into our backward intelligences. We never pause for a moment's consideration, but we admit it as an axiom. An enthusiast sways humanity exactly by disregarding this great truth, and dinning it into our ears that this or that question has only one possible solution; and your enthusiast is a fine florid fellow, dominates things for awhile and shakes the world out of a doze; but when once he is gone, an army of quiet and uninfluential people set to work to remind us of the other side and demolish the generous imposture. While Calvin is putting everybody exactly right in his *Institutes,* and hot-headed Knox is thundering in the pulpit, Montaigne is already looking at the other side in his library in Perigord, and predicting that they will find as much to quarrel about in the Bible as they had found already in the Church. Age may have one side, but assuredly Youth has the other. There is nothing more certain than that both are right, except perhaps that both are wrong. Let them agree to differ; for who knows but what agreeing to differ may not be a form of agreement rather than a form of difference?

I suppose it is written that any one who sets up for a bit of a philosopher, must contradict himself to his very face. For here have I fairly talked myself into thinking that we have the whole thing before us at last; that there is no answer to the mystery, except that there are as many as you please; that there is no centre to the maze because, like the famous sphere, its centre is everywhere; and that agreeing to differ with every ceremony of politeness, is the only "one undisturbed song of pure concent" to which we are ever likely to lend our musical voices.

—Robert Louis Stevenson

Though it is hard to find single poems that sum it all up with Stevenson's rich acceptance of contradiction, the fact is that all the great poets seem to have attempted some air of wisdom in their later years, and all of them have been hailed, as Santayana hails Dante, Lucretius, and Goethe, as creators not just of beauty but also of wisdom. For some, achievement of wisdom in "this world"— the discovery of just how one's fate relates to the whole of things —is sufficient in itself. For Wallace Stevens, this world is enough —*if* it has poetry in it.

A PASTORAL NUN

Finally, in the last year of her age,
Having attained a present blessedness,
She said poetry and apotheosis are one.

This is the illustration that she used:
If I live according to this law I live
In an immense activity, in which

Everything becomes morning, summer, the hero,
The enraptured woman, the sequestered night,
The man that suffered, lying there at ease,

Without his envious pain in body, in mind,
The favorable transformations of the wind
As of a general being or human universe.

There was another illustration, in which
The two things compared their tight resemblances:
Each matters only in that which it conceives.

For others, like Petrarch in one of his many "Canzoniere," "Italia Mia," the achievement of wisdom is both essential "here below" and as preparation for life after death.

> Lords; see how time flies
> how life flies,
> and how Death is at our backs.
> You are here now; think of your departure;
> for to that perilous passage the soul will come,
> naked and alone.
> As you pass through this valley
> put away, I beg you, hatred and scorn . . .
> and let the time now spent in causing pain
> be turned to some worthier action of hand or mind,
> to some fair work of praise or noble study;
> and so find both happiness here below
> and the way open to Heaven.

For others still, like our hero Yeats in what is to me his most admirable "solution," wisdom lies in following Stevenson's acceptance of the ambiguities—in effect a kind of deeper return to the virtue of humility.

AMONG SCHOOL CHILDREN

I

I walk through the long schoolroom questioning;
A kind old nun in a white hood replies;
The children learn to cipher and to sing,
To study reading-books and history,
To cut and sew, be neat in everything
In the best modern way—the children's eyes
In momentary wonder stare upon
A sixty-year-old smiling public man.

II

I dream of a Ledaean body, bent
Above a sinking fire, a tale that she
Told of a harsh reproof, or trivial event
That changed some childish day to tragedy—
Told, and it seemed that our two natures blent
Into a sphere from youthful sympathy,
Or else, to alter Plato's parable,
Into the yolk and white of the one shell.

III

And thinking of that fit of grief or rage
I look upon one child or t'other there
And wonder if she stood so at that age—
For even daughters of the swan can share
Something of every paddler's heritage—
And had that colour upon cheek or hair,
And thereupon my heart is driven wild:
She stands before me as a living child.

IV

Her present image floats into the mind—
Did Quattrocento finger fashion it
Hollow of cheek as though it drank the wind
And took a mess of shadows for its meat?
And I though never of Ledaean kind
Had pretty plumage once—enough of that,
Better to smile on all that smile, and show
There is a comfortable kind of old scarecrow.

V

What youthful mother, a shape upon her lap
Honey of generation had betrayed,
And that must sleep, shriek, struggle to escape
As recollection or the drug decide,
Would think her son, did she but see that shape
With sixty or more winters on its head,
A compensation for the pang of his birth,
Or the uncertainty of his setting forth?

VI

Plato thought nature but a spume that plays
Upon a ghostly paradigm of things;
Solider Aristotle played the taws
Upon the bottom of a king of kings;
World-famous golden-thighed Pythagoras
Fingered upon a fiddle-stick or strings
What a star sang and careless Muses heard:
Old clothes upon old sticks to scare a bird.

VII

Both nuns and mothers worship images,
But those the candles light are not as those
That animate a mother's reveries,
But keep a marble or a bronze repose.
And yet they too break hearts—O Presences
That passion, piety or affection knows,
And that all heavenly glory symbolise—
O self-born mockers of man's enterprise;

VIII

Labour is blossoming or dancing where
The body is not bruised to pleasure soul,
Nor beauty born out of its own despair,
Nor blear-eyed wisdom out of midnight oil.
O chestnut tree, great rooted blossomer,
Are you the leaf, the blossom or the bole?
O body swayed to music, O brightening glance,
How can we know the dancer from the dance?

—W. B. Yeats

Neither Yeats nor Stevens thought of themselves as conventionally religious (there is in fact a current hot debate about whether Stevens on his deathbed "repented" and accepted Holy Communion). But their notions of wisdom move us ever closer to a subordination of Self to the Whole that can only be called religious. Over the centuries and throughout all cultures I know anything about, a large majority of the most serious consolers and celebrators have put their aspirations to wisdom in religious terms. Indeed, most of the poems of consolation we have seen, especially those of resignation, relinquishment, or reconciliation, could be viewed as prayers. Even the most overtly secular say something like "I've suffered, we all suffer, but we can hope for, pray for, peace at the end—*provided* that we have learned to school our egos properly." And that can be translated into the specifically religious terms that many would repudiate: "*provided* we have learned to worship not our selves but—to put it in terms as ecumenical as possible—Whatever It Is from Which We Came and to Which We Return: God/Allah/Nature." For Robert Penn Warren, the word we seek is "Truth," with a capital T.

The Whole Question

You'll have to rethink the whole question. This
Getting born business is not as simple as it seemed,
Or midwife thought, or doctor deemed. It is,
Time shows, more complicated than either—or you—ever
     dreamed.

If it can be said that you dreamed anything
Before what's called a hand slapped blazing breath
Into you, snatched your dream's lulling nothing-
ness into what Paul called the body of this death.

You had not, for instance, previsioned the terrible thing called
     love,
Which began with a strange, sweet taste and bulbed softness
     while
Two orbs of tender light leaned there above.
Sometimes your face got twisted. They called it a smile.

You noticed how faces from outer vastness might twist, too.
But sometimes different twists, with names unknown,
And there were noises with no names you knew,
And times of dark silence when you seemed nothing—or gone.

Years passed, but sometimes seemed nothing except the same.
You knew more words, but they were words only, only—
Metaphysical midges that plunged at the single flame
That centered the infinite dark of your skull; or lonely,

You woke in the dark of real night to hear the breath
That seemed to promise reality in the vacuum
Of the sleepless dream beginning when underneath
The curtain dawn seeps, and on wet asphalt wet tires hum.

Yes, you must try to rethink what is real. Perhaps
It is only a matter of language that traps you. You
May yet find a new one in which experience overlaps
Words. Or find some words that make the Truth come true.

—Robert Penn Warren, in his late seventies

The structure of explicitly religious works is much like that of the great Christian oratorios: Let's face the reality—all flesh is grass, this world is full of pain along with the joys, we cannot control our lot, which is likely to get worse though it may get better. It's in your hands, Lord, so: *Dona nobis pacem,* give us peace, here and hereafter. As the "atheist" Forster put it for us earlier, "How peaceful it is here!"

GOD'S GRANDEUR

The world is charged with the grandeur of God.
    It will flame out, like shining from shook foil;
    It gathers to a greatness, like the ooze of oil
Crushed. Why do men then now not reck his rod?
Generations have trod, have trod, have trod;
    And all is seared with trade; bleared, smeared with toil,
    And wears man's smudge and shares man's smell: the soil
Is bare now, nor can foot feel, being shod.

And for all this, nature is never spent;
    There lives the dearest freshness deep down things;
And though the last lights off the black West went
    Oh, morning, at the brown brink eastward, springs—
Because the Holy Ghost over the bent
    World broods with warm breast and with ah ! bright wings.

—Gerard Manley Hopkins

THE FLOWER

How fresh, O Lord, how sweet and clean
Are Thy returns! ev'n as the flowers in Spring,
   To which, besides their own demean,
The late-past frosts tributes of pleasure bring;
      Grief melts away
      Like snow in May,
   As if there were no such cold thing.

   Who would have thought my shrivel'd heart
Could have recover'd greennesse? It was gone
   Quite under ground; as flowers depart
To see their mother-root, when they have blown,
      Where they together
      All the hard weather,
   Dead to the world, keep house unknown.

   These are Thy wonders, Lord of power,
Killing and quickning, bringing down to Hell
   And up to Heaven in an houre;
Making a chiming of a passing-bell.
      We say amisse
      This or that is;
   Thy word is all, if we could spell.

   O that I once past changing were,
Fast in Thy Paradise, where no flower can wither;
   Many a Spring I shoot up fair,
Offring at Heav'n, growing and groning thither;
      Nor doth my flower
      Want a Spring-showre,
   My sinnes and I joyning together.

But while I grow in a straight line,
Still upwards bent, as if Heav'n were mine own,
   Thy anger comes, and I decline;
What frost to that? what pole is not the zone
     Where all things burn,
     When Thou dost turn,
   And the least frown of Thine is shown?

And now in age I bud again,
After so many deaths I live and write;
   I once more smell the dew and rain,
And relish versing: O, my onely Light,
     It cannot be
     That I am he
On whom Thy tempests fell all night.

These are Thy wonders, Lord of love,
To make us see we are but flow'rs that glide;
   Which when we once can find and prove,
Thou hast a garden for us where to bide;
     Who would be more,
     Swelling through store,
Forfeit their Paradise by their pride.

                  —George Herbert

We should end, then, not with an embrace of any one dogma about how to grow older, but with a recognition that aging in our time has goaded us, pretty much as sudden death goaded our ancestors, into a serious confrontation with ultimate questions. And it has incited many of our best poets into undisguised prayers, prayers that celebrate the gift of life as coming from a gracious source far above and beyond our petty efforts at complaint or consolation. (Call it, if you object to religious terms, the "nature of things" that Burke thanked for his friendship with Cowley [pages 194–95]).

Up-Hill

Does the road wind up-hill all the way?
    Yes, to the very end.
Will the day's journey take the whole long day?
    From morn to night, my friend.

But is there for the night a resting-place?
    A roof for when the slow dark hours begin.
May not the darkness hide it from my face?
    You cannot miss that inn.

Shall I meet other wayfarers at night?
    Those who have gone before.
Then must I knock, or call when just in sight?
    They will not keep you standing at that door.

Shall I find comfort, travel-sore and weak?
    Of labor you shall find the sum.
Will there be beds for me and all who seek?
    Yea, beds for all who come.

                    —Christina Rossetti

    I'm tired, but God will finally give me a bed to sleep in—that may seem like slim comfort, but it is a far cry (the cliché seems appropriate here) from the mere *wish* that one could believe, and thus pray—the wish that can be detected behind many of the lamentations in Part I.

    Are we, then—we who were born somewhat earlier than those "others"—living in a "belated" time? Maybe, maybe not. As compared to when? What we can say with confidence, though, looking back on all these splendid gifts collected here, is that we live late enough to be the heirs to a fabulous range of *recorded* human experience: Our forebears have felt deeply and left a rich record of their feelings. What I have preserved here is only a tiny fragment of what you will find if you decide, after tasting this sample, that such friends offer real support in your own pilgrimage.

Whatever else we might say about our troubled times, we who are growing older *now* are in this one respect more fortunate than any previous generation: the past few decades, partly because poets have become aware of the facts covered in those statistics I quoted at the beginning, have more than doubled our heritage of literary musings on this special topic. And we have found here that when we dip into modern, aging poets' "Last Poems" or "Thoughts in Winter," they write as well about the losses and gains of aging as they wrote, when young, about youthful fire and angst. In doing so, whether we think of them as lamenting or celebrating, they offer us a range of experience and companionship that life itself, when we were younger, could not supply.

PART III

A Further Harvest

The dry branch burns more fiercely than the green.
—Elder Olson, in his mid-seventies

I am more myself than ever before.
—May Sarton, at seventy

*In the past few years, I have made a thrilling
discovery . . . that until one is over sixty, one can
never really learn the secret of living. One can then
begin to live, not simply with the intense part of
oneself, but with one's entire being.*
—Ellen Glasgow

*We are all happier in many ways when we are old
than when we were young. The young sow wild oats.
The old grow sage.*
—Winston Churchill

*Forgive, O Lord, my little jokes on Thee
And I'll forgive Thy great big one on me.*
—Robert Frost, in his late eighties

Amo ergo sum. . . . Senesco sed amo.
(I love, therefore I am. . . . I am getting old, but
I love.)
—Ezra Pound, in his early sixties, Canto LXXX

*Though our outer nature is wasting away, our inner
nature is being renewed every day.*
—2 Corinthians 4:16

SONNET: ON HIS BLINDNESS

When I consider how my light is spent,
　E're half my days, in this dark world and wide,
　And that one Talent which is death to hide,
　Lodg'd with me useless, though my Soul more bent
To serve therewith my Maker, and present
　My true account, lest he returning chide,
　　"Doth God exact day-labour, light deny'd?"
　　I fondly ask. But Patience, to prevent
That murmur, soon replies: "God doth not need
　Either man's work or his own gifts. Who best
　Bear his milde yoak, they serve him best. His State
Is Kingly. Thousands at his bidding speed
　And post o'er Land and Ocean without rest:
　　They also serve who only stand and waite."

　　　　　　　　　　　　　　　　—John Milton

　　　　In winter in the woods alone
　　　　Against the trees I go.
　　　　I mark a maple for my own
　　　　And lay the maple low.

　　　　At four o'clock I shoulder axe
　　　　And in the afterglow
　　　　I link a line of shadowy tracks
　　　　Across the tinted snow.

　　　　I see for Nature no defeat
　　　　In one tree's overthrow
　　　　Or for myself in my retreat
　　　　For yet another blow.

　　　　　　　　—Robert Frost, in his late
　　　　　　　　　　　　eighties

[The happiest age is that] between sixty and eighty; by this time a man's reputation is made. He no longer has any ambition or desires; he enjoys what he has sown. It is the age of harvest-home.

—Bernard de Fontenelle

Lying there suspended in time, without pressure, I began to see what a rich summer it has proved to be, a litany of friends old and new, a few great events like my reading at the Unitarian Assembly and the appearance of the book of criticism and my visit to Orland, a constant ebb and flow of life coming and going—and, not the least, three birthdays to celebrate, Eleanor's eighty-eighth, Marguerite's ninetieth, and Laurie's ninety-first, three great women all in full possession of their powers—seventy is not old, after all, and if I can be like them at the end of two more decades I shall have reason to be happy.

What better way in fact to celebrate a seventieth year than with a feast of friends? And if I had imagined this year as one with time for reflection, it is always a mistake to try to order one's life in such an arbitrary way. Time for reflection will come when time is ripe. And right now I realize that just three days' rest and holiday are all that I need to reset my course, as happy and free as a sailor putting out again into the ocean after anchoring in a sheltered bay.

Next week, adventure!

—May Sarton, at seventy

The Silence Now

These days the silence is immense.
It is there deep down, not to be escaped.
The twittering flight of goldfinches,
The three crows cawing in the distance
Only brush the surface of this silence
Full of mourning, the long drawn-out
Tug and sigh of waters never still—
The ocean out there, and the inner ocean.

Only animals comfort because they live
In the present and cannot drag us down
Into those caverns of memory full of loss.
They pay no attention to the thunder
Of distant waves. My dog's eager eyes
Watch me as I sit by the window, thinking.

At the bottom of the silence what lies in wait?
Is it love? Is it death? Too early or too late?
What is it I can have that I still want?

My swift response is to what cannot stay,
The dying daffodils, peonies on the way.
Iris just opening, lilac turning brown
In the immense silence where I live alone.

It is the transient that touches me, old,
Those light-shot clouds as the sky clears,
A passing glory can still move to tears,
Moments of pure joy like some fairy gold
Too evanescent to be kept or told.
And the cat's soft footfall on the stair
Keeps me alive, makes Nowhere into Here.
At the bottom of the silence it is she
Who speaks of an eternal Now to me.

—May Sarton, at seventy-six

OLD LOVERS AT THE BALLET

In the dark theatre lovers sit
Watching the supple dancers weave
A fugue, motion and music melded.
There on the stage below, brilliantly lit
No dancer stumbles or may grieve;
Their very smiles are disciplined and moulded.

And in the dark old lovers feel dismay
Watching the ardent bodies leap and freeze,
Thinking how age has changed them and has mocked.
Once they were light and bold in lissome play,
Limber as willows that could bend with ease—
But as they watch a vision is unlocked.

Imagination springs the trap of youth.
And in the dark motionless, as they stare,
Old lovers reach new wonders and new answers
As in the mind they leap to catch the truth,
For young the soul was awkward, unaware,
That claps its hands now with the supple dancers.

And in the flesh those dancers cannot spare
What the old lovers have had time to learn,
That the soul is a lithe and serene athlete
That deepens touch upon the darkening air.
It is not energy but light they burn,
The radiant powers of the Paraclete.

—May Sarton, approaching eighty

THE FIRST SNOW OF THE YEAR

The old man, listening to the careful
Steps of his old wife as up she came,
Up, up, so slowly, then her slippered
Progress down the long hall to their door—

Outside the wind, wilder suddenly,
Whirled the first snow of the year; danced
Round and round with it, coming closer
And closer, peppering the panes; now here she was—

Said "Ah, my dear, remember?" But his tray
Took all of her attention, having to hold it
Level. "Ah, my dear, don't you remember?"
"What?" "That time we walked in the white woods."

She handed him his napkin; felt the glass
To make sure the milk in it was warm;
Sat down; got up again; brought comb and brush
To tidy his top hair. "Yes, I remember."

He wondered if she saw now what he did.
Possibly not. An afternoon so windless,
The huge flakes rustled upon each other,
Filling the woods, the world, with cold, cold—

They shivered, having a long way to go,
And then their mittens touched; and touched again;
Their eyes, trying not to meet, did meet;
They stopped, and in the cold held out their arms

Till she came into his: awkwardly,
As girl to boy that never kissed before.
The woods, the darkening world, so cold, so cold,
While these two burned together. He remembered,

And wondered if she did, how like a sting,
A hidden heat it was; while there they stood
And trembled, and the snow made statues of them.
"Ah, my dear, remember?" "Yes, I do."

She rocked and thought: he wants me to say something.
But we said nothing then. The main thing is,
I'm with him still; he calls me and I come.
But slowly. Time makes sluggards of us all.

"Yes, I do remember." The wild wind
Was louder, but a sweetness in her speaking
Stung him, and he heard. While round and round
The first snow of the year danced on the lawn.

—Mark Van Doren

NIGHT THOUGHTS IN AGE

Light, that out of the west looked back once more
Through lids of cloud, has closed a sleepy eye;
The heaven of stars bends over me its silence,
A harp through which the wind of time still whispers
Music some hand has hushed but left there trembling—
Conceits of an aging man who lies awake
Under familiar rafters, in this leafy
Bird-singing, haunted, green, ancestral spot
Where time has made such music! For often now,
In this belovèd country whose coastal shores
Look seaward, without limit, to the south—
Land of flung spume and spray, sea-winds and -voices,
Where the gull rides the gale on equal wing,
With motionless body and downward-bending head,
Where, in mid-summer days, offshore, the dolphin
Hurdles the water with arching leap and plunge—
I meditate, lying awake, alone,
On the sea's voice and time's receding music,

Felt ebbing in the heart and shrunken vein—
How time, that takes us all, will at the last,
In taking us, take the whole world we are dreaming:
Sun, wind and sea, whisper of rain at night,
The young, hollow-cheeked moon, the clouds of evening
Drifting in a great solitude—all these
Shall time take away, surely, and the face
From which the eyes of love look out at us
In this brief world, this horror-haunted kingdom
Of beauty and of longing and of terror,
Of phantoms and illusion, of appearance
And disappearance—magic of leger-de-main,
Trick of the prestidigitator's wand—
The huge phantasmagoria we are dreaming:
This shall time take from us, and take forever,
When we are taken by that receding music.
O marvel of things, fabulous dream, too soon,
Too soon will the wild blood cry out and death
Quell, with one blow, the inscrutable fantasy!
Shall prayer change this? Youth is the hour for prayer,
That has so much to pray for; a man's life,
Lived howsoever, is a long reconcilement
To the high, lonely, unforgiving truth,
Which will not change for his or any prayer,
Now or hereafter: in that reconcilement
Lies all of wisdom. Age is the hour for praise,
Praise that is joy, praise that is acquiescence,
Praise that is adoration and gratitude
For all that has been given and not been given.
Night flows on. The wind, that all night through
Quickened the treetops with a breath of ocean,
Veers inland, falls away, and the sea's voice,
Learned in lost childhood, a remembered music,
By day or night, through love, through sleep, through dream,
Still breathing its perpetual benediction,
Has dwindled to a sigh. By the west window,

In the soft dark the leaves of the sycamore
Stir gently, rustle, and are still, are listening
To a silence that is music. The old house
Is full of ghosts, dear ghosts on stair and landing,
Ghosts in chamber and hall; garden and walk
Are marvellous with ghosts, where so much love
Dwelt for a little while and made such music,
Before it too was taken by the tide
That takes us all, of time's receding music.
Oh, all is music! All has been turned to music!
All that is vanished has been turned to music!
And these familiar rafters, that have known
The child, the young man and the man, now shelter
The aging man who lies here, listening, listening—
All night, in a half dream, I have lain here listening.

—John Hall Wheelock, in his late seventies

FERN HILL

Now as I was young and easy under the apple boughs
About the lilting house and happy as the grass was green,
        The night above the dingle starry,
            Time let me hail and climb
        Golden in the heydays of his eyes,
And honored among wagons I was prince of the apple towns
And once below a time I lordly had the trees and leaves
            Trail with daisies and barley
        Down the rivers of the windfall light.

And as I was green and carefree, famous among the barns
About the happy yard and singing as the farm was home,
        In the sun that is young once only,
            Time let me play and be
        Golden in the mercy of his means,
And green and golden I was huntsman and herdsman, the calves

Sang to my horn, the foxes on the hills barked clear and cold,
    And the sabbath rang slowly
   In the pebbles of the holy streams.

All the sun long it was running, it was lovely, the hay
Fields high as the house, the tunes from the chimneys, it was air
   And playing, lovely and watery
     And fire green as grass.
   And nightly under the simple stars
As I rode to sleep the owls were bearing the farm away,
All the moon long I heard, blessed among stables, the night-jars
   Flying with the ricks, and the horses
    Flashing into the dark.

And then to awake, and the farm, like a wanderer white
With the dew, come back, the cock on his shoulder: it was all
   Shining, it was Adam and maiden,
    The sky gathered again
   And the sun grew round that very day.
So it must have been after the birth of the simple light
In the first, spinning place, the spellbound horses walking warm
   Out of the whinnying green stable
    On to the fields of praise.

And honored among foxes and pheasants by the gay house
Under the new made clouds and happy as the heart was long,
   In the sun born over and over,
    I ran my heedless ways,
   My wishes raced through the house high hay
And nothing I cared, at my sky blue trades, that time allows
In all his tuneful turning so few and such morning songs
   Before the children green and golden
    Follow him out of grace,

Nothing I cared, in the lamb white days, that time would take me
Up to the swallow thronged loft by the shadow of my hand,
   In the moon that is always rising,
    Nor that riding to sleep

I should hear him fly with the high fields
And wake to the farm forever fled from the childless land.
Oh as I was young and easy in the mercy of his means,
            Time held me green and dying
        Though I sang in my chains like the sea.

            —Dylan Thomas, still green but already "dying," at thirty-one

GRASSES

Undulant across the slopes
a gloss of purple
day by day arrives to dim
the green, as grasses

I never learned the names of—
numberless, prophetic,
transient—put on a flowering
so multiform, one

scarcely notices: the oats grow tall,
their pendent helmetfuls
of mica-drift, examined stem
by stem, disclose

alloys so various, enamelings
of a vermeil so
craftless, I all but despair of
ever reining in a

metaphor for: even the plebeian
dooryard plantain's
every homely cone-tip earns a
halo, a seraphic

hatband of guarantee that
dying, for
the unstudied, multitudinously,
truly lowly,

has no meaning, is nothing
if not flowering's
swarming reassurances of one
more resurrection.

—Amy Clampitt, turning seventy

FIZZLE 3:
A far a bird

Ruinstrewn land, he has trodden it all night long, I gave up,
hugging the hedges, between road and ditch, on the scant
grass, little slow steps, no sound, stopping ever and again,
every ten steps say, little wary steps, to catch his breath, then
listen, ruinstrewn land, I gave up before birth, it is not possible
otherwise, but birth there had to be, it was he, I was inside,
now he stops again, for the hundredth time that night say,
that gives the distance gone, it's the last, hunched over his
stick, I'm inside, it was he who wailed, he who saw the light,
I didn't wail, I didn't see the light, one on top of the other the
hands weigh on the stick, the head weighs on the hands, he
has caught his breath, he can listen now, the trunk horizontal,
the legs asprawl, sagging at the knees, same old coat, the
stiffened tails stick up behind, day dawns, he has only to raise
his eyes, open his eyes, raise his eyes, he merges in the hedge,
afar a bird, a moment past he grasps and is fled, it was he had
a life, I didn't have a life, a life not worth having, because of
me, it's impossible I should have a mind and I have one,
someone divines me, divines us, that's what he's come to,
come to in the end, I see him in my mind, there divining us,
hands and head a little heap, the hours pass, he is still, he seeks
a voice for me, it's impossible I should have a voice and I have
none, he'll find one for me, ill beseeming me, it will meet the
need, his need, but no more of him, that image, the little heap
of hands and head, the trunk horizontal, the jutting elbows,
the eyes closed and the face rigid listening, the eyes hidden
and the whole face hidden, that image and no more, never

changing, ruinstrewn land, night recedes, he is fled, I'm inside, he'll do himself to death, because of me, I'll live it with
him, I'll live his death, the end of his life and then his death,
step by step, in the present, how he'll go about it, it's impossible I should know, I'll know, step by step, it's he will die, I
won't die, there will be nothing of him left but bones, I'll be
inside, nothing but a little grit, I'll be inside, it is not possible
otherwise, ruinstrewn land, he is fled through the hedge, no
more stopping now, he will never say I, because of me, he
won't speak to anyone, no one will speak to him, he won't
speak to himself, there is nothing left in his head, I'll feed it all
it needs, all it needs to end, to say I no more, to open its
mouth no more, confusion of memory and lament, of loved
ones and impossible youth, clutching the stick in the middle
he stumbles bowed over the fields, a life of my own I tried, in
vain, never any but his, worth nothing, because of me, he said
it wasn't one, it was, still is, the same, I'm still inside, the
same, I'll put faces in his head, names, places, churn them all
up together, all he needs to end, phantoms to flee, last phantoms to flee and to pursue, he'll confuse his mother with
whores, his father with a roadman named Balfe, I'll feed him
an old curdog, a mangy old curdog, that he may love again,
lose again, ruinstrewn land, little panic steps

—Samuel Beckett, in his early eighties

FROM "A CATCH OF SHY FISH"

garbageman: the man with the orderly mind

What do you think of us in fuzzy endeavor, you whose directions
  are sterling, whose lunge is straight?
Can you make a reason, how can you pardon us who memorize
  the rules and never score?
Who memorize the rules from your own text but never quite
  transfer them to the game,
Who never quite receive the whistling ball, who gawk, begin to
  absorb the crowd's own roar.

Is earnestness enough, may earnestness attract or lead to light;
Is light enough, if hands in clumsy frenzy, flimsy whimsicality,
  enlist;
Is light enough when this bewilderment crying against the dark
  shuts down the shades?
Dilute confusion. Find and explode our mist.

sick man looks at flowers

You are sick and old, and there is a closing in—
The eyes gone dead to all that would beguile.
Echoes are dull and the body accepts no touch
Except its pain. Mind is a little isle.

But now invades this impudence of red!
This ripe rebuke, this burgeoning affluence
Mocks me and mocks the desert of my bed.

old people working (garden, car)

Old people working. Making a gift of garden.
Or washing a car, so some one else may ride.
A note of alliance, an eloquence of pride.
A way of greeting or sally to the world.

weaponed woman

Well, life has been a baffled vehicle
And baffling. But she fights, and
Has fought, according to her lights and
The lenience of her whirling-place.

She fights with semi-folded arms,
Her strong bag, and the stiff
Frost of her face (that challenges "When" and "If.")
And altogether she does Rather Well.

old tennis player

Refuses
To refuse the racket, to mutter No to the net.
He leans to life, conspires to give and get
Other serving yet.

—Gwendolyn Brooks

A Prayer for Old Age

God guard me from those thoughts men think
In the mind alone;
He that sings a lasting song
Thinks in a marrow-bone;

From all that makes a wise old man
That can be praised of all;
O what am I that I should not seem
For the song's sake a fool?

I pray—for fashion's word is out
And prayer comes round again—
That I may seem, though I die old,
A foolish, passionate man.

—William Butler Yeats, around seventy

From My Diary

"She was," my father said (in an aside),
"A great beauty, forty years ago."
Out of my crude childhood, I stared at
Our tottering hostess, tremulous
In her armchair, pouring tea from silver—
Her grey silk dress, her violet gaze.
I only saw her being seventy,
I could not see the girl my father saw.

Now that I'm older than my father then was
I go with lifelong friends to the same parties
Which we have gone to always.
We seem the same age always
Although the parties sometimes change to funerals
That sometimes used to change to christenings.

Faces we've once loved
Fit into their seven ages as Russian dolls
Into one another. My memory
Penetrates through successive layers
Back to the face which first I saw. So when the last
Exterior image is laid under its lid,
Your face first seen will shine through all.

—Stephen Spender

Wide Awake, Full of Love

Being in this stage
I look to the last,
see myself returning:
the seamed face
as of a tired rider
upon a tired horse
coming up . . .

What of your dish-eyes
that have seduced
me? Your voice
whose cello notes
upon the theme have led
me to the music?

I see your neck scrawny
your thighs worn
your hair thinning,
whose round brow
pushes it aside, and
turn again upon
the thought: To migrate

to that South to hop
again upon the shining
grass there
half ill with love
and mope and
will not startle for
the grinning worm

—William Carlos Williams

AFTER THE PERSIAN

I

I do not wish to know
The depths of your terrible jungle:
From what nest your leopard leaps
Or what sterile lianas are at once your serpents' disguise and
    home.

I am the dweller on the temperate threshold,
The strip of corn and vine,
Where all is translucence (the light!)
Liquidity, and the sound of water.
Here the days pass under shade
And the nights have the waxing and the waning moon.
Here the moths take flight at evening;
Here at morning the dove whistles and the pigeons coo.
Here, as night comes on, the fireflies wink and snap
Close to the cool ground,
Shining in a profusion
Celestial or marine.

Here it is never wholly dark but always wholly green,
And the day stains with what seems to be more than the sun
What may be more than my flesh.

II

I have wept with the spring storm;
Burned with the brutal summer.
Now, hearing the wind and the twanging bow-strings,
I know what winter brings

The hunt sweeps out upon the plain
And the garden darkens.
They will bring the trophies home
To bleed and perish
Beside the trellis and the lattices,
Beside the fountain, still flinging diamond water,
Beside the pool
(Which is eight-sided, like my heart).

III

All has been translated into treasure:
Weightless as amber,
Translucent as the currant on the branch,
Dark as the rose's thorn.

Where is the shimmer of evil?
This is the shell's iridescence
And the wild bird's wing.

IV

Ignorant, I took up my burden in the wilderness.
Wise with great wisdom, I shall lay it down upon flowers.

V

Goodbye, goodbye!
There was so much to love, I could not love it all;
I could not love it enough.

Some things I overlooked, and some I could not find.
Let the crystal clasp them
When you drink your wine, in autumn.

—Louise Bogan

THE PLAIN SENSE OF THINGS

After the leaves have fallen, we return
To a plain sense of things. It is as if
We had come to an end of the imagination,
Inanimate in an inert savoir.

It is difficult even to choose the adjective
For this blank cold, this sadness without cause.
The great structure has become a minor house.
No turban walks across the lessened floors.

The greenhouse never so badly needed paint.
The chimney is fifty years old and slants to one side.
A fantastic effort has failed, a repetition
In a repetitiousness of men and flies.

Yet the absence of the imagination had
Itself to be imagined. The great pond,
The plain sense of it, without reflections, leaves,
Mud, water like dirty glass, expressing silence

Of a sort, silence of a rat come out to see,
The great pond and its waste of the lilies, all this
Had to be imagined as an inevitable knowledge,
Required, as a necessity requires.

                    —Wallace Stevens, at seventy-three

NADIRS

There were the clerks of the zenith and the figures,
There were winter-type clouds over the winter
There were summer-type clouds over the summer figures
And to speak to each there was a way, the same.
I went up to the clerk of the nadir and said See me
In noctions of one kind or another
Under a winter sun, and see safely to the zenith
How I welter under a blooming moon.
All is mine, but I like it
By each gesture toward the other or one.
So besit, said the clerks of the nadir
And the zenith as they turned to their own
Accounting of afternoon—
They were busy. How busy were they?
They required waiting in line
For the sun to go down over the eastern figures
And the moon to arise over the western figures
Moving from plane to plane.

                    —Josephine Miles

BRIM

Less of time than the world allows
A repeated task, sinews not taking
Supposed messages, where will we be
Under the reign of senex? I absolve him
Of many miseries.

Curry another time, other worldly,
But here at home
Turn to skies in their wheeling
A simple crowded passage across the brim.

—Josephine Miles

STROKE

I should like to hurry to get back into the world.
I am so far from it, eyes, ears blurred,
Memory forsaken.
Rumors of what's going on
I would urge to be longer, stronger.

What did you say? I say
The voices I hear
Ring out from a round bell from far away,
Hurry up! What is your hurry?
Strike me back into the world.

—Josephine Miles

CROSSING THE BAR

Sunset and evening star,
    And one clear call for me!
And may there be no moaning of the bar,
    When I put out to sea,

But such a tide as moving seems asleep,
    Too full for sound and foam,
    When that which drew from out the boundless deep
    Turns again home.

Twilight and evening bell,
    And after that the dark!
And may there be no sadness of farewell,
    When I embark;

For though from out our bourne of Time and Place
    The flood may bear me far,
I hope to see my Pilot face to face
    When I have crossed the bar.

                —Alfred Lord Tennyson, at about eighty

HALCYON DAYS

Not from successful love alone,
Nor wealth, nor honor'd middle age, nor victories of politics
    or war;
But as life wanes, and all the turbulent passions calm,
As gorgeous, vapory, silent hues cover the evening sky,
As softness, fulness, rest, suffuse the frame, like fresher,
    balmier air,
As the days take on a mellower light, and the apple at last
    hangs really finish'd and indolent-ripe on the tree,
Then for the teeming quietest, happiest days of all!
The brooding and blissful halcyon days!

                —Walt Whitman, at seventy

OLD WOMEN

Arthritically bent, in black, spindle-legged,
They move, leaning on canes, to the altar where the Pantocrator
In a dawn of gilded rays lifts his two fingers.
The mighty, radiant face of the All-Potent
In whom everything was created, whatever is on the earth and in
    Heaven,
To whom are submitted the atom and the scale of galaxies,
Rises over the heads of His servants, covered with their shawls
While into their shriveled mouths they receive His flesh.

A mirror, mascara, powder, and cones of carmine
Lured every one of them and they used to dress up
As themselves, adding a brighter glow to their eyes,
A rounder arch to their brows, a denser red to their lips.
They opened themselves, amorous, in the riverside woods,
Carried inside the magnificence of the beloved,
Our mothers whom we have never repaid,
Busy, as we were, with sailing, crossing continents.
And guilty, seeking their forgiveness.

He who has been suffering for ages rescues
Ephemeral moths, tired-winged butterflies in the cold,
Genetrixes with the closed scars of their wombs,
And carries them up to His human Theotokos,
So that the ridicule and pain change into majesty
And thus it is fulfilled, late, without charms and colors,
Our imperfect, earthly love.

—Czeslaw Milosz, at seventy-five

BREAKFAST TIME

I've had my morning tea already,
two cups;
to be precise, I've had my morning tea twice:
I prefer to be, you know, precise.
I've placed the newspaper ready for him
at his end of the table.
And how are you today? I say. How's your back?
His decaffeinated coffee's in the coffee maker.
I've put his skimmed milk in the white china mug
with two white Sweetex sweeteners.

That salix is double the width it was, you know, double!

I'm sure I put his sweeteners in,
just after I took the polyunsaturated soya margarine out of
    the fridge.

Just look at that variegated hosta, just look!

Flotsa's cat-flap clacks.

That hosta's sensational!

The cappuccino coffee maker hisses.
Yesterday I opened the broom cupboard for a tin of
    sardines
and stared at the brooms before shifting to a different
    door.

I've never had eschscholzia like it! Never!

We had three days away last week
—Dimitri next door did the watering
but I can't remember where we went.

I hope his coffee's sweet.
Have your pill-ule, I say, merrily,
handing over a fish-oil capsule as big as a suppository.
I simply can't remember where we went last week.
Alzheimer's. Maybe.

I must, simply must, get more bedding plants today.

When his fingers are too stiff to bed plants,
Will I look in the sweetener jar for slug bait?
Or among the shoe polish tins to find the garden trowel?
Will I?
We'll go to Cruise Hill, I say; I like those nurseries best.
Let's make the most of the sun.
Toast? or d'you fancy some porridge?

—Betty Rosen

THINKING OF THE LOST WORLD

This spoonful of chocolate tapioca
Tastes like—like peanut butter, like the vanilla
Extract Mama told me not to drink.
Swallowing the spoonful, I have already traveled
Through time to my childhood. It puzzles me
That age is like it.
                    Come back to that calm country
Through which the stream of my life first meandered,
My wife, our cat, and I sit here and see
Squirrels quarreling in the feeder, a mockingbird
Copying our chipmunk, as our end copies
Its beginning.
                    Back in Los Angeles, we missed
Los Angeles. The sunshine of the Land
Of Sunshine is a gray mist now, the atmosphere
Of some factory planet: when you stand and look

You see a block or two, and your eyes water.
The orange groves are all cut down . . . My bow
Is lost, all my arrows are lost or broken,
My knife is sunk in the eucalyptus tree
Too far for even Pop to get it out,
And the tree's sawed down. It and the stair-sticks
And the planks of the tree house are all firewood
Burned long ago; its gray smoke smells of Vicks.

Twenty Years After, thirty-five years after,
Is as good as ever—better than ever,
Now that D'Artagnan is no longer old—
Except that it is unbelievable.
I say to my old self: "I believe. Help thou
Mine unbelief."
                I believe the dinosaur
Or pterodactyl's married the pink sphinx
And lives with those Indians in the undiscovered
Country between California and Arizona
That the mad girl told me she was princess of—
Looking at me with the eyes of a lion,
Big, golden, without human understanding,
As she threw paper-wads from the back seat
Of the car in which I drove her with her mother
From the jail in Waycross to the hospital
In Daytona. If I took my eyes from the road
And looked back into her eyes, the car would—I'd be—

Or if only I could find a crystal set
Sometimes, surely, I could still hear their chief
Reading to them from Dumas or *Amazing Stories;*
If I could find in some Museum of Cars
Mama's dark blue Buick, Lucky's electric,
Couldn't I be driven there? Hold out to them,
The paraffin half picked out, Tawny's dewclaw—
And have walk to me from among their wigwams

My tall brown aunt, to whisper to me: "Dead?
They told you I was dead?"
                         As if you could die!
If I never saw you, never again
Wrote to you, even, after a few years,
How often you've visited me, having put on,
As a mermaid puts on her sealskin, another face
And voice, that don't fool me for a minute—
That are yours for good . . . All of them are gone
Except for me; and for me nothing is gone—

The chicken's body is still going round
And round in widening circles, a satellite
From which, as the sun sets, the scientist bends
A look of evil on the unsuspecting earth.
Mama and Pop and Dandeen are still there
In the Gay Twenties.
                         The Gay Twenties! You say
The Gay Nineties . . . But it's all right: they *were* gay,
O so gay! A certain number of years after,
Any time is Gay, to the new ones who ask:
"Was that the first World War or the second?"
Moving between the first world and the second,
I hear a boy call, now that my beard's gray:
"Santa Claus! Hi, Santa Claus!" It *is* miraculous
To have the children call you Santa Claus.
I wave back. When my hand drops to the wheel,
It is brown and spotted, and its nails are ridged
Like Mama's. Where's my own hand? My smooth
White bitten-fingernailed one? I seem to see
A shape in tennis shoes and khaki riding-pants
Standing there empty-handed; I reach out to it
Empty-handed, my hand comes back empty,
And yet my emptiness is traded for its emptiness,
I have found that Lost World in the Lost and Found

Columns whose gray illegible advertisements
My soul has memorized world after world:
LOST—NOTHING. STRAYED FROM NOWHERE. NO
   REWARD.
I hold in my own hands, in happiness,
Nothing: the nothing for which there's no reward.

                         —Randall Jarrell

ECCLESIASTES, CHAPTER 3

To every thing there is a season, and a time to every purpose
under the heaven:

   2 A time to be born, and a time to die; a time to plant,
and a time to pluck up that which is planted;

   3 A time to kill, and a time to heal; a time to break down,
and a time to build up;

   4 A time to weep, and a time to laugh; a time to mourn,
and a time to dance;

   5 A time to cast away stones, and a time to gather stones
together; a time to embrace, and a time to refrain from em-
bracing;

   6 A time to get, and a time to lose; a time to keep, and a
time to cast away;

   7 A time to rend, and a time to sew; a time to keep
silence, and a time to speak;

   8 A time to love, and a time to hate; a time of war, and a
time of peace.

   9 What profit hath he that worketh in that wherein he
laboreth?

   10 I have seen the travail, which God hath given to the
sons of men to be exercised in it.

   11 He hath made every thing beautiful in his time: also he
hath set the world in their heart, so that no man can find out
the work that God maketh from the beginning to the end.

   12 I know that there is no good in them, but for a man to
rejoice, and to do good in his life.

13 And also that every man should eat and drink, and enjoy the good of all his labor, it is the gift of God.

14 I know that, whatsoever God doeth, it shall be for ever: nothing can be put to it, nor any thing taken from it: and God doeth it, that men should fear before him.

15 That which hath been is now; and that which is to be hath already been; and God requireth that which is past.

16 And moreover I saw under the sun the place of judgment, that wickedness was there; and the place of righteousness, that iniquity was there.

17 I said in mine heart, God shall judge the righteous and the wicked: for there is a time there for every purpose and for every work.

18 I said in mine heart concerning the estate of the sons of men, that God might manifest them, and that they might see that they themselves are beasts.

19 For that which befalleth the sons of men befalleth beasts; even one thing befalleth them: as the one dieth, so dieth the other; yea, they have all one breath; so that a man hath no preeminence above a beast: for all is vanity.

20 All go unto one place; all are of the dust, and all turn to dust again.

21 Who knoweth the spirit of man that goeth upward, and the spirit of the beast that goeth downward to the earth?

22 Wherefore I perceive that there is nothing better, than that a man should rejoice in his own works; for that is his portion: for who shall bring him to see what shall be after him?

ECCLESIASTES, CHAPTER 10

Dead flies cause the ointment of the apothecary to send forth a stinking savor: so doth a little folly him that is in reputation for wisdom and honor.

2 A wise man's heart is at his right hand; but a fool's heart at his left.

3 Yea also, when he that is a fool walketh by the way, his wisdom faileth him, and he saith to every one that he is a fool.

4 If the spirit of the ruler rise up against thee, leave not thy place; for yielding pacifieth great offences.

5 There is an evil which I have seen under the sun, as an error which proceedeth from the ruler:

6 Folly is set in great dignity, and the rich sit in low place.

7 I have seen servants upon horses, and princes walking as servants upon the earth.

8 He that diggeth a pit shall fall into it; and whoso breaketh an hedge, a serpent shall bite him.

9 Whoso removeth stones shall be hurt therewith; and he that cleaveth wood shall be endangered thereby.

10 If the iron be blunt, and he do not whet the edge, then must he put to more strength: but wisdom is profitable to direct.

11 Surely the serpent will bite without enchantment; and a babbler is no better.

12 The words of a wise man's mouth are gracious; but the lips of a fool will swallow up himself.

13 The beginning of the words of his mouth is foolishness: and the end of his talk is mischievous madness.

14 A fool also is full of words: a man cannot tell what shall be; and what shall be after him, who can tell him?

15 The labor of the foolish wearieth every one of them, because he knoweth not how to go to the city.

16 Woe to thee, O land, when thy king is a child, and thy princes eat in the morning!

17 Blessed art thou, O land, when thy king is the son of nobles, and thy princes eat in due season, for strength, and not for drunkenness!

18 By much slothfulness the building decayeth; and through idleness of the hands the house droppeth through.

19 A feast is made for laughter, and wine maketh merry: but money answereth all things.

20 Curse not the king, no not in thy thought; and curse not the rich in thy bedchamber: for a bird of the air shall carry the voice, and that which hath wings shall tell the matter.

Psalm 90

Lord, thou hast been our dwelling place in all generations.

2 Before the mountains were brought forth, or ever thou hadst formed the earth and the world, even from everlasting to everlasting, thou art God.

3 Thou turnest man to destruction; and sayest, Return, ye children of men.

4 For a thousand years in thy sight are but as yesterday when it is past, and as a watch in the night.

5 Thou carriest them away as with a flood; they are as a sleep: in the morning they are like grass which groweth up.

6 In the morning it flourisheth, and groweth up; in the evening it is cut down, and withereth.

7 For we are consumed by thine anger, and by thy wrath are we troubled.

8 Thou hast set our iniquities before thee, our secret sins in the light of thy countenance.

9 For all our days are passed away in thy wrath: we spend our years as a tale that is told.

10 The days of our years are threescore years and ten; and if by reason of strength they be fourscore years, yet is their strength labor and sorrow; for it is soon cut off, and we fly away.

11 Who knoweth the power of thine anger? even according to thy fear, so is thy wrath.

12 So teach us to number our days, that we may apply
our hearts unto wisdom.

13 Return, O Lord, how long? and let it repent thee concerning thy servants.

14 O satisfy us early with thy mercy; that we may rejoice
and be glad all our days.

15 Make us glad according to the days wherein thou hast
afflicted us, and the years wherein we have seen evil.

16 Let thy work appear unto thy servants, and thy glory
unto their children.

17 And let the beauty of the Lord our God be upon us:
and establish thou the work of our hands upon us; yea, the
work of our hands establish thou it.

Hymn to God My God, in My Sickness

Since I am coming to that holy room
    Where, with Thy choir of saints for evermore,
I shall be made Thy music; as I come
    I tune the instrument here at the door,
    And what I must do then, think here before.

Whilst my physicians by their love are grown
    Cosmographers, and I their map, who lie
Flat on this bed, that by them may be shown
    That this is my southwest discovery
    Per fretum febris, by these straits to die,

I joy, that in these straits, I see my West;
    For, though their currents yield return to none,
What shall my West hurt me? As West and East
    In all flat maps (and I am one) are one,
    So death doth touch the resurrection.

Is the Pacific Sea my home? Or are
    The Eastern riches? Is Jerusalem?
Anyan, and Mágellan, and Gíbraltar,
    All straits, and none but straits, are ways to them,
    Whether where Japhet dwelt, or Cham, or Shem.

We think that Paradise and Calvary,
    Christ's cross, and Adam's tree, stood in one place;
Look, Lord, and find both Adams met in me;
    As the first Adam's sweat surrounds my face,
    May the last Adam's blood my soul embrace.

So, in his purple wrapped, receive me, Lord;
    By these his thorns give me his other crown;
And, as to others' souls I preached Thy word,
    Be this my text, my sermon to mine own:
    Therefore that he may raise the Lord throws down.

—John Donne

What Are Years?

What is our innocence,
  what is our guilt? All are
    naked, none is safe. And whence
is courage: the unanswered question,
the resolute doubt,—
dumbly calling, deafly listening—that
in misfortune, even death,
          encourages others
          and in its defeat, stirs

    the soul to be strong? He
sees deep and is glad, who
    accedes to mortality
and in his imprisonment rises
upon himself as
the sea in a chasm, struggling to be
free and unable to be,
          in its surrendering
          finds its continuing.
    So he who strongly feels,
behaves. The very bird,
    grown taller as he sings, steels
his form straight up. Though he is captive,
his mighty singing
says, satisfaction is a lowly
thing, how pure a thing is joy.
          This is mortality,
          this is eternity.

—Marianne Moore

Notes and Sources

Where full publication information is not provided, please see notation in the Acknowledgments of Permissions, pages 319–327.

INTRODUCTION: FEELING OLDER

21. **Bly:** Carol Bly, Foreword to *Full Measure: Modern Short Stories on Aging,* ed. Dorothy Sennett (St. Paul: Graywolf Press, 1988).
21. **Blythe:** Ronald Blythe, *The View in Winter: Reflections on Old Age,* p. 10. This fine book has been a helpful guide to some of my own collecting.
21. **Woolf:** Virginia Woolf (1882–1941), *Mrs. Dalloway,* p. 119.
21. **Plato:** (427–347 B.C.), *The Republic,* trans. Francis MacDonald, p. 4.
21. **Eliot:** T. S. Eliot (1888–1965), "East Coker," *Four Quartets.*
21. **Scott-Maxwell:** Florida Scott-Maxwell, as quoted in Blythe, *The View in Winter,* p. 12.
24. **Montaigne:** (1533–1592), *Essays, The Complete Works,* trans. Donald M. Frame, pp. 236–37.
24. **Minois:** Georges Minois *History of Old Age: From Antiquity to the Renaissance,* trans. Sarah Hanbury Tenison, p. 294. This book is full of splendid quotations, especially revealing about antiquity.
25. **Donne:** John Donne (1572–1631), "Death Be Not Proud," widely reprinted, with variant punctuation. Reprinted here from *John Donne: The Divine Poems,* ed. Helen Gardner (Oxford: Oxford University Press, 1978), p. 9.
27. **Howe:** Irving Howe (1920–1993), *A Margin of Hope: An Intellectual Journey.*
29. **actuarial reports:** Population statistics have shifted through this century from a "population pyramid," with far more ten-year-olds alive than forty-year-olds, and even fewer at the apex, to a "populations rectangle," with as many seniors as infants. See, for example, Alan Pifer and Lydia Bronte, "Introduction: Squaring the Pyramid," in their collection, *Our Aging Society: Paradox and Promise* (New York: W. W. Norton & Company, 1986): "Since 1900 . . . our life expectancy has increased by twenty-eight years, from forty-seven to seventy-five. . . . [By 2035] every fifth, and possibly every fourth, American will be 'elderly'—if sixty-five and over continues to be the definition of that term. By the middle of the next century there will be some 16 million people over the age of eighty-five. . . . A majority of Americans at the age of fifty today still have a third to half of their life spans ahead of them," p. 12.

30. **Yeats:** William Butler Yeats (1865–1939), lines from "The Tower," *The Poems of W. B. Yeats: A New Edition.*

30. **Yeats:** W. B. Yeats, First stanza of "Sailing to Byzantium," *The Poems of W. B. Yeats: A New Edition*, p. 194.

31. **Cherry:** Kelly Cherry, "Lines Written on the Eve of a Birthday," *Natural Theology*, p. 41.

32. **Final Exit:** Derek Humphry, *Final Exit: Self-deliverance and Assisted Suicide for the Dying* (Eugene, OR: The Hemlock Society, 1991).

32–33. **Swift:** Jonathan Swift (1667–1745), *Gulliver's Travels*, Book III.

33. **modern man:** Or, if you prefer, "post-modern." As they say in "Peanuts," whatever.

33. **Shaw:** George Bernard Shaw (1856–1950), Preface to *Buoyant Billions*, as quoted in John Updike, *Self-Consciousness: A Memoir.*

35. **Shakespeare:** "Life . . . is a tale . . . ," *Macbeth*, act 5, scene 5, lines 20 ff.

36. **Shakespeare:** *As You Like It*, act 2, scene 7, lines 157–65.

37. **Milton:** John Milton (1608–1674), *Poetical Works*, p. 431.

37. **Larkin:** Philip Larkin (1922–1985), "On Being Twenty-six," *Collected Poems*, pp. 24–25. His own anthology, *The Oxford Book of Twentieth-Century English Verse*, is—no doubt partly because of his own obsession with aging—richly laden with the poetry of aging.

38. **Byron:** George Gordon, Lord Byron (1788–1824), "On This Day I Complete My Thirty-sixth Year," from "Occasional Pieces," 1807–1924, *Byron: Poetical Works*, p. 112.

38. **Yeats:** W. B. Yeats, "The Wild Old Wicked Man," *W. B. Yeats: The Poems*, p. 311.

39. **Cicero:** (106–43 B.C.), *On Old Age and On Friendship*, ed. and trans. Frank O. Copely.

40. **Warren:** Robert Penn Warren (1905–1989), "Last Walk of the Season," *New and Selected Poems: 1923–1985.*

PART I: FACING THE FACTS

43. **Bacon:** Francis Bacon (1561–1626). Yes, your suspicion is justified: Some of my quotations come from sources that did not identify *their* sources, and I refuse to spend my life hunting through Bacon's vast corpus to verify five words.

43. **Shakespeare:** "The Passionate Pilgrim," Poem 12. David Bevington tells us that the poem, with its clichéd "Crabbed age and youth cannot live together. / Youth is full of pleasance, age is full of care," may be by Shakespeare, but it shows "no unequivocal sign of Shakespeare's genius." Should that worry us here?

43. **Egyptian papyrus:** As quoted in Joseph T. Freeman, *Aging: Its History and Literature* (New York: Human Sciences Press, 1979), p. 21.

43. **Van Doren:** Mark Van Doren (1894–1972), "Last Housecleaning," *Collected and New Poems: 1924–1963*, p. 521.

43. **Beckett:** Samuel Beckett (1906–1989), "Addenda," *Watt*, p. 247.

45. **Going Like Sixty:** *Going Like Sixty*, Richard Armour, 1974; *Golden Age Exercises*, Frances King and William F. Herzig, 1968; *Aging Successfully*, George Lawton, 1946; *How to Make the Rest of Your Life the Best of Your Life*, Henry Legler, 1969; *Live Longer and Enjoy It*, Peter J. Steincrohn, 1972.

45. **Browning:** Robert Browning (1812–1889), "Rabbi Ben Ezra," *Robert Browning's Poetry*, pp. 246–47.

46. **Pope:** Alexander Pope (1688–1744), "Thoughts on Various Subjects." Also attributed to Swift. No doubt somebody knows which is right.

47. **Burke:** Kenneth Burke (1897–1993), *The Selected Correspondence of Kenneth Burke and Malcolm Cowley: 1915–1981*, p. 329.

47. **Berryman:** John Berryman (1914–1972), as quoted in Paul Mariani, *Dream Song: The Life of John Berryman* (New York: William Morrow, 1990), pp. 163–64.

48. **Chateaubriand's claim:** As quoted in Simone de Beauvoir, *The Coming of Age*, p. 299. I have found this book on the whole the best single discussion of aging—not an easy confession for me, since I am less than enthusiastic about much of her other work, *The Second Sex* excepted. *Age* combines some literary quotations with her own strong feelings about aging and current scientific knowledge about it.

48. **Genesis:** 24:1.

49. **Cowley:** Malcolm Cowley (1898–1989), *The View from Eighty*, pp. 3–4.

51. **Villon:** François Villon (1431–1463?), trans. Paul J. Archambault, as quoted in Prisca von Dorotka Bagnell and Patricia Spencer Soper, eds., *Perceptions of Aging in Literature: A Cross-Cultural Study, Contributions to the Study of Aging*, p. 52. A useful, broad-ranging collection.

51. **Juvenal:** (c. 60–127), Satire X, quoted widely.

54. **Seneca:** (4 B.C.–A.D. 65), *Epistolae morales*, trans. R. M. Gummere.

55. **dirty, sallow complexion:** Terms assembled by Maria S. Haynes, as quoted in Minois, *History of Old Age*, p. 95.

55–56. **Chaucer:** Geoffrey Chaucer (1340?–1400), *The Canterbury Tales: An Illustrated Selection*, trans. Nevill Coghill, pp. 112, 313.

57–58. **Rich:** Adrienne Rich (1929–   ), poems numbered 18 and 16, *Your Native Land, Your Life*, pp. 100, 98.

58. **Bishop:** Elizabeth Bishop (1927–1979), "One Art," *The Collected Poems 1927–1979*, p. 178.

59. **Updike:** John Updike (1932–   ), *Self-Consciousness: A Memoir*, pp. 252, 259.

60. **Johnson:** Samuel Johnson (1709–1784), "The Vanity of Human Wishes," *Complete English Poems*, J. D. Fleeman, ed. (New York: St. Martin's Press, 1971), pp. 89–91.

62. **Larkin:** Philip Larkin, "Dear Charles, My Muse, asleep or dead," *Collected Poems*," pp. 217–18.

63. **Ruskin:** John Ruskin (1819–1900), chap. 11, "The Place of Dragons," *St. Mark's Rest*, in E. T. Cook and Alexander Wedderburn, eds., *The Works of John Ruskin* (London: George Allen, 1906), vol. 24: 370–71.

64. **Landor:** Walter Savage Landor (1775–1864), "Yes; I write verses now and

then," *The Works and Life of Walter Savage Landor* (London: Chapman and Hall, 1876), vol. 8: 90–91.

65. **Cherry:** Kelly Cherry, "Used: The Mind-Body Problem," *Natural Theology.*

66. **Whitman:** Walt Whitman (1819–1892), "Sands at Seventy," in "First Annex" to *Leaves of Grass,* written in 1888–89, and included in Philadelphia edition of 1891–92.

70. **Burke:** Kenneth Burke, *The Selected Correspondence of Kenneth Burke and Malcolm Cowley: 1915–1981,* pp. 282–83.

70. **Cowley:** Malcolm Cowley, *The Selected Correspondence of Kenneth Burke and Malcolm Cowley: 1915–1981,* p. 341.

72. **Lerner:** Laurence Lerner, "It Is Time," *Rembrandt's Mirror,* pp. 17–19.

74. **Wordsworth:** William Wordsworth (1770–1850), "Extempore Effusion Upon the Death of James Hogg," written November 1835, from "Epitaphs and Elegiac Pieces." Reprinted widely.

76. **Byron:** George Gordon, Lord Byron, "What is the worst of woes that wait on age?" *Childe Harold's Pilgrimage,* Canto 2, stanza 98.

76. **Lamb:** Charles Lamb (1775–1834) "The Old Familiar Faces," *The Works of Charles and Mary Lamb,* ed. E. V. Lucas, 7 vols. (London: Methuen, 1912), vol. 4, pp. 25–26.

77. **Burke:** Kenneth Burke, on the death of his wife, *The Selected Correspondence of Kenneth Burke and Malcolm Cowley: 1915–1981,* p. 368.

78. **Browning:** Robert Browning, "A Toccata of Galuppi's," stanza 15, *Robert Browning's Poetry,* p. 116.

78. **Hardy:** Thomas Hardy (1840–1928), "Faithful Wilson," *The Complete Poems of Thomas Hardy,* p. 892.

79. **Graves:** Robert Graves (1895–1985), "The Face in the Mirror," *Collected Poems,* p. 187.

79. **Hardy:** Thomas Hardy, "I Look into My Glass," *The Complete Poems of Thomas Hardy,* p. 81.

80. **Arnold:** Matthew Arnold (1822–1888), "Growing Old," *New Poems,* 1867.

81. **Samuel:** Barzillai. 2 Samuel 19:32–39, King James Version.

82. **Menander:** (342?–291 B.C.), as quoted in Minois, *History of Old Age,* p. 52.

82. **Ptah Hotep:** As quoted in Minois, *History of Old Age,* pp. 14–15.

83. **James:** Alice James (1848–1892), "February 2nd [1892]" and "March 4th [1892]," *The Diary of Alice James,* pp. 976–79.

85. **Egyptian papyrus:** As quoted in Minois, *History of Old Age,* p. 15.

85. **James:** Henry James (1843–1916), letter to W. Morton Fullerton, "February 25th, 1897," *Selected Letters,* pp. 302–3.

86. **Jonson:** Ben Jonson (1573–1637), "My Picture Left in Scotland," *Ben Jonson,* p. 324.

87. **Milton:** John Milton, *Paradise Lost,* chap. 11, lines 526–46.

87. **Rossetti:** Christina Rossetti (1830–1894), "Song ['Oh roses for the flush of youth']," *The Complete Poems of Christina Rossetti,* vol. 1, p. 40.

88. **al-Haydari:** Buland al-Haydari (1926–   ), "Old Age," *An Anthology of Modern Arabic Poetry,* pp. 129–31.

89. **Mimnermus:** *Greek Lyrics,* trans. Richmond Lattimore, p. 29.
89. **Euripides:** (c. 485–406 B.C.), "Chorus," *Herakles,* as quoted in Minois, *History of Old Age,* p. 50.
90. **Sophocles:** (c. 495–406 B.C.), *Oedipus at Colonus,* as quoted in Prisca von Dorotka Bagnell and Patricia Spencer Soper, eds., *Perceptions of Aging in Literature,* p. 24.
91. **Hoffman:** Daniel Hoffman (1923–   ), "Jogger," *Hang-Gliding from Helicon: New and Selected Poems, 1948–1988,* p. 183.
92. **Colette:** (1873–1934), Letter to Pierre Moreno, "December 29, 1949," *Letters from Colette,* trans. Robert Phelps, p. 194.
92. **Van Doren:** Mark Van Doren (1894–1972), "Last Houseclearning," *Collected and New Poems: 1924–1963,* p. 521.
92. **Sarton:** May Sarton (1912–1995), *As We Are Now,* pp. 108, 115.
93 **Ecclesiastes 1:** King James Version.
95. **Stevens:** Wallace Stevens (1879–1955), "Lebensweisheitspielerei," *Collected Poems,* p. 504.

PART II: CURES, CONSOLATIONS, CELEBRATIONS

101. **Amiel:** Henri Frédéric Amiel (1821–1881). My failure to identify yet another quotation could become embarrassing, if I did not know that *you* know how hard it is to locate the origins of one-liners like this one.
101. **Stein:** Gertrude Stein (1874–1946), "Stanzas in Meditation," *The Yale Gertrude Stein,* p. 452.
101. **Matisse:** Henri Matisse (1869–1954), "April 8, 1941," letter to Albert Marquet, *Matisse,* by Pierre Schneider (New York: Rizzoli International, 1984), p. 738.
101. **Holmes:** Oliver Wendell Holmes (1809–1894), "On the Seventieth Birthday of Julia Ward Howe," *The Complete Poetical Works of Oliver Wendell Holmes.*
101. **Glasgow:** Ellen Glasgow (1874–1945), *The Woman Within* (New York: Harcourt Brace Jovanovich, 1954), p. 282.
101. **Yeats:** W. B. Yeats, "Quarrel in Old Age," *The Poems of W. B. Yeats: A New Edition,* p. 253.
101. **Goethe:** Johann Wolfgang von Goethe (1749–1832), *Conversations with Goethe in the Last Years of His Life,* by Johann Peter Eckermann, trans. S. M. Fuller (Boston: Hilliard, Gray and Company, 1839).
103. **Neugarten:** Bernice L. Neugarten (1916–   ), ed., *Middle Age and Aging: A Reader in Social Psychology* (Chicago: University of Chicago Press, 1968).
103. **"Age Concern" survey:** reported in Blythe, *The View in Winter,* p. 13.
104. **Bly:** Carol Bly, Foreword to *Full Measure: Modern Short Stories on Aging.*
104. **Rich:** Adrienne Rich, "One Life," *Times Power: Poems, 1985–1988,* p. 42.
109. **Rossetti:** Christina Rossetti (1830–1894), "Dead Before Death," *The Complete Poems of Christina Rossetti.*
109. **Yusuf al-Khal:** Yusuf al-Khal (1917–   ), "Old Age," *An Anthology of Modern Arabic Poetry,* pp. 53–55.
111. **Life begins at forty:** A best-seller in 1932, by Walter A. Pitkin, was called

Life Begins at Forty. Modern Maturity magazine has been using "Life Begins at Fifty" as a slogan in their advertising. Surely the ten-year jump shows that we are all growing older?

112. **Seneca:** As quoted in Theodore Groene, *The Harvest Years,* p. 121.

114. **Hodapp:** Minnie Iverson Hodapp (1889–1986), "I Haven't Lost My Marbles Yet!"

115. **Holmes:** Oliver Wendell Holmes (1809–1894), "The Old Player," *The Complete Poetical Works of Oliver Wendell Holmes.*

115. **Cornaro:** Caterina Cornaro (1454–1510), as quoted in Beauvoir, *The Coming of Age,* p. 305.

116. **"I am growing old":** As quoted in Prisca von Dorotka Bagnell and Patricia Spencer Soper, eds., *Perceptions of Aging in Literature.*

116. **the old joke:** Joke borrowed from Gail Godwin's *A Southern Family.* Incidentally, Godwin's novel offers shrewd observations on what it means to grow old—about how to celebrate the life that includes aging.

117. **Twain:** Mark Twain (1835–1910), *The Adventures of Huckleberry Finn,* chap. 17, "The Grangerfords Take Me In."

118. **Merrill:** James Merrill (1926–1995), "Losing the Marbles," *The Inner Room,* pp. 84–90.

125. **affirmers live longer:** See O. Carl Simonton, M.D., et al., *Getting Well Again . . . Revolutionary Lifesaving Self-Awareness Techniques,* 1978; and Norman Cousins, *Head First: The Biology of Hope,* 1989.

126. **Berryman:** John Berryman (1914–1972), "No," *Collected Poems, 1937–1971,* p. 250.

127. **Parker:** Dorothy Parker (1893–1967), "Résumé," *The Portable Dorothy Parker,* p. 99.

127. **Hughes:** Langston Hughes (1902–1967), "Life Is Fine," *Selected Poems.*

129. **Beauvoir:** Simone de Beauvoir (1908–1986), *The Coming of Age,* pp. 540–41.

129. **Skinner:** B. F. Skinner (1904–1970), and M. E. Vaughan, *Enjoy Old Age: A Program of Self-Management,* p. 86.

130. **Johnson:** Samuel Johnson (1709–1784), writing to John Taylor, *The Letters of Samuel Johnson,* pp. 395–96.

130. **Mannes:** The process of maturing, Marya Mannes, *More in Anger* (Philadelphia: Lippincott, 1958).

131. **Cicero:** *On Old Age and On Friendship,* pp. 6, 32.

132. **Frost:** Robert Frost (1874–1963), "Provide, Provide," *The Poetry of Robert Frost,* p. 404.

134. **Housman:** A. E. Housman (1859–1936), "IV," *More Poems,* p. 165.

135. **Hardy:** Thomas Hardy (1840–1928), "He Never Expected Much, or, A Consideration on My Eighty-sixth Birthday," *The Complete Poems of Thomas Hardy,* p. 886.

136. **Blythe:** Ronald Blythe, *The View in Winter,* pp. 22–33.

136. **Skinner:** B. F. Skinner, *Enjoy Old Age,* pp. 133–34.

137. **Swift:** Jonathan Swift (1667–1745), "Resolutions When I Come to Be Old," *Jonathan Swift,*" p. 23. His "Resolutions" can be found in almost every anthology about aging. The Latin phrase in the resolution number 15 trans-

lates roughly as "and to disdain and avoid those who lie in wait for their inheritance."

139. **Davies:** Robertson Davies (1913–1996), "You're Not Getting Older, You're Getting Nosier," introduction to *Vital Signs: International Stories on Aging.*

141. **Eliot:** T. S. Eliot, line from "East Coker," *Four Quartets.*

141. **Forster:** E. M. Forster (1879–1970), "Going to Bits," *Commonplace Book,* p. 224.

143. **Boyle:** Kay Boyle (1902–1992), "Poets," *This Is Not a Letter,* pp. 20–22.

146. **political dreams:** On political disillusionment, see Beauvoir's report on Anatole France and H. G. Wells in *The Coming of Age,* pp. 413–15.

146. **Boyle:** Kay Boyle, "A Poem About Black Power," *Testament for My Students and Other Poems,* pp. 31–32.

148. **Marvell:** Andrew Marvell (1621–1678), "To His Coy Mistress," to be found in almost every anthology of English poetry.

150. **Spenser:** Edmund Spenser (1552–1599), *The Faerie Queene,* section 2, chap. 12, line 75.

150. **Wilde:** Oscar Wilde (1854–1900), quotation *not* from *Lady Windemere's Fan,* but from *Lord Arthur Saville's Crimes,* 1877.

150. **Gide:** André Gide (1869–1951), *Ainsi soit-il,* in *Journal, 1939–49: Souvenirs,* Bibliothèque de la Pléiade (Paris: Gallimard, 1954), p. 1169.

150. **Montaigne:** As quoted in Beauvoir, *The Coming of Age,* p. 159.

151. **Anacreon:** (c. 570–c. 480 B.C.), "Defiance Of Age," trans. Thomas Moore (1779–1852).

152. **Falstaff:** Shakespeare (1564–1616), Hal to Falstaff, *Henry IV, Part I.*

152. **Powys:** John Cowper Powys (1872–1963), as quoted in Blythe's introduction to *The View in Winter.* Blythe's interviews contain a great deal on this subject.

152. **Berenson:** Bernard Berenson (1865–1959), *Sunset and Twilight: From the Diaries of Bernard Berenson, 1947–1958,* ed. Nicky Mariana (New York: Harcourt Brace Jovanovich, 1963).

153. **"Today":** "Today"—the version I learned as a child. The new Mormon hymnal has made the song even more aggressively work-oriented, by changing the final line to "Prepare for tomorrow by working today."

154. **Yeats:** W. B. Yeats (1865–1939), "Sailing to Byzantium," stanzas 1–4, *The Poems of W. B. Yeats: A New Edition,* p. 194.

155–58. **Woolf:** Virginia Woolf (1882–1941), *To the Lighthouse.*

158. **Rilke:** Rainer Maria Rilke (1875–1926), "*Du musst dein Leben ändern,*" final line of "*Archaischer Torso Apollos,*" from *Neue Gedichte: 1907–08.*

159. **Beauvoir:** Simone de Beauvoir, *The Coming of Age,* pp. 490–91.

159. **Brontë:** Emily Brontë (1818–1848), "No coward soul is mine" and "Riches I hold in light esteem," in *Collected Poems.* It was her sister Charlotte who said "No coward soul" was her last poem.

160. **Millay:** Edna St. Vincent Millay (1892–1950), "The Courage That My Mother Had," *Collected Poems.*

162. **Wylie:** Elinor Wylie (1885–1928), "Let No Charitable Hope" and "Nadir," *Collected Poems,* 1932.

163. **James:** William James (1842–1910), June 4, 1910, letter to Henry P. Bowditch, *The Letters of William James,* ed. Henry James (Millwood, NY: Kraus Reprint, 1920), pp. 341–42.

165. **Wu Yü-pi:** As quoted in Prisca von Dorotka Bagnell and Patricia Spencer Soper, eds., *Perceptions of Aging in Literature,* p. 157.

166. **Thomas:** Dylan Thomas (1914–1953), "Do Not Go Gentle into That Good Night," *Poems of Dylan Thomas,* p. 128.

168. **James:** Henry James, "29 August 1915 Sunday" and "12 September 1915 Sunday," *The Complete Notebooks of Henry James,* pp. 430–31.

169. **Roethke:** Theodore Roethke (1908–1963), "The Decision," *The Collected Poems of Theodore Roethke,* p. 245.

169. **Boyle:** Kay Boyle, "Advice to the Old (including myself)," *This Is Not a Letter,* p. 29.

171. **Selden:** John Selden (1584–1654), *Table Talk,* 1689.

171. **The View in Winter:** As quoted in Blythe, *The View in Winter,* p. 40.

172. **Rich:** Adrienne Rich, Poem 28, *Times Power: Poems,* p. 110.

172. **Sappho:** (c. 610–c. 565 b.c.), "Age and Light," *Sappho: A New Translation,* trans. Mary Barnard, p. 93.

173. **Beckett:** Samuel Beckett (1906–1989), *Happy Days* (New York: Grove Press, 1961), p. 64.

173. **Kael:** Pauline Kael, *Hooked: Film Writing,* 1985–1988.

174. **Forster:** E. M. Forster (1879–1970), *Commonplace Book,* pp. 256, 234.

175. **Seneca:** "Letter XII," *Letters to Lucilius,* as quoted in Minois, *History of Old Age,* p. 101.

175–76. **Landor:** Walter Savage Landor (1775–1864), "Leaf after leaf drops off" and "Death stands above me, whispering low," *The Works and Life of Walter Savage Landor,* vol. 8: 183, 178.

176. **Landor:** Walter Savage Landor (1775–1864), "Dying Speech of an Old Philosopher," *Poems by Walter Savage Landor,* Geoffrey Grigson, ed. (Carbondale, IL: Southern Illinois University Press, 1965), p. 172.

177. **Forster:** E. M. Forster, *Commonplace Book,* pp. 257–58.

178. **Plato:** *The Republic,* pp. 4–5.

179–80. **Yeats:** W. B. Yeats, "From 'Oedipus at Colonus,'" and "The Tower," *The Poems of W. B. Yeats: A New Edition.*

181. **Roethke:** Theodore Roethke, "The Restored," *The Collected Poems of Theodore Roethke,* p. 249.

182. **Wharton:** Edith Wharton (1862–1932), letter from *The Letters of Edith Wharton.*

183. **Blythe:** Ronald Blythe, *The View in Winter,* pp. 45–46.

183. **Nodier:** Charles Nodier (1780–1844), as quoted in Beauvoir, *The Coming of Age,* p. 370.

183. **Beauvoir:** Old woman, as quoted in *The Coming of Age,* p. 372.

183. **Aunt Relva:** I'm not making this up. See my privately published edition of her autobiography, *The Autobiography of Relva Booth Ross,* ed. Wayne C. Booth (Provo, UT), 1971.

184. **Beauvoir on Memory:** Beauvoir, *The Coming of Age,* pp. 364–65.

185. **the creation:** A Catholic friend, David Tracy, has taken part over several years in ecumenical meetings of representatives of the major world faiths, attempting to find what they have in common. He returned from one conference to announce what may be the most paradoxical triumph in the history of conferences: They all agreed, finally, that something went radically wrong with creation!

186. **Pitter:** Ruth Pitter (1897–1992), "Yorkshire Wife's Sage," *Collected Poems*, pp. 181–82.

187. **Kumin:** Maxine Kumin (1925–   ), "The Envelope," *The Retrieval System*, p. 40.

188. **Hugo:** Victor Hugo (1802–1885), "The Contented Exile," loosely translated by Ida J. Lemon, *The Poems of Victor Hugo* (New York: The Athenaeum Society, 1909), vol. 2: 767–68. The French goes somewhat better:

> Qu'est-ce cette terre? Une tempête d'âmes.
> Dans cette ombre, où, nochers errants, nous n'abordâmes
> Jamais qu'à des ecueils, les prenant pour des ports;
> Dans l'orage des cris, des désirs, des transports,
> Des amours, des douleurs, des voeux, tas de nuées;
> Dans les furants baisers de ces prostituées
> Que nous nommons fortune, ambition, succès;
> Devant Job, qui, souffrant, dit: Qu'est-ce que je sais?
> Et Pascal qui, tremblant, dit: Qu'est-ce que je pense? . .
> Dans ce néant qui mord, dans ce chaos qui ment,
> Ce qui l'homme finit par voir distinctement,
> C'est pas-dessus nos deuils, nos chutes, nos descentes,
> La souverainté des choses innocentes, . . .
> Certe, il est salutaire et bon pour le pensée, ...
> De contempler parfois, . . .
> Une profonde paix toute faite d'étoiles;
> C'est à cela que Dieu songeait quand il a mis
> Les poètes auprès des enfants endormis.
> (*L'Art d'être grandpère*, Paris, 1884)

189. **"Georges and Jeanne":** This one was translated by N. Y. Tyerman, pp. 769–70. Again, I find the French less sentimental:

> Moi qu'un petit enfant rend tout à fait stupide,
> J'en ai deux, Georges et Jeanne; et je prends l'un pour guide
> Et l'autre pour lumière, et j'accours à leur voix
> Vu que Georges a deux ans et que Jeanne a dix mois.
> Leurs essais d'exister sont divinement gauches;
> On croit, dans leur parole où tremblent des ébauches,
> Voir un rest de ciel que se dissipe et fuit;
> Et moi qui suis le soir, et moi qui suis la nuit,
> Moi dont le destin pâle et froid se décoloré,

J'ai l'attendrissement de dire: Ils sont l'aurore.
Georges songe aux gâteaux, aux beaux jouets étrange,
Au chien, au coq, au chat; et Jeanne pense aux anges.
Puis, au réveil, leurs yeux s'ouvrent, pleins de rayons.
Ils arrivent, hélas, à l'heure où nous fuyons.

189. **Wordsworth:** William Wordsworth, "Ode: Intimations of Immortality from Recollections of Early Childhood," stanza 5.

192. **Eliot:** T. S. Eliot, "Burnt Norton," *Four Quartets.*

193. **James:** Henry James, "August 21, 1913," letter to Hugh Walpole, *Selected Letters,* p. 413.

194. **Burke:** Kenneth Burke, *The Selected Correspondence of Kenneth Burke and Malcolm Cowley: 1915–1981,* pp. 379–80. A further example of a friendship sustained into later years is found in *The Letters of Evelyn Waugh and Diana Cooper,* ed. Artemis Cooper (New York: Ticknor and Fields, 1992); many more can be sampled in *The Oxford Book of Friendship,* ed. D. J. Enright and David Rawlinson (New York: Oxford University Press, 1991).

198. **Arnold:** Matthew Arnold (1822–1888), "Dover Beach," *Matthew Arnold,* pp. 135–36. "Dover Beach" recently won the "National Association of Overworked Anthologists' Prize" for Most Frequent Appearance in Anthologies.

199. **"When you and I were young, Maggie":** words by George W. Johnson, music by James Butterfield (Chicago: J. A. Butterfield, 1866), as quoted in Howard P. Chudacoff, *How Old Are You?: Age Consciousness in American Culture* (Princeton: Princeton University Press, 1989), p. 142.

199. **"The Old Folks":** Words and music by T. H. Hinton (Syracuse, N.Y.: Clemons and Redington, 1867), as quoted in Chudacoff, *How Old Are You?,* p. 142.

200. **Burns:** Robert Burns (1759–1796), "John Anderson My Jo," *Complete Poetical Works of Robert Burns,* p. 223.

201. **Roethke:** Theodore Roethke, "Wish for a Young Wife," *The Collected Poems of Theodore Roethke,* p. 217.

201. **Browning:** Elizabeth Barrett Browning (1806–1861), Sonnet 43, reprinted everywhere.

202. **Machiavelli:** Niccolo Machiavelli (1469–1527). Another one I can't locate!

203. **"Life Begins at 80":** Frank C. Laubach, "Life Begins at 80," appeared in Ann Landers's column on December 29, 1990, in *The Chicago Tribune.*

204. **Landor:** Walter Savage Landor (1775–1864), "The burden of an ancient rhyme," *The Works and Life of Walter Savage Landor,* vol. 8: 74.

205. **Cousins:** Norman Cousins (1915–1990), *Anatomy of an Illness, as Perceived by the Patient: Reflections on Healing and Regeneration,* pp. 39–40.

205. **Naylor:** James Ball Naylor (1860–1945), "David and Solomon." Another one that I can't track down.

207. **Bliven:** Bruce Bliven (1889–1977), as quoted in John Kotre and Elizabeth Hall, *Seasons of Life: Our Dramatic Journey from Birth to Death* (Boston: Little, Brown & Company, 1990), p. 370.

207. **Betjeman:** John Betjeman (1906–1984), "The Last Laugh," *A Nip in the Air*, p. 62.

208. **Armour:** Richard Armour (1906–1989), *Going Like Sixty* (New York: McGraw-Hill, 1975).

208. **Olson:** Elder Olson (1909–1992), lines from "Conversation Pieces," *Last Poems*, p. 22.

208. **Twain:** Mark Twain (1835–1910), "Mark Twain's Seventieth Birthday," *Mark Twain Speaking,* ed. Paul Fatout (Iowa City: University of Iowa Press, 1976), pp. 462–67.

216. **Nash:** Ogden Nash (1902–1971), "Crossing the Border," in *Verses from 1929 On* (Boston: Little, Brown, 1959), p. 522.

216–17. **Lear:** Edward Lear (1812–1888), "There Was an Old Man Who Supposed" and "There Was an Old Man with a Beard," *The Book of Nonsense*.

217. **Carroll:** Lewis Carroll (1832–1898), "Advice from a Caterpillar," *Alice's Adventures in Wonderland*

218. **Jonson:** Ben Jonson, *Volpone*, act 1, scene 4, lines 145–59, in *Ben Jonson*, pp. 21–22.

219. **Beckett:** Samuel Beckett, *Watt*, pp. 68–69.

221. **Burke:** Kenneth Burke, *The Selected Correspondence of Kenneth Burke and Malcolm Cowley: 1915–1981*, p. 371.

221. **Landor:** Walter Savage Landor (1775–1864), "Epigram XXVI," *The Works and Life of Walter Savage Landor*, vol. 8: 164.

222. **Auden:** W. H. Auden, (1907–1973), "Doggerel by a Senior Citizen," *W. H. Auden: Collected Poems*, pp. 37–38.

225. **Confucius:** (551–478 B.C.), *Confucian Analects (Lun-yu)*, trans. J. Legge, *The Four Books* (Shanghai, 1933).

225. **Bacon:** Francis Bacon, as quoted in E. M. Forster, *Commonplace Book*, p. 200.

226. **Schopenhauer:** Arthur Schopenhauer (1788–1860), "The Ages of Life," *Counsels and Maxims*, trans. T. B. Saunders (St. Clair Shores: Scholarly Press, 1970), pp. 151–52.

227. **Beauvoir:** Simone de Beauvoir, *The Coming of Age*, p. 491.

227. **Updike:** John Updike, *Self-Consciousness: A Memoir*, p. 260.

229. **Beethoven:** Ludwig von Beethoven (1770–1827), String Quartet in F Major (London: Ernst Eulenburg, n.d.).

230. **Forster:** E. M. Forster, *Commonplace Book*, p. 246.

230. **Mencken:** H. L. Mencken (1880–1956).

230. **Sainte-Beuve:** As quoted in Beauvoir, *The Coming of Age*, p. 380.

231. **cummings:** e. e. cummings (1894–1962), poem numbered 62 "now does our world descend," *Complete Poems, 1913–1962*, p. 834.

232. **Montaigne:** As quoted in Beauvoir, *The Coming of Age*, pp. 158–60.

235. **Landor:** Walter Savage Landor (1775–1864), "To Age," *The Works and Life of Walter Savage Landor*, vol. 8: 221–22.

236. **Psalms 144 and 90:** Composite compiled for a Koved funeral described in chapter 5 of Barbara Myerhoff's *Number Our Days*, facing p. 1.

236. **Diogenes Laertius:** (c. third century A.D.), *Lives of Eminent Philosophers,* X.122, as quoted in Minois, *History of Old Age,* p. 54.

237. **Eliot:** T. S. Eliot, "East Coker," end of section 2, *Four Quartets.*

237. **Goethe:** T. S. Eliot, "Goethe as the Sage," lecture delivered in May 1955 at Hamburg University.

237. **King Lear:** Shakespeare, *King Lear,* act 5, scene 3, lines 8–19.

238. **Russell:** Bertrand Russell (1872–1970), *Autobiography of Bertrand Russell,* vol. 3, *1944–1969* (New York: Simon & Schuster, 1969).

238. **Whitman:** Walt Whitman (1819–1892), "To Get the Final Lilt of Songs," "First Annex" to *Leaves of Grass,* Philadelphia edition of 1891–92.

240. **Fisher:** M. F. K. Fisher (1908–1992), *Sister Age,* pp. 234–39.

246. **Stevenson:** Robert Louis Stevenson, (1850–1894), "Crabbed Age and Youth," in *Virginibus Puerisque* (New York: Charles Scribner's Sons, 1911), pp. 86–102.

255. **Stevens:** Wallace Stevens, "A Pastoral Nun," *Collected Poems,* pp. 378–79.

256. **Petrarch:** Francesco Petrarch (1304–1374), #128 in "The Canzoniere," "Italia mia," trans. Kenelm Foster, *Petrarch: Poet and Humanist,* p. 58.

256. **Yeats:** W. B. Yeats, "Among School Children," *The Poems of W. B. Yeats: A New Edition,* pp. 215–17.

260. **Warren:** Robert Penn Warren, "The Whole Question," *New and Selected Poems: 1923–1985,* p. 54.

261. **Hopkins:** Gerard Manley Hopkins (1844–1889), "God's Grandeur," in *The Poems of Gerard Manley Hopkins,* p. 66.

262. **Herbert:** George Herbert (1593–1633), "The Flower."

264. **"Up-Hill":** Christina Rossetti, "Up-Hill," in *The Collected Poems of Christina Rossetti.*

PART III: A FURTHER HARVEST

269. **Olson:** Elder Olson (1909–1992), "Himself in Age," *Last Poems.*

269. **Glasgow:** Ellen Glasgow (1873–1945) *The Woman Within* (New York: Harcourt Brace Jovanovich, 1954), p. 282.

269. **Frost:** Robert Frost, Epigraph, *In the Clearing,* p. 39.

269. **Pound:** Ezra Pound (1885–1972), "Canto LXXX," *The Cantos.*

271. **Milton:** John Milton (1608–1674), "On His Blindness," Sonnet XVI.

271. **Frost:** Robert Frost, untitled poem, "In winter in the woods alone," *In the Clearing,* p. 101.

272. **Fontenelle:** Bernard de Fontenelle (1657–1757), as quoted in Beauvoir, *The Coming of Age,* p. 306.

272–74. **Sarton:** May Sarton, *At Seventy: A Journal,* p. 136; "The Silence Now," *The Silence Now,* p. 16; "Old Lovers at the Ballet," *Halfway to Silence,* p. 51.

275. **Van Doren:** Mark Van Doren, "The First Snow of the Year," *Collected and New Poems: 1924–1963,* pp. 533–34.

276. **Wheelock:** John Hall Wheelock (1886–1978), "Night Thoughts in Age," *Poems New and Old.*

278. **Thomas:** Dylan Thomas, "Fern Hill," *Poems of Dylan Thomas.*

280. **Clampitt:** Amy Clampitt (1920–1994), "Grasses," *Westward,* pp. 33–34.

282. **Beckett:** Samuel Beckett, "Fizzle 3: Afar a Bird," *Fizzles,* pp. 25–27.

283. **Brooks:** Gwendolyn Brooks (1917–1996), "A Catch of Shy Fish," *Blacks* (Chicago: Third World Press, 1991).

284. **Yeats:** W. B. Yeats, "A Prayer for Old Age," *W. B. Yeats: The Poems,* p. 282.

285. **Spender:** Stephen Spender, (1909–   ), "From My Diary," *Collected Poems, 1928–1985,* p. 162.

285. **Williams:** William Carlos Williams (1883–1963), "Wide Awake, Full of Love," *Collected Poems of William Carlos Williams, 1939–1962,* vol. 2, p. 207.

286. **Bogan:** Louise Bogan (1897–1970), "After the Persian," stanzas II, III, IV, and V, *Collected Poems, 1923–1953,* pp. 123, 124.

288. **Stevens:** Wallace Stevens, "The Plain Sense of Things," *Collected Poems,* pp. 502–3.

289–90. **Miles:** Josephine Miles (1911–1985), "Nadirs," "Brim," and "Stroke," *Collected Poems,* pp. 229, 228, 245.

291. **Tennyson:** Alfred, Lord Tennyson (1809–1892), "Crossing the Bar."

291. **Whitman:** Walt Whitman, "Halcyon Days," "Second Annex" to *Leaves of Grass,* Philadelphia edition of 1891–92.

292. **Milosz:** Czeslaw Milosz, "Old Women," *The Collected Poems, 1931–1987,* p. 454.

293. **Rosen:** Betty Rosen, "Breakfast Time," previously unpublished.

294. **Jarrell:** Randall Jarrell (1914–1965), "Thinking of the Lost World," *The Lost World,* pp. 67–69.

297. **Ecclesiastes:** 3, 8, 10, King James Version.

300. **Psalm 90:** King James Version.

301. **Donne:** John Donne, "Hymn to God My God, in My Sickness," reprinted widely.

303. **Moore:** Marianne Moore (1887–1972), "What Are Years?," *Collected Poems,* p. 175. Ezra Pound read this poem aloud at Marianne Moore's funeral.

Some Books That Provide Lists
of Books About Aging

Bagnell, Prisca von Dorotka, and Patricia Spencer Soper. *Perceptions of Aging in Literature: A Cross-Cultural Study.* Westport, CT: Greenwood Press, 1989.

Chudakoff, Howard P. *How Old Are You?: Age Consciousness in American Culture.* Princeton: Princeton University Press, 1989.

Cole, Thomas R., and Mary G. Winkler. *The Oxford Book of Aging: Reflections on the Journey of Life.* Oxford: Oxford University Press, 1994.

Fowler, Margaret, and Priscilla McCutcheon. *Songs of Experience: An Anthology of Literature on Growing Old.* New York: Ballantine Books, 1991.

Kotre, John, and Elizabeth Hall. *Seasons of Life: Our Dramatic Journey from Birth to Death.* Boston: Little, Brown, 1990.

Laslett, Peter. *A Fresh Map of Life: The Emergence of the Third Age.* London: Weidenfeld and Nicolson, 1989.

Minois, Georges. *History of Old Age: From Antiquity to the Renaissance.* Translated by Sarah Hanbury Tenison. Chicago: The University of Chicago Press, 1989. French original, 1987. No bibliography, but notes provide a rich guide to literature of aging (mainly European), century by century.

Neugarten, Bernice, ed. *Middle Age and Aging: A Reader in Social Psychology.* Chicago: The University of Chicago Press, 1968.

Pifer, Alan, and Lydia Bronte. *Our Aging Society: Paradox and Promise.* New York: Norton, 1986.

Schmidt, Mary Gwynne. *Negotiating a Good Old Age: Challenges of Residential Living in Late Life.* San Francisco: Jossey-Bass, 1990.

Woodward, Kathleen. *Aging and Its Discontents: Freud and Other Fictions.* Bloomington: Indiana University Press, 1991.

Acknowledgments of Permissions

Grateful acknowledgment is made to the following publishers, publications, and individuals for permission to include material in this work. Every attempt has been made to locate the proper grantor for each selection used. If an error or omission is found, the publisher would appreciate hearing about it and will make the appropriate correction in the next edition.

al-Haydari, Buland: "Old Age," from *An Anthology of Modern Arabic Poetry*, edited by M. A. Khouri and H. Algar, University of California Press. Copyright © 1974 The Regents of the University of California.

al-Khal, Yusuf: "Old Age" from *An Anthology of Modern Arabic Poetry*, edited by M. A. Khouri and H. Algar, University of California Press. Copyright © 1974 The Regents of the University of California.

Arnold, Matthew: "Dover Beach," from *Matthew Arnold*, Oxford Standard Authors series, edited by Miriam Allott and Robert H. Sugar, published in 1986. Reprinted by permission of Oxford University Press, Oxford.

Auden, W. H.: "Doggerel by a Senior Citizen," from *W. H. Auden: Collected Poems*, by W. H. Auden, edited by Edward Mendelson. Copyright © 1969 by W. H. Auden. Reprinted by permission of Random House, Inc.

Beauvoir, Simone de: Reprinted by permission of The Putnam Publishing Group from *The Coming of Age*, by Simone de Beauvoir. Copyright © 1972 by Andre Deutsch Ltd.

Beckett, Samuel: "Fizzle 3: Afar a Bird," from *Fizzles*, by Samuel Beckett. Copyright © 1976 by Samuel Beckett, *Watt*, by Samuel Beckett. Copyright © 1953 by Samuel Beckett. Used by permission of Grove Press, Inc.

Berryman, John: "No," from *Collected Poems, 1937–1971*, by John Berryman. Copyright © 1989 by Kate Donahue Berryman. Reprinted by permission of Farrar, Straus & Giroux, Inc.

Betjeman, John: "The Last Laugh" is reprinted from *A Nip in the Air*, by John Betjeman, by permission of W. W. Norton & Company, Inc. Copyright © 1974 by John Betjeman.

Bishop, Elizabeth: "One Art," from *The Complete Poems: 1927–1979*, by Elizabeth Bishop. Copyright © 1979, 1983 by Alice Helen Methfessel. Reprinted by permission of Farrar, Straus & Giroux, Inc.

Blythe, Ronald: Excerpts from *The View in Winter: Reflections on Old Age*, copyright © 1979 by Ronald Blythe, reprinted by permission of Harcourt Brace Jovanovich, Inc.

Bogan, Louise: "After the Persian II, III, IV, V," copyright © 1923, 1929, 1930, 1931, 1933, 1934, 1935, 1936, 1937, 1938, 1941, 1949, 1951, 1952, 1957, 1958, 1962, 1963, 1964, 1965, 1966, 1967, 1968, by Louise Bogan. From *The Blue Estuaries, Poems 1923–1968,* by Louise Bogan. First published by The Ecco Press in 1977. Reprinted by permission.

Boyle, Kay: "A Poem About Black Power," from *Testament for My Students and Other Poems,* by Kay Boyle. Copyright © 1970 by Kay Boyle. Used by permission of Doubleday, a division of Bantam Doubleday Dell Publishing Group, Inc. "Poets" and "Advice to the Old (including myself)," reprinted from Kay Boyle, *This Is Not a Letter and Other Poems* (Los Angeles: Sun & Moon Press, 1985). © Kay Boyle, 1985, Reprinted by permission of the publisher.

Brontë, Emily: "No coward soul is mine" and "Riches I hold in light esteem," from *Complete Poems of Emily Brontë,* edited by C. W. Hatfield, 1941, © Columbia University Press, New York. Reprinted by permission of the publishers.

Brooks, Gwendolyn: "A Catch of Shy Fish," from *Blacks,* copyright © by Gwendolyn Brooks, 1991. Published by The David Company, Chicago, 1987; reissued by Third World Press, Chicago, 1991. Reprinted by permission of Gwendolyn Brooks.

Browning, Robert: The lines from "A Toccata of Galuppi's" and "Rabbi Ben Ezra" are reprinted from *Robert Browning's Poetry,* A Norton Critical Edition, Selected and Edited by James F. Loucks, by permission of W. W. Norton & Company, Inc. Copyright © 1979 by W. W. Norton & Company, Inc.

Burke, Kenneth: From *Selected Correspondence,* by Kenneth Burke and Malcolm Cowley; Paul Jay, editor. Copyright © 1988 by Malcolm Cowley, Paul Jay, and Kenneth Burke. Used by permission of Viking Penguin, a division of Penguin Books USA Inc.

Burns, Robert: "John Anderson, My Jo," from *The Complete Poetical Works of Robert Burns,* by Robert Burns, published in 1987 by Houghton Mifflin Company.

Byron, George Gordon, Lord: "On This Day I Complete My Thirty-sixth Year," from *Byron: Poetical Works,* published in 1945. Reprinted by permission of Oxford University Press, Oxford.

Chaucer, Geoffrey: From *The Canterbury Tales: An Illustrated Selection,* by Geoffrey Chaucer, translated by Nevill Coghill (Allen Lane, 1977), copyright © Nevill Coghill, 1951, 1958, 1960, 1977. Reproduced by permission of Penguin Books Ltd.

Cherry, Kelly: "Lines Written on the Eve of a Birthday" and "The Mind-Body Problem," from *Natural Theology: Poems by Kelly Cherry.* Copyright © 1973, 1975, 1976, 1977, 1978, 1979, 1980, 1981, 1982, 1983, 1988 by Kelly Cherry. Reprinted by permission of Louisiana State University Press.

Cicero: "Cato: On Old Age," from *On Old Age and On Friendship,* translated and with an Introduction by Frank O. Copley. Copyright © 1967 by the University of Michigan. Reprinted by permission of the University of Michigan Press.

Clampitt, Amy: "Grasses," from *Westward,* by Amy Clampitt. Copyright © 1990 by Amy Clampitt. Reprinted by permission of Alfred A. Knopf, Inc.

Colette: Excerpt from Colette's letter to Pierre Moreno, from *Letters from Colette,* translated by Robert Phelps. Translation copyright © 1980 by Farrar, Straus & Giroux, Inc. Reprinted by permission of Farrar, Straus & Giroux, Inc.

Cousins, Norman: Reprinted from *Anatomy of an Illness, as Perceived by the Patient,* by Norman Cousins, by permission of W. W. Norton & Company, Inc. Copyright © by W. W. Norton & Company, Inc.

Cowley, Malcolm: Excerpt from *The View from 80,* by Malcolm Cowley. Copyright © 1976, 1978, 1980 by Malcolm Cowley. Used by permission of Viking Penguin, a division of Penguin Books USA Inc. Letters to Kenneth Burke from *Selected Correspondence,* by Kenneth Burke and Malcolm Cowley, Paul Jay, editor. Copyright © 1988 by Malcolm Cowley, Paul Jay, and Kenneth Burke. Used by permission of Viking Penguin, a division of Penguin Books USA Inc.

   cummings, e. e.: "now does our world descend" is reprinted from *Complete Poems, 1913–1962,* by E. E. Cummings, by permission of Liveright Publishing Corporation. Copyright © 1923, 1925, 1931, 1935, 1938, 1939, 1940, 1944, 1945, 1946,1947, 1948, 1949, 1950, 1951, 1952, 1953, 1954, 1955, 1956, 1957, 1958, 1959, 1960, 1961, 1962 by the Trustees for the E. E. Cummings Trust. Copyright © 1961, 1963, 1968 by Marion Morehouse Cummings.

Davies, Robertson: Introduction, copyright © 1991 by Robertson Davies. Reprinted from *Vital Signs,* edited by Dorothy Sennett with Anne Czarniecki, with the permission of Graywolf Press, Saint Paul, Minnesota.

Eliot, T.S.: Excerpt from "East Coker" in *Four Quartets,* copyright 1943 by T. S. Eliot and renewed 1981 by Esmé Valerie Eliot, reprinted by permission of Harcourt Brace Jovanovich, Inc.

Fisher, M. F. K.: From *Sister Age,* by M. F. K. Fisher. Copyright © 1983 by M. F. K. Fisher. Reprinted by permission of Alfred A. Knopf, Inc.

Forster, E. M.: Reprinted from *Commonplace Book,* by E. M. Forster, edited by Philip Gardner, with the permission of the publishers, Stanford University Press. Copyright © 1978 and 1985 by The Provost and Scholars of King's College, Cambridge. Introduction, Notes and other Editorial Matter, Copyright © Philip Gardner 1985.

Frost, Robert: "Provide, Provide," from *The Poetry of Robert Frost,* edited by Edward Connery Lathem. Copyright © 1969 by Holt, Rinehart and Winston. Copyright © 1936 by Robert Frost. Copyright © 1964 by Lesley Frost Ballantine. "Epigram" and untitled poem, from *The Poetry of Robert Frost,* edited by Edward Connery Lathem. Copyright © 1962 by Robert Frost. Copyright © 1969 by Holt, Rinehart and Winston. Reprinted by permission of Henry Holt and Company, Inc.

Graves, Robert: "The Face in the Mirror," from *Collected Poems,* by Robert Graves. Copyright © 1975 by Robert Graves. Reprinted by permission of Oxford University Press, Inc.

Guisewite, Cathy: CATHY copyright 1990 Cathy Guisewite. Reprinted with permission of UNIVERSAL PRESS SYNDICATE. All rights reserved.

Hardy, Thomas: "Faithful Wilson," "He Never Expected Much," and "I Look into My Glass," reprinted with permission of Macmillan Publishing Company from *The Complete Poems of Thomas Hardy,* edited by James Gibson. Copyright

© 1928 by Florence E. Hardy and Sydney E. Cockerell, renewed 1956 by Lloyds Bank Ltd.

Hoffman, Daniel: "Jogger," from *Hang-Gliding from Helicon: New and Selected Poems, 1948–1988,* by Daniel Hoffman. Copyright © 1974, 1975, 1977, 1978, 1979, 1980, 1982, 1983, 1984, 1986, 1987, 1988 by Daniel Hoffman. Reprinted by permission of Louisiana State University Press.

Holmes, Oliver Wendell: Lines from "On the Seventieth Birthday of Julia Ward Howe" and "The Old Player," from *The Complete Poetical Works of Oliver Wendell Holmes,* published in 1975 by Houghton Mifflin Company.

Hopkins, Gerard Manley: "God's Grandeur," from *The Poems of Gerard Manley Hopkins,* 4th Edition, edited by W. H. Gardner and N. H. Mackenzie, Oxford University Press, Oxford, 1970.

Housman, A. E.: "I to My Perils," from *More Poems,* by A. E. Housman. Copyright © 1936 by Barclays Bank Ltd. Copyright © 1964 by Robert E. Symons. Reprinted by permission of Henry Holt and Company, Inc.

Howe, Irving: Excerpt from *A Margin of Hope,* copyright © 1982 by Irving Howe, reprinted by permission of Harcourt Brace Jovanovich, Inc.

Hughes, Langston: "Life Is Fine," from *Selected Poems,* by Langston Hughes. Copyright © 1948 by Alfred A. Knopf, Inc. Reprinted by permission of the publisher.

James, Alice: "February 2nd (1892) [This Long Slow Dying]" and "March 4th (1892) [Physical Pain]," from *The Diaries of Alice James,* edited by Leon Edel. Reprinted by permission of the William Morris Agency, Inc. on behalf of the author. Copyright © 1964 by Leon Edel.

James, Henry: Letter to Henry Bowditch reprinted by permission of the publishers from Henry James, *Selected Letters,* Leon Edel, editor, Camridge, Mass.: The Belknap Press of Harvard University Press. Copyright © 1974, 1975, 1980, 1984, 1987, Leon Edel, Editorial copyright © 1974, 1975, 1980, 1984, 1987 by Alexander R. James, James copyright material. Notebook entries from *The Complete Notebooks of Henry James,* edited by Leon Edel and Lyall H. Powers. Copyright © 1986 by Leon Edel and Lyall H. Powers. Reprinted by permission of Oxford University Press, Inc.

Jarrell, Randall: "Thinking of the Lost World," copyright © 1965 by Randall Jarrell from *The Lost World,* reprinted in *The Complete Poems of Randall Jarrell,* Farrar Straus & Giroux, 1989. Permission granted by Rhoda Weyr Agency, New York.

Johnson, Samuel: Excerpt from *The Letters of Samuel Johnson,* edited by Bruce Redford. Copyright © 1992 by Princeton University Press. Reprinted by permission of Princeton University Press.

Jonson, Ben: "My Picture Left in Scotland" and "Volpone," Act 1, reprinted from *Ben Jonson,* Oxford Standard Authors series, edited by Ian Donaldson, published in 1985. Reprinted by permission of Oxford University Press, Oxford.

Kael, Pauline: From *Hooked* by Pauline Kael. Copyright © 1985, 1988, 1989, by Pauline Kael. All material in this book appeared originally in *The New Yorker.* Used by permission of the publisher, Dutton, an imprint of New American Library, a division of Penguin Books USA Inc.

Koestler, Arthur: From *Arthur Koestler: The Story of a Friendship*, by George Mikes. Copyright © 1983 by George Mikes. Reprinted by permission of Andre Deutsch Ltd.

Kumin, Maxine: "The Envelope," from *The Retrieval System*, by Maxine Kumin. Copyright © 1978 by Maxine Kumin. Used by permission of Viking Penguin, a division of Penguin Books USA Inc.

Larkin, Philip: "Dear CHARLES, My Muse, asleep or dead" and excerpt from "On Being Twenty-six," from *Collected Poems*, by Philip Larkin. Copyright © 1988, 1989 by the Estate of Philip Larkin. Reprinted by permission of Farrar, Straus & Giroux, Inc.

Lattimore, Richmond: Translation of Mimnermus from *Greek Lyrics*, by Richmond Lattimore. Copyright © 1949, 1955, and 1960 by Richmond Lattimore. Reprinted by permission of the University of Chicago Press.

Laubach, Frank C.: "Life Begins at 80," reprinted by permission of Bob Laubach.

Lear, Edward: "There Was an Old Man with a Beard" and "There Was an Old Man Who Supposed," from *The Book of Nonsense*, by Edward Lear. Introduction by Bryan Holme. Copyright © 1980 by the Metropolitan Museum of Art and Viking Penguin. Used by permission of Viking Penguin, a division of Penguin Books USA Inc.

Lerner, Laurence: "It Is Time," in *Rembrandt's Mirror*, by Laurence Lerner. Copyright © Laurence Lerner 1987. Reprinted by permission of Martin Secker and Warburg Limited.

Merrill, James: "Losing the Marbles," from *The Inner Room*, by James Merrill. Copyright © 1988 by James Merrill. Reprinted by permission of Alfred A. Knopf, Inc.

Miles, Josephine: "Brim," "Nadirs," and "Stroke" from *Collected Poems*, by Josephine Miles. Copyright © 1983 by Josephine Miles. Reprinted by permission of the University of Illinois Press.

Millay, Edna St. Vincent: "The Courage That My Mother Had," by Edna St. Vincent Millay. From *Collected Poems*, Harper & Row. Copyright © 1954, 1982 by Norma Millay Ellis. Reprinted by permission of Elizabeth Barnett, literary executor.

Milosz, Czeslaw: "Old Women," copyright © 1988 by Czeslaw Milosz Royalties, Inc. From *The Collected Poems, 1931–1987*, by Czeslaw Milosz, first published by The Ecco Press in 1988. Reprinted by permission.

Milton, John: Text from *Poetical Works*, edited by Helen Darbishire, Oxford Standard Authors series, published in 1958. Reprinted by permission of Oxford University Press, Oxford.

Minois, Georges: Excerpts from *History of Old Age: From Antiquity to the Renaissance*, by Georges Minois, translated by Sarah Hanbury Tenison. Originally published as *Histoire de la vieillesse: De l'Antiquité à la Renaissance*, © 1987, Librairie Arthème Fayard. Copyright © 1989 by Polity Press, the University of Chicago Press. Reprinted by permission of the University of Chicago Press.

Montaigne: Reprinted from "Of Age," *The Complete Works*, translated by

Donald M. Frame, published by Stanford University Press in 1958, with permission of the publisher.

Moore, Marianne: "What Are Years?" reprinted with permission of Macmillan Publishing Company, from *The Collected Poems of Marianne Moore.* Copyright © 1941, and renewed 1969, by Marianne Moore.

Myerhoff, Barbara: From *Number Our Days,* by Barbara Myerhoff. Copyright © 1978 by Barbara Myerhoff. Used by permission of the publisher, Dutton, an imprint of New American Library, a division of Penguin Books USA Inc.

Nash, Ogden: "Crossing the Border," from *Verses from 1929 On,* by Ogden Nash. Copyright © 1956 by Ogden Nash. Copyright © renewed by Frances Nash, Isabel Nash Eberstadt, and Linell Nash Smith. First appeared in *The New Yorker.* Reprinted by permission of Little, Brown and Company.

Olson, Elder: Lines from "Conversation Pieces" and "Himself in Age," from *Last Poems,* published by the University of Chicago Press in 1984 and reprinted by permission of the author and the University of Chicago Press.

Parker, Dorothy: "Résumé," copyright 1926, 1928, renewed 1954, © 1956 by Dorothy Parker, from *The Portable Dorothy Parker,* by Dorothy Parker, Introduction by Brendan Gill. Used by permission of Viking Penguin, a division of Penguin Books USA Inc.

Petrarch: From "Italia mia, #128 in "The Canzoniere," quoted and translated by Kenelm Foster in *Petrarch: Poet and Humanist* (Edinburgh: Edinburgh University Press, 1984), p. 58. © Edinburgh University Press (1984).

Pitter, Ruth: "Yorkshire Wife's Saga," from *Collected Poems,* by Ruth Pitter. Copyright © 1968 by Ruth Pitter. Reprinted by permission of the publisher, Barrie & Jenkins, and Random Century Group.

Plato: Excerpt from *The Republic,* translated by Francis MacDonald Cornford, 1945, reprinted by permission of Oxford University Press, Oxford.

Pound, Ezra: Excerpt from Canto LXXX, from *The Cantos,* by Ezra Pound, reprinted by permission of New Directions Publishing Corporation.

Rich, Adrienne: Poem #16, "It's true, these last few years I've lived," Poem #18, "The problem, unstated till now, is how," and Poem #28, "This high summer we love will pour its light" are reprinted from *Your Native Land, Your Life, Poems by Adrienne Rich,* by permission of W. W. Norton & Company, Inc. Copyright © 1986 by Adrienne Rich. "One Life" is reprinted from *Time's Power: Poems, 1985–1988,* by Adrienne Rich, by permission of W. W. Norton & Company, Inc. Copyright © 1989 by Adrienne Rich.

Roethke, Theodore: "The Decision," copyright © 1958 by Beatrice Roethke, Administratrix of the Estate of Theodore Roethke; "The Restored," copyright © 1960 by Beatrice Roethke, Administratrix of the Estate of Theodore Roethke; "Wish for a Young Wife," copyright © 1963 by Beatrice Roethke, Administratrix of the Estate of Theodore Roethke; from *The Collected Poems of Theodore Roethke,* by Theodore Roethke. Used by permission of Doubleday, a division of Bantam Doubleday Dell Publishing Group, Inc.

Rosen, Betty: "Breakfast Time," reprinted by permission of the author.

Rossetti, Christina: "Song ['Oh roses for the flush of youth']," "Dead Before Death," and "Up-Hill" from *The Complete Poems of Christina Rossetti,* A Variorum

Edition, Volume I. Edited, with Textual Notes and Introductions, by R. W. Crump. Copyright © 1979 by Louisiana State University Press. Reprinted by permission of Louisiana State University Press.

Russell, Bertrand: From *Autobiography of Bertrand Russell*, Volume 3: 1944–1969, reprinted by permission of The Bertrand Russell Peace Foundation Ltd.

Sappho: "Age and Light" is reprinted from *Sappho: A New Translation*, by Mary Barnard. Copyright © 1958 by The Regents of the University of California; © renewed 1984 by Mary Barnard. Used by permission of the University of California Press.

Sarton, May: Excerpt reprinted from *As We Are Now, A Novel*, by May Sarton, by permission of W. W. Norton & Company, Inc. Copyright © 1973 by May Sarton; "Old Lovers at the Ballet" is reprinted from *Halfway to Silence, New Poems by May Sarton*, by permission of W. W. Norton & Company, Inc. Copyright © 1980 by May Sarton; passage reprinted from *At Seventy, A Journal*, by May Sarton, by permission of W. W. Norton & Company, Inc. Copyright 1984 by May Sarton; "The Silence Now," is reprinted from *The Silence Now, New and Uncollected Earlier Poems*, by May Sarton, by permission of W. W. Norton & Company, Inc. Copyright © 1988 by May Sarton.

Seneca: Excerpt on page 54 reprinted by permission of the publishers and the Loeb Classical Library from *Seneca: Epistolae Morales*, Vol(s). IV–VI, translated by R. M. Gummere, Cambridge, Mass.: Harvard University Press, 1917, 1920, 1925. Excerpt on page 178 reprinted by permission of the publishers from *The Harvest Years*, by Theodor Groene. Copyright © 1966 by the Christopher Publishing House.

Skinner, B. F.: Reprinted from *Enjoy Old Age: A Program of Self-Management*, by B. F. Skinner and M. E. Vaughan, by permission of W. W. Norton & Company, Inc. Copyright © 1983 by B. F. Skinner and Margaret E. Vaughan.

Sophocles: Excerpt from *Oedipus at Colonus*, reprinted by permission of Greenwood Publishing Group, Inc., Westport, CT, from *Perceptions of Aging in Literature: A Cross-Cultural Study*, edited by Prisca von Dorotka Bagnell and Patricia Spencer Soper. Copyright by and published in 1989 by Greenwood Press.

Spender, Stephen: "From My Diary," from *Collected Poems: 1928–1985*, by Stephen Spender. Copyright © 1986 by Stephen Spender. Reprinted by permission of Random House, Inc.

Stein, Gertrude: "Stanzas in Meditation" is reprinted from *The Yale Gertrude Stein*, by permission of Yale University Press. Copyright © 1980 by Yale University.

Stevens, Wallace: "Lebensweisheitspielerei," from *Collected Poems*, by Wallace Stevens. Copyright © 1952 by Wallace Stevens. "A Pastoral Nun," from *Collected Poems*, by Wallace Stevens. Copyright © 1947 by Wallace Stevens. "The Plain Sense of Things," from *Collected Poems*, by Wallace Stevens. Copyright © 1952 by Wallace Stevens. Reprinted by permission of Alfred A. Knopf, Inc.

Swift, Jonathan: "When I Come to be Old," from *Jonathan Swift*, Oxford Standard Authors series, edited by Angus Ross and David Woolley, published in 1984. Reprinted by permission of Oxford University Press, Oxford.

Thomas, Dylan: "Do not go gentle into that good night" and "Fern Hill," from Dylan Thomas: *Poems of Dylan Thomas.* Copyright © 1945 by The Trustees for the Copyrights of Dylan Thomas. Reprinted by permission of New Directions Publishing Corporation.

Twain, Mark: "Mark Twain's 70th Birthday Speech" is reprinted from *Mark Twain Speaking,* by Paul Fatout, by permission of The Mark Twain Foundation.

Updike, John: Excerpts from *Self-Consciousness,* by John Updike. Copyright © 1989 by John Updike. Reprinted by permission of Alfred A. Knopf, Inc.

Van Doren, Mark: "Last Housecleaning" and "The First Snow of the Year," from *Collected and New Poems: 1924–1963,* by Mark Van Doren. Copyright © 1963 by Mark Van Doren, renewal copyright © 1991 by Dorothy G. Van Doren. Reprinted by permission of Hill and Wang, a division of Farrar, Straus & Giroux, Inc.

Villon, François: Excerpt reprinted by permission of Greenwood Publishing Group, Inc., Westport, CT, from *Perceptions of Aging in Literature: A Cross-Cultural Study,* edited by Prisca von Dorotka Bagnell and Patricia Spencer Soper. Copyright by and published in 1989 by Greenwood Press. Originally from *The Poems of François Villon,* translated with an introduction by Galway Kinnell. Copyright © 1965, 1977 by Galway Kinnell. Reprinted by permission of Houghton Mifflin Company. All rights reserved.

Warren, Robert Penn: "The Whole Question," from *New and Selected Poems: 1923–1985,* by Robert Penn Warren. Copyright © 1985 by Robert Penn Warren. Reprinted by permission of Random House, Inc.

Wharton, Edith: Reprinted with permission of Charles Scribner's Sons, an imprint of Macmillan Publishing Company, from *The Letters of Edith Wharton,* edited by R. W. B. Lewis, Nancy Lewis, and William R. Tyler. Copyright © 1988 by R. W. B. Lewis, Nancy Lewis, and William R. Tyler.

Wheelock, John Hall: "Night Thoughts in Age," reprinted with permission of Charles Scribner's Sons, an imprint of Macmillan Publishing Company, from *Poems Old and New,* by John Hall Wheelock. Copyright © 1955 by John Hall Wheelock. Originally appeared in *The New Yorker.*

Williams, William Carlos: "Wide Awake, Full of Love," from *The Collected Poems of William Carlos Williams, 1939–1962,* vol. 2. Copyright © 1950 by William Carlos Williams. Reprinted by permission of New Directions Publishing Corporation.

Woolf, Virginia: Excerpts from *Mrs. Dalloway,* by Virginia Woolf, copyright 1925 by Harcourt Brace Jovanovich, Inc. and renewed 1953 by Leonard Woolf, reprinted by permission of the publisher. Excerpt from *To the Lighthouse,* by Virginia Woolf, copyright 1927 by Harcourt Brace Jovanovich, Inc., and renewed 1954 by Leonard Woolf, reprinted by permission of the publisher.

Wu Yü-pi: Excerpt reprinted by permission of Greenwood Publishing Group, Inc., Westport, CT, from *Perceptions of Aging in Literature: A Cross-Cultural Study,* edited by Prisca von Dorotka Bagnell and Patricia Spencer Soper. Copyright by and published in 1989 by Greenwood Press. In *The Personal Reflections on the Pursuit of Sagehood: The Life and Journal of Wu Yü-pi,* translated by M. Theresa Kelleher. Ph.D. dissertation M. Theresa Kelleher, Columbia University, 1982.

Wylie, Elinor: "Let No Charitable Hope" and "Nadir," from *Collected Poems,* by Elinor Wylie. Copyright © 1932 by Alfred A. Knopf, Inc. and renewed 1960 by Edwina C. Rubenstein. Reprinted by permission of the publisher.

Yeats, W. B.: Lines from "The Tower," "Sailing to Byzantium," and "Among School Children," reprinted with permission of Macmillan Publishing Company from *The Poems of W. B. Yeats: A New Edition,* edited by Richard J. Finneran. Copyright 1928 by Macmillan Publishing Company, copyright renewed 1956 by Georgie Yeats. "A Prayer for Old Age," reprinted with permission of Macmillan Publishing Company from *The Poems of W. B. Yeats: A New Edition,* edited by Richard J. Finneran. Copyright 1934 by Macmillan Publishing Company, renewed 1962 by Bertha Georgie Yeats.

Index

0308

ABOUT THE AUTHOR

Wayne Booth is George M. Pullman Professor of English Emeritus at the University of Chicago. His books include *The Vocation of a Teacher* and the widely influential *The Rhetoric of Fiction*. Currently he is writing his autobiography and learning thumb position on the cello.

DISCARDED